I0124776

Locke's Political Thought
and the Oceans

Locke's Political Thought and the Oceans

Pirates, Slaves, and Sailors

Sarah Pemberton

LEXINGTON BOOKS
Lanham • Boulder • New York • London

Published by Lexington Books
An imprint of The Rowman & Littlefield Publishing Group, Inc.
4501 Forbes Boulevard, Suite 200, Lanham, Maryland 20706
www.rowman.com

Unit A, Whitacre Mews, 26-34 Stannary Street, London SE11 4AB

Copyright © 2017 by Lexington Books

All rights reserved. No part of this book may be reproduced in any form or by any electronic or mechanical means, including information storage and retrieval systems, without written permission from the publisher, except by a reviewer who may quote passages in a review.

British Library Cataloguing in Publication Information Available

Library of Congress Cataloging-in-Publication Data Available

ISBN 978-1-4985-3821-3 (cloth : alk. paper)
ISBN 978-1-4985-3823-7 (pbk. : alk. paper)
ISBN 978-1-4985-3822-0 (electronic)

Table of Contents

Acknowledgments

This project began as a conference paper in 2012 and grew inexorably into a book. Throughout the process I have received the encouragement and help of many colleagues, friends, and family members, and I am deeply grateful to them all.

This book would not have been possible without the support and funding provided by Ohio University and the University of South Florida. I have been lucky to work with colleagues who were generous with their time and their insights. In the course of this project many of my colleagues provided invaluable advice and comments, and my thanks go especially to Mark Amen, Susan Burgess, Darcie Fontaine, Judith Grant, Cheryl Hall, Brandon Kendhammer, Sarah Poggione, Manu Samnotra, Scott Solomon, Kathleen Sullivan, Steven Tauber, Debra Thompson, Stephen Turner, Myra Waterbury, and Julie White. The archival research involved in this book was enabled by grants from the University of South Florida and by research leave during autumn 2014, which made it possible for me to accept a Visiting Fellowship at the Centre for the Study of the History of Political Thought at Queen Mary University of London. I am grateful to the Centre's members Georgios Varouxakis and Quentin Skinner for the encouragement and counsel that they provided.

During the past four years I have presented draft versions of several chapters at a number of conferences and meetings, and this book benefited greatly from the questions, suggestions, and provocations that I received. I am very grateful to the following scholars for the feedback that they provided: Clare Anderson, Lorna Bracewell, Alec Dinnin, Vicki Hsueh, Jane Anna Gordon, Jennie Jeppesen, Hamish Maxwell-Stewart, Anita Rupprecht, and Thomas Smith. My thanks also go to Jonathan Havercroft, Tracy Strong, and the other members of the University of Southampton Department of

Politics and International Relations for inviting me to present to their department seminar and for providing rich and insightful comments. I also benefited from discussing this project with attendees at the Seminar in the History of Political Ideas organized by the Institute for Historical Research at the University of London.

This project owes particular debts to two exceptional Locke scholars: Barbara Arneil and David Armitage. As my PhD supervisor at the University of British Columbia, Barbara provided unfailing support, encouragement, and advice. Although this project began after my PhD, it was nonetheless shaped by Barbara's wonderful teaching and research. Early in this project David Armitage played an equally vital role by generously sharing his copy and transcription of "Pyracy 97," and his scans of Locke's colonial papers.

It was a pleasure to work with Joseph Parry at Lexington Books, and I am grateful for his support and wisdom in guiding me through the publication process. I also received valuable commentary on my draft manuscript from three anonymous reviewers who provided wide-ranging, incisive, and detailed comments. I learned much from their different and complementary perspectives, and this book is much stronger as a result. All remaining errors are, of course, my own.

I dedicate this book to my family. My partner, Greg, provided encouragement and comments at every stage in the process. The ultimate inspiration for the book came from my mum, who hails from a family of sailors and is as fierce as any pirate. She insisted that I learned to sail and ensured that there was a safe harbor to which I could return.

Introducing Locke's
Maritime Political Thought

In September 1695 a gang of English pirates pulled off one of the biggest heists in history when they ambushed an Indian pilgrim fleet traveling from Surat to Mocha. The pirates captured two ships and stole treasure worth over £150,000,[1] equivalent to more than twenty million pounds today.[2] Each pirate received over a thousand pounds in proceeds,[3] which was a fortune in a period when most sailors earned less than twenty pounds per year.[4] Word of these riches quickly spread in English colonies and inspired other sailors to become pirates, causing a surge in maritime crime. The raid also sparked a diplomatic crisis, because the captured ships belonged to a prominent Indian merchant and to Aurangzeb, the Mughal Emperor of India. Not only had Aurangzeb lost his ship and treasure, but his granddaughter was on board and had been sexually assaulted by the pirates.[5] The Indian authorities were furious that Englishmen had attacked Indian ships and responded by imprisoning the staff of the East India Company, suspending trade with England, and demanding that the English bring the pirates to justice.[6] The following year John Locke was appointed to England's new Board of Trade, and the Board began working to tackle the problem of piracy. Locke himself proposed a new English piracy law and a multilateral piracy treaty, supported the deployment of English naval ships to fight pirates, and advocated the removal of colonial governors who failed to arrest pirates. The Board's work led to a new piracy law in 1700 that expanded the definition of piracy, introduced more severe penalties, and authorized the English navy to capture and try pirates anywhere on the world's seas. The Board also proposed political reforms to suppress piracy in English colonies, and these reforms gave the English Crown and Parliament more centralized control over the American colonies. Taken collectively, the Board's work on piracy contributed to the development of the eighteenth-century British empire on land and at sea.

Piracy was only one of many issues tackled by the Board of Trade during Locke's tenure, but it helps to illustrate both Locke's contribution to English policymaking and the relationship between his political theory and his work on the Board. This book examines Locke's political thought about the oceans by considering his arguments in the *Two Treatises*, Locke's other political writings including unpublished essays and letters, and his activity on the Board of Trade. The Board worked on a huge range of economic and colonial issues that often have no direct bearing on Locke's political thought, so I will not attempt to summarize all Locke's activity on the Board. Instead, I provide a close examination of Locke's Board of Trade work on three issues that are related both to the maritime world and to important aspects of his political theory: piracy, forced naval service (also known as naval impressment), and the transportation of English convicts to the colonies for sale into forced labor. The piracy policies that Locke proposed to the Board are based on his empirical understanding of piracy and his underlying views about crime, punishment, and the legal status of the oceans, which are part of his normative political theory. Locke's work on convict transportation as a member of the Board was influenced both by his practical understanding of English colonialism and migration, and by his theoretical views about natural rights, slavery, and forced labor. Similarly, the issue of forced naval service is related both to Locke's theoretical arguments about military service in the *Two Treatises* and to his knowledge of English military policy and colonial governance. Analyzing Locke's writing and activity about piracy, convict transportation, and forced naval service enables us to understand his views about three maritime issues that were under debate during the 1690s and that are each connected to areas of Locke's political theory that are of continued interest for political theorists.

In studying Locke's political thought about the seas I use a combination of textual, philosophical, and contextual analysis. Using textual analysis, I examine what Locke wrote about the seas in the *Two Treatises*, his other political texts, and unpublished writings such as letters and draft policy proposals. This analysis shows that the maritime world is a recurrent theme in Locke's writing from the 1650s to the 1690s, including in the *Two Treatises*. Close textual analysis also reveals how Locke's arguments are developed within each text, for example by showing how the theory of property in Locke's *Second Treatise* builds on passages in the *First Treatise* that discuss theories of natural law at sea. I then use philosophical analysis to examine the logical relationships between Locke's arguments about the seas, including by identifying points of ambiguity or inconsistency. For example, philosophical analysis shows how the agriculturalist theory of property in the *Second Treatise* leads Locke to the conclusion that the oceans have not been privately appropriated and therefore remain a "Common of Mankind."[7] Contextual analysis of Locke's life, activity, and historical setting is then used to shed light on the intended meaning and significance of his writing about the seas. This contextual analysis often shows what concerns or events Locke was responding to when he wrote a text, so it can help us to understand the intended meaning and significance of his writing. For example, contextual analysis shows that Locke's unpublished "Pyracy 97" manuscript was written in response to Board of Trade discussions about piracy originating from England's American colonies, and that Locke sought to implement his proposals through a new English piracy law. By combining textual, philosophical, and contextual approaches we can see what Locke wrote about the seas, how his claims support or contradict each other, and form a better understanding of what Locke intended these arguments to mean and what political consequences he wanted them to have.

LOCKE'S POLITICAL ACTIVITY

Locke initially became involved in English politics and colonial government through his work for Anthony Ashley Cooper, later the Earl of Shaftesbury.[8] Shaftesbury was one of the Lords Proprietors of the Carolinas colony, and in 1668 Locke became Secretary to the Lords Proprietors which made him responsible for handling the colony's official correspondence and for helping the Lords Proprietors to implement their colonial vision. As Secretary Locke played some role in drafting the 1669 *Fundamental Constitutions of Carolina,* but it is unclear if he had much influence over its content and several of its provisions conflict with his arguments in the *Two Treatises.*[9] For example, the 1669 constitution grants legislative authority to hereditary nobles known as landgraves,[10] whereas Locke argues in the *Two Treatises* that the legislative should be established by the consent of the majority.[11] *The Fundamental Constitutions of Carolina* were revised in 1682 and Locke also contributed to these revisions.[12] Locke's involvement in the Carolinas colony has been examined in detail by scholars who argue that attention to this context helps us to understand passages in the *Two Treatises* relating to property,[13] warfare,[14] and indigenous peoples.[15] The existing history of political thought literature therefore suggests that analysis of Locke's early work on English colonial governance can help us to understand the origins and intended meaning of his arguments in the *Two Treatises.*

In 1672 Shaftesbury persuaded Charles II to establish a committee overseeing England's international trade and colonies, which was termed the Council of Trade and Foreign Plantations.[16] Shaftesbury was the first President of the Council,[17] and in October 1673 Locke became its Secretary and Treasurer. The Council of Trade and Foreign Plantations was responsible for collecting information and issuing advice about international trade and the administration of English colonies. In this period there were three categories of English colonies: proprietary colonies governed by Lords Proprietors, such as Carolina; charter colonies whose legal basis lay in a charter granted by the English Crown, such as Rhode Island and Massachusetts; and Crown colonies that were under the direct authority of the English Crown and ruled by a governor appointed by the monarch, such as Virginia, Jamaica, and Barbados. The Council had the most direct influence over Crown colonies, including the power to advise their governors and to approve or deny laws passed by their local councils.[18] As Secretary, Locke read and recorded the letters that the Council received, and drafted letters and advice from the Council to colonial governors, merchants, and the King. During Locke's tenure the Council received letters on issues such as the supply of black slaves to England's Caribbean colonies[19] and the problems posed by priva- teer raids on English traders,[20] and composed advice on subjects ranging from the religious policies of colonial governors[21] to the best way to recap- ture New York from the Dutch.[22] Locke's work for the Council of Trade and Foreign Plantations has received little scholarly attention, but it contributed to his knowledge of English trade and colonialism, his political experience, and probably to his theoretical views. Prior to serving as Secretary of the Council Locke's writings centered on politics and religion, but after his appointment Locke also began to discuss economics and to argue that nation- al success depends on international trade. This case for the importance of trade is first presented in Locke's 1674 essay "Trade,"[23] but appears in the *Two Treatises* when Locke claims that trade motivates people to acquire large amounts of land or cattle and thereby contributes to economic growth.[24] In the *Two Treatises* Locke also argues that international trade underpins the domestic economy, explaining that English bread production indirectly in- volves "Pitch, Tar, Masts, Ropes, and all the Materials made use of in the Ship, that brought any of the Commodities made use of by any of the Work- men, to any part of the Work."[25] Without his experience on the Council of Trade and Foreign Plantations it is unclear whether Locke would have devel- oped these views about political economy.

Locke also had a personal stake in English colonialism during the 1670s through his investments in the Bahamas Company and the Royal African Company.[26] The Royal African Company held a monopoly on trade between Africa and England or English colonies, including the trade in African slaves, so Locke's investment in the company has been scrutinized by schol- ars seeking to understand his views on race and slavery.[27] In the *Two Treatises* Locke argues that individuals have a natural right to freedom, and that slavery is legitimate only for those who have used aggressive violence towards another individual or state.[28] However, by the 1670s the African slave trade had already led to systems of racialized chattel slavery in England's Caribbean colonies and some mainland American colonies, as Locke knew from his colonial work.[29] In response to the apparent tension between Locke's theoretical stance on slavery in the *Two Treatises* and his earlier investment in the African slave trade, scholars have proposed several explanations. One possibility is that Locke intended the just war theory of slavery in the *Two Treatises* to justify slave trading by the Royal African Company, as Peter Laslett and Jennifer Welchman argue.[30] Alternatively, James Farr maintains that Locke's discussion of slavery in the *Two Treatises* was written in response to political tyranny in England, and was not intended to justify the enslavement of Africans.[31] A third approach is provided by John Dunn who argues that African slavery was not justified according to the *Two Treatises*, but suggests that Locke was evasive about racialized practices of slavery.[32] Whatever Locke's views about the Royal African Company, scholars now tend to interpret the theory of slavery in the *Two Treatises* as inconsistent with practices of racialized chattel slavery in English colonies, and many scholars argue that Locke did not hold racist views about non-Europeans.[33]

By December 1674 Shaftesbury had fallen out of favor with the King, who responded by dissolving the Council of Trade and Foreign Plantations and transferring its powers to the Privy Council.[34] Although Shaftesbury no longer held government office he was active in Parliament, and for the next few years Shaftesbury and Locke focused their attentions on Whig politics.[35] In 1676 Shaftesbury's calls for more regular parliamentary elections led to his temporary imprisonment, but Locke was in France at the time.[36] By July 1681 hostility between the Whigs and the King had worsened, and Shaftesbury was re-arrested.[37] At trial Shaftesbury was acquitted by a sympathetic jury, but afterwards he began to meet with other prominent Whigs to discuss the possibility of armed rebellion against the King.[38] Historical scholarship suggests that these Whig discussions about rebellion against Charles II formed the immediate political backdrop for Locke's authorship of the *Two Treatises,* which probably took place between 1681 and 1683.[39] Fearing arrest again, Shaftesbury left England for Holland in late 1682 and in January 1683 he died there.[40] Within months the Whig plots against the King were discovered and the government began to arrest those involved, including Locke's friend and fellow political theorist Algernon Sydney.[41] By the summer of 1683 Locke also feared arrest so he hid his drafts for the *Two Treatises* and left for Holland.[42] In Holland Locke developed friendships with other English radicals in exile, including agents working for William of Orange.[43] When Locke finally returned to England in early 1689 he traveled on the same ship as Princess Mary and reportedly at her invitation.[44]

Locke's extensive political experience and his good connections to William and Mary meant that he was well placed to shape English policy after the Glorious Revolution. King William's trust and confidence in Locke is clear from the fact that he repeatedly offered Locke diplomatic posts, including to Vienna, Brandenburg, and Paris.[45] Locke declined these foreign postings, but continued to be involved in politics within England. During the early 1690s Locke contributed to political debates on interest rates and re-coinage, including by publishing several essays[46] and meeting with government ministers and MPs.[47] In May 1696 Locke's influence over English economic policy was formalized when King William created a Board of Trade and appointed Locke as one of its eight founding members. The Board was tasked with "promoting the trade of the Kingdom and for inspecting and improving the Plantations," and was also instructed "to consider methods of employing the poor."[48] Over the next four years much of Locke's activity was devoted to work for the Board, including by collecting information from colonists and merchants, drafting instructions for colonial governors, developing policy proposals, and lobbying the government and MPs to adopt these policies.

As the leading Whig on the Board of Trade Locke exercised considerable influence over English colonial policy, but his views often clashed with those of the leading Tory William Blathwayt. Blathwayt was an experienced and powerful civil servant who served as Secretary of War under King William, and had many allies in the colonies.[49] These opposing partisan and ideological views produced starkly different visions of political order and colonial governance: Blathwayt sought to increase the executive power of the Crown, whereas Locke argued for the rule of law, the power of Parliament, and the protection of property rights.[50] Partisan loyalties were also expressed through political appointments, including by defending colonial governors associated with their party, criticizing colonial governors associated with the opposite party, and trying to appoint their friends to prominent posts. Locke was skilled at this wrangling over appointments and arranged for his former Secretary William Popple to become the Board's Secretary; for Blathwayt's associate Benjamin Fletcher to be removed as governor of New York and replaced by the Whig Lord Bellomont; and for Blathwayt's friend Edmund Andros to resign as governor of Virginia and be replaced by Francis Nicholson.[51] Despite their political disagreements, Locke and Blathwayt rarely came into direct conflict during Board meetings because they both attended seasonally and rarely coincided. Locke suffered from respiratory problems that became worse in London during winter, so he only attended Board of Trade meetings in person during summer and autumn. By contrast, Blathwayt's duties as Secretary of War meant that he was usually only present at the Board in winter and spring. This pattern of attendance meant that the balance of power on the Board of Trade shifted seasonally, and that the outcome of a decision could depend on the time of year that it took place.

Locke personally drafted several policy proposals for consideration by the Board and two of these documents have received particular attention from political theorists: his 1697 "Essay on the Poor Law" and 1697–8 "Essay on Virginia." The "Essay on the Poor Law" has been studied for insights about Locke's views on socioeconomic inequality and the rights of the poor, and both C. B. Macpherson and Nancy Hirschmann argue that the essay shows Locke views the poor as less rational and therefore ineligible for full political participation.[52] By contrast, scholars have used the "Essay on Virginia" to help understand Locke's views about topics such as the public good,[53] the separation of powers,[54] and the intended referents of the theory of slavery in the *Two Treatises*.[55] Other proposals that Locke wrote for the Board have been largely neglected by scholars, including an unpublished manuscript about piracy written in 1697. The Board also made decisions about many issues where we have no single document outlining Locke's views, and Locke's stance on these issues can often be identified by consulting his minor writings and Board of Trade records.[56] For example, in 1697 the Board approved the practice of transporting criminal convicts from England to English colonies for sale into forced labor as indentured servants, and Locke's support for this practice can be identified both from his signature on the Board's decision and from his advocacy of convict transportation in the "Essay on Virginia." On many issues, a fuller picture of Locke's political views can therefore be gained by examining his activity and writing on the Board of Trade alongside his other political texts.

LOCKE'S MARITIME POLITICAL THOUGHT

Although there is a huge and wide-ranging body of literature on Locke's political theory, little attention has been paid to Locke's thought about the seas. This inattention to maritime themes in Locke's work is regrettable, because the oceans were central to the politics and colonial expansion of European states during the modern era and this was reflected in theoretical debates about the status of the oceans. For European colonization in the Americas to be legitimate it was necessary to justify the acquisition and control of land, and the prior travel by sea. If all or some of the Atlantic was part of the exclusive property or jurisdiction of Native Americans then they might have the right to exclude Europeans from those waters, in which case European colonists might have acted unlawfully before even reaching the American coast. Alternately, if all or some of the Atlantic was part of the exclusive property or jurisdiction of one European state then they might have had the right to prohibit the citizens of other European states from using those waters. In the early modern period both Spain and Portugal claimed exclusive rights over regions of the Atlantic, arguing that the pope had given Spain exclusive rights to the western Atlantic and Portugal exclusive rights to the eastern Atlantic and to seas east of Africa. If other European states had accepted this Iberian view of maritime law then they would have been excluded from trading or establishing colonies in the Americas, the Caribbean, Africa, and Asia. Instead, several European states challenged the Iberian view of maritime law, and the alternative theories developed by figures such as Grotius have shaped our current understandings of law, property, and statehood. The status of the seas remained important after a colony in the Americas had been established, because the ongoing success of the colony depended on maritime trade, transatlantic migration, and naval defense. In order to provide a theoretical justification for English colonialism and empire it was therefore necessary to establish rights to use the oceans for trade and migration, and rights to engage in self-defense and law enforcement at sea.

This book examines Locke's maritime political thought by providing a broad account of Lockean natural law theory and the seas, followed by detailed analysis of Locke's views about piracy, forced naval service, and the forced transportation and sale of English criminals. In addition to making detailed claims about specific aspects of Locke's political thought, such as slavery, this book makes three overarching arguments that are respectively thematic, conceptual, and methodological. Thematically, the book argues that Locke's political writings contain a systematic political theory of the seas that responds to earlier theories of maritime law and shows how important Lockean concepts such as natural rights apply at sea. My analysis suggests that the innovative theory of property in the *Two Treatises of Government* provides a new theoretical justification for universal rights to unrestricted oceanic travel, trade, and fishing, while Locke's natural law theory prohibits theft, violence, and tyranny at sea. The oceans are also a recurrent theme in Locke's other political writing. The first composition that Locke ever published is a poem celebrating the end of the 1654 Anglo-Dutch naval war, and in it he portrays England as a maritime nation whose merchant shipping has a positive influence on the world:

> Our ships are now most beneficial grown,
> Since they bring home no spoils but what's their own.
> Unto these branchless pines our forward spring
> Owes better fruit than autumn's wont to bring;
> Which gives not only gems and Indian ore,
> But adds at once whole nations to the store:
> Nay, if to make a world's but to compose
> The difference of things, and make them close
> In mutual amity, and cause peace to creep
> Out of the jarring chaos of the deep,
> Our ships do this; so that, whilst others' take
> Their course about the world, ours a world make. [57]

Here, Locke advocates a system of maritime trade based on lawful property ownership and peaceful exchange, but he also presents an expansionist political vision in which English merchant ships are tasked with acquiring foreign nations and turning chaos into peace and order. There is clear continuity between this vision and Locke's arguments in the *Two Treatises,* where he prohibits aggression and the seizure of land through conquest, and argues that English colonization of the Americas should be peaceful, lawful, and bring civilizational benefits to the indigenous people. Locke's enthusiasm for English maritime trade is repeated in his writings on political economy, including the 1674 essay "Trade" and 1693 paper "For a General Naturalisation."[58] Locke's engagement with and contribution to early modern theories of maritime law and international relations deserve wider recognition, and my analysis lends support to David Armitage's call for Locke to be seen as part of the "historical canon of international thought."[59]

This book also seeks to make a conceptual contribution to scholarship in the history of political thought by arguing that Locke's political writing and activity enabled English empire, not just English colonialism. Work by Barbara Arneil, James Tully, Bhikhu Parekh, and others has shown that Locke's involvement in English colonial governance shaped his political theory, and that the *Two Treatises* promoted English colonialism by justifying the farming, appropriation, settlement, and control of land in the Americas.[60] This literature on Locke and colonialism is part of a wider body of scholarship that examines how Western political theorists conceptualized colonialism and empire during the modern period.[61] Although this existing literature has generated many important insights about Locke's work, it has focused on the extension of political power over land while largely ignoring the oceans.[62] By contrast, focusing on Locke's maritime political thought calls attention to a notable difference between colonialism and empire, namely that colonialism centers on control of land whereas empire also involves the exercise of power at sea. The distinction I am drawing here between colonialism and empire involves the type of space that power is extended over, the forms of power that can be exerted there, and the justifications for exerting such power. While the existing scholarly literature shows how Locke contributed to English colonialism by justifying English ownership and sovereignty over American land, this book shows that Locke also enabled English political power at sea by justifying maritime trade, migration, and the deployment of the English navy. Making a conceptual shift from colonialism to empire therefore involves expanding the scope of analysis by examining both land and seas, and paying attention to the different types and justifications of power in these spaces. Considering Locke's political theory about the seas alongside his arguments about land shows that he enabled the extension of English political power through claims about the establishment of private property and sovereignty in some spaces, such as American land,

and through claims about the absence of private property and sovereignty in other spaces, such as the world's oceans. In other words, the conceptual shift from colonialism to empire shows that European imperialism was justified by political theories that strategically claimed ownership and the lack of ownership, exclusive political control and the absence of such control. Like Grotius before him, Locke enabled his state's imperialism by arguing that land could be appropriated and governed, but that the world's oceans could not.

Methodologically, this book seeks to make a minor contribution by suggesting that attention to Locke's writing and activity as a member of the Board of Trade can help us to better understand the intended meaning of passages in the *Two Treatises*. Like earlier history of political thought scholars such as Peter Laslett, Richard Ashcraft, and David Armitage I suggest that contextual information sheds light on the intended meaning and significance of Locke's political writings.[63] However, scholars who engage in contextual analysis of the *Two Treatises* have tended to use information about Locke's life and work before writing the text to understand how he developed the views expressed in the *Two Treatises* and what he intended those arguments to achieve. For example, Arneil and Armitage argue that Locke's involvement in the Carolinas during the 1670s influenced his views about Native Americans and colonialism, thereby shaping his theory of property in the *Two Treatises*.[64] In this book I take a slightly different approach by examining contextual information about Locke's political activity both before and after he wrote and published the *Two Treatises*. I suggest that this inclusive approach enables scholars to gain a more complete picture of Locke's theoretical and practical politics, and of the consistency (or lack thereof) in his views between different texts and over time.[65] Moreover, I argue that analyzing Locke's political work after the *Two Treatises* is particularly helpful for understanding how he may have intended his mature theoretical views to be applied in practice, and for understanding Locke's own political commitments, as opposed to the commitments of those who paid him to perform political work. I will briefly expand on these points below.

Locke's involvement in English politics and colonial governance during the 1660s and 1670s is an important part of the historical context surrounding the *Two Treatises*, but the nature of Locke's political work in that period also creates interpretive problems for scholars. When Locke served as Secretary for the Carolinas his role centered on providing administrative help and advice to the Lords Proprietors, who in turn made the major decisions. Similarly, as Secretary and Treasurer for the Council of Trade and Foreign Plantations Locke provided administrative help to the Council members, but was not formally empowered to participate in the Council's decision-making. Locke also performed political work for the Earl of Shaftesbury, but the records of this work are patchy and it is often difficult to distinguish Locke's own views from those of his employer.[66] If some of the documents that Locke helped to draft during the 1660s and 1670s conflict with his later political writings then the divergence may be explained by the fact that Locke was an employee acting under the instruction of powerful men whose views sometimes differed from his own. Even if Locke's early political work reflected his own views at the time and not the views of his employers, then it is unclear if Locke had yet developed the political views outlined in the *Two Treatises*. Locke's political beliefs were in transition during the 1670s as he shifted away from the support for royal prerogative and non-democratic rule expressed in the *First Tract on Government* and *Second Tract on Government,* and began to develop the Whig views later outlined in the *Second Treatise*. If some of Locke's early political activity and writing seem to be in tension with his arguments in the *Second Treatise* then this may be due to Locke changing his mind in the interim. As a result, Locke's early political and colonial work may prove an unreliable guide to understanding his mature political views.

By contrast, Locke was appointed to the Board of Trade as a member and decision-maker in his own right, which gave him direct and explicit influence over the Board's policy direction. Locke's formal role in policymaking means that it is often possible to identify his personal stances from archival records about his proposals, arguments, and votes on the Board. Moreover, Locke's appointment to the Board of Trade occurred after he had developed his mature political views and recently published the *Two Treatises*. We know that Locke significantly changed his political views in the twenty years preceding the publication of the *Two Treatises,* but it is less likely that his views underwent such a change between publishing the *Two Treatises* in 1690 and serving on the Board from 1696 to 1700. If Locke's political views did significantly change following the initial publication of the *Two Treatises* then one might expect to find evidence of the change in his revisions of the *Two Treatises* for re-publication in 1694 and 1698, but in fact his revisions focused on correcting printers' errors.[67] Overall, there is good reason to expect more consistency between the political views that Locke expresses in the *Two Treatises* and his work on the Board of Trade than between the *Two Treatises* and his administrative political work during the 1670s. Moreover, Locke's role on the Board gave him a chance to translate his political theory into actual policy, so it is an obvious place for scholars to look for insights about how Locke intended his theoretical ideas to be applied in practice. Those seeking to understand Locke's theoretical views on issues such as slavery or colonialism by reference to his political activity might therefore find it productive to examine Board of Trade records, as well as earlier contextual information such as Locke's investments and involvement in the Carolinas colony.

The examination of Locke's maritime political thought in this book is divided into roughly two parts: a broad account of Lockean natural law theory and the seas, followed by detailed analysis of Locke's views about piracy, forced naval service, and the forced transportation and sale of English criminals. Chapter One considers how Locke's theories of property and sovereignty apply to the oceans, and compares his arguments to two influential alternative accounts: the free seas theory presented by Hugo Grotius in *Mare Liberum* and the closed sea theory of John Selden in *Mare Clausum*. This analysis shows that Locke's *Two Treatises* provides a compelling new justification for common ownership of and access to the seas, which enables Locke to justify English maritime trade and empire. Chapter Two extends this analysis by considering Locke's theory of crime and law enforcement at sea, with a focus on the archetypal maritime crime of piracy. I argue that Locke's natural law theory prohibits piracy and justifies the punishment of pirates, and that he also empowers states to pass and enforce laws that prohibit their citizens from engaging in piracy. The first two chapters therefore explain the basics of how the political theory of the *Two Treatises* applies to the oceans, laying the foundation for more detailed analysis of particular issues and for examination of how Locke's theoretical views compared to his work on the Board of Trade.

The second part of the book considers how the account of political theory and the seas in the *Two Treatises* compares to Locke's writing and activity on three maritime policy issues as a member of the Board of Trade. Chapter Three examines Locke's views about the problem of piracy in the 1690s by consulting Locke's unpublished "Pyracy 97" manuscript, his letters, and Board of Trade records. Using these sources, I argue that Locke successfully advocated a new and more severe piracy law for all English jurisdictions, and that he supported English naval expansion to fight pirates. Locke's efforts to suppress piracy were pursued in the name of enforcing law and protecting trade, which is consistent with his arguments in the *Two Treatises*, but I suggest that the piracy policy Locke advocated also contributed to building English empire on land and at sea. Chapters Four and Five then examine examples of how Locke's ideas about freedom and slavery apply at sea. In Chapter Four I use Board of Trade records and Locke's later political writings to show that Locke advocated penal slavery and convict transportation for English criminals, and I suggest that Locke intended the theory of slavery in the *Two Treatises* to justify penal slavery for English convicts. Chapter Five then investigates Locke's views on naval manning, and finds that he supported the selective use of forced naval service in the "Essay on the Poor Law" and as a member of the Board. Despite Locke's theoretical defense of individual freedom in the *Two Treatises*, I argue that on the issue of naval service Locke prioritized English economic interests over the freedom of impressed sailors. It may seem contradictory to proclaim individual rights to freedom and support the practice of forced naval service, but Locke was not alone in doing so and ideological inconsistency over forced naval service was a common and recurrent theme in English politics for much of the next two centuries.[68]

In the course of studying Locke's maritime political thought I have engaged with some of the existing literature about his life and work, but other areas have inevitably been omitted. Locke is justly famous for writing on a huge variety of subjects ranging from natural sciences to religion, education, and the philosophy of mind. Even within the realm of Locke's political thought there is a huge amount of primary material including Locke's published essays, unpublished notes, drafts, letters, and thousands of archival records. Moreover, there is a rich and extensive secondary literature about Locke's political thought by scholars from a range of academic disciplines. No single book could do justice to this wealth of primary and secondary material, so I have had to be selective. Where a primary or secondary text has little or no direct bearing on Locke's political thought about the oceans I have usually taken the view that it falls outside the scope of this book, and as a result many important ideas are either omitted or mentioned only briefly. For example, in Chapter One I discuss how the theory of property in the *Two Treatises* applies to the oceans, but I do not delve into the extensive scholarly debates about how this theory applies to land and goods, or the debates about the merits of this theory of property. At various points in the book I examine particular aspects of Locke's arguments in the *Two Treatises*, and in each case the intent is to elucidate Locke's political theory about the oceans and not to fundamentally re-interpret these passages or ideas. In short, this book does not aim to provide a new reading of Locke's political thought about a well-established subject such as property or religious toleration; instead it seeks to outline and then examine the previously neglected area of Locke's political thought about the oceans.

Lastly, a brief note about language. When quoting archival sources I have chosen to preserve the character and style of the text by retaining the original spelling and grammar. This decision to use the original form of expression means that readers may notice some stylistic oddities, such as inconsistency in how Locke and the Board of Trade spell the word "piracy." A more substantive stylistic question arises over gendered language. In his political writing Locke often refers to "man" or "mankind," and scholars have debated whether the people described by these terms are all male or if women are also included.[69] The meaning of these terms depends on the passages where they are used, but in relation to Locke's maritime political thought I have generally assumed that "man" and "mankind" refer to all human beings. For example, I interpret Locke's description of the oceans as a "Common of Mankind"[70] as a statement that the oceans are commonly owned by all humans, regardless of gender. I have echoed this interpretation in my own use of the terms "man" and "mankind" to refer to all human beings. On the occasions when the gender of a person or persons is particularly important to either my reading of Locke or my analysis then their gender is stated explicitly, as occurs in the discussion of female convicts in Chapter Four.

NOTES

1. Bradley P. Nutting, "The Madagascar Connection: Parliament & Piracy, 1690–1709," *American Journal of Legal History* 22, no. 3 (1978): 205; Robert C. Ritchie, *Captain Kidd and the War Against the Pirates* (Cambridge, MA: Harvard University Press, 1986), 88–9; Mark G. Hanna, *Pirate Nests and the Rise of the British Empire, 1570–1740* (Chapel Hill: University of North Carolina Press, 2015), 189.

2. The present-day monetary value of the treasure was calculated using the economic history website https://www.measuringworth.com/ukcompare/relativevalue.php.

3. Ritchie, *Captain Kidd*, 89.

4. In 1700 the mean annual pay for common seamen has been estimated at no more than sixteen pounds per year, but pay was higher in wartime, see Marcus Rediker, *Between the Devil and the Deep Blue Sea: Merchant Seamen, Pirates and the Anglo-American Maritime World* (New York: Cambridge University Press, 1987), 304.

5. Hanna, *Pirate Nests,* 189.

6. For a more detailed account of the events see Nutting, "Madagascar Connection," 205–6 and Philip Stern, *The Company State: Corporate Sovereignty and the Early Modern Foundations of the British Empire in India* (New York: Oxford University Press, 2011), 134–41.

7. John Locke, *Two Treatises of Government,* ed. Peter Laslett (Cambridge: Cambridge University Press, 1988), II §30 289.

8. See H. R. Fox Bourne, *The Life of John Locke*, Volume 1 (New York: Harper and Brothers Publishers, 1876), 196 and Maurice Cranston, *John Locke: A Biography* (London: Longmans, Green & Co Ltd, 1968), 111–4.

9. Cranston, *John Locke,* 119; Barbara Arneil, *John Locke and America: The Defence of English Colonialism* (New York: Oxford University Press, 1996), 118–30.

10. John Locke and others, "The Fundamental Constitutions of Carolina" in *Locke: Political Essays*, John Locke and ed. Mark Goldie (Cambridge: Cambridge University Press, 1997), 163 and 180.

11. Locke, *Two Treatises*, II §132 354.

12. David Armitage, "John Locke, Carolina, and the *Two Treatises of Government,*" *Political Theory* 32, no. 5 (2004): 613–5.

13. Barbara Arneil, *John Locke and America*, 122–6; Armitage, "John Locke, Carolina," 602–27.

14. Arneil, *John Locke and America*, 121–30; Brad Hinshelwood, "The Carolinian Context of Locke's Theory of Slavery," *Political Theory* 41, no. 4 (2013): 562–90; Vicki Hsueh, "Cultivating and Challenging the Common: Lockean Property, Indigenous Traditionalisms, and the Problem of Exclusion," *Contemporary Political Theory* 5, no. 2 (2006): 193–214.

15. James Farr, "Locke, 'Some Americans,' and the Discourse on 'Carolina,'" *Locke Studies* 9 (2009), available at http://www.lockestudies.org/wp-content/uploads/2013/10/FarrLS9.pdf; Hinshelwood, "Carolinian Context."

16. Cranston, *John Locke,* 146.

17. *Ibid*, 145–6.

18. Ralph Paul Bieber, "The British Plantation Councils of 1670–4," *The English Historical Review* 40, no. 157 (1925): 93–106; Cranston, *John Locke,* 155.

19. Great Britain Public Record Office (GBPRO), *Calendar of State Papers Colonial: America and West Indies, Volume 7, 1669–1674*, ed. W. Noel Sainsbury (London, 1889), 540, 552, and 572–3.

20. *Ibid*, 537–8.

21. In December 1673 the Council advised the new governor of Barbados to exercise religious toleration in the colony, but to practice the authorized Protestant religion in his own home, see *Ibid*, 542.

22. The Council's advice to the government about how to recapture New York is signed by Locke in the margin, see *Ibid*, 530–1.

23. John Locke, "Trade" in *Locke: Political Essays*, 221–2.

24. Locke, *Two Treatises*, II §48 301.

25. *Ibid*, II §43 298.

26. Cranston, *John Locke,* 155.

27. See Wayne Glausser, "Three Approaches to Locke and the Slave Trade," *Journal of the History of Ideas* 51, no. 2 (1990): 200–2; David Armitage, "John Locke: Theorist of Empire?" in *Empire and Modern Political Thought,* ed. Sankar Muthu (Cambridge: Cambridge University Press, 2012), 89.

28. Locke, *Two Treatises of Government*, II §23 284.

29. In addition to Locke's involvement in the Carolinas, there is abundant evidence of racialized slavery in the records he used as Secretary of the Council of Trade and Foreign Plantations, which had jurisdiction over England's Caribbean slave colonies. The correspondence received by the Council during Locke's appointment includes a list specifying that seventeen Royal African Company ships carrying over five thousand black slaves had arrived in Jamaica, Barbados, Virginia, and the island of Nevis by January 1674, see GBPRO, *Calendar of State Papers Colonial,* vol. 7, 552. It was part of Locke's job description to record the letters received by the Council, and this document would have left him in no doubt about the scale of slave trading by the Royal African Company or about the reliance on slave labor in these colonies.

30. See Locke, *Two Treatises*, II §24 284–5 n; Jennifer Welchman, "Locke on Slavery and Inalienable Rights," *Canadian Journal of Philosophy* 25, no. 1 (1995): 67–81.

31. James Farr, "'So Vile and Miserable an Estate': The Problem of Slavery in Locke's Political Thought," *Political Theory* 14, no. 2 (1986): 263–9; James Farr, "Locke, Natural Law, and New World Slavery," *Political Theory* 36, no. 4 (2008): 495–522.

32. John Dunn, *The Political Thought of John Locke: An Historical Account of the Argument of the 'Two Treatises of Government'* (Cambridge: Cambridge University Press, 1969), 174–5.

33. Many history of political thought scholars have drawn a distinction between ethnocentric views that portray some cultures and societies as inferior to others, and racist views that portray some individuals as innately inferior to others. For example, James Tully, Bhikhu Parekh, Barbara Arneil, and Bruce Buchan argue that Locke's theories of property and sovereignty are Eurocentric and culturally biased against indigenous peoples. However, Arneil, Parekh, and Armitage argue that Locke was not racist against indigenous peoples because he did not view indigenous individuals as innately irrational or inferior to Europeans. Such a distinction between ethnocentrism and racism is common but not uniformly accepted, and Charles Mills argues that Locke's condemnation of non-European ways of life suggests that he saw non-Europeans as less rational and was therefore implicitly racist. See James Tully, *An Approach to Political Philosophy: Locke in Contexts* (Cambridge and New York: Cambridge University Press, 1993), 137–76; Bhikhu Parekh, "Liberalism and Colonialism: A Critique of Locke and Mill" in *Decolonization of Imagination*, eds. J. Nederveen Pieterse and B. Parekh (London, UK: Zed Books, 1995), 81–98; Arneil, *John Locke and America;* Bruce Buchan, "The Empire of Political Thought: Civilization, Savagery and Perceptions of Indigenous Government," *History of the Human Sciences* 18, no. 2 (2005): 1–22; Armitage, "Locke: Theorist of Empire"; Charles Mills, *The Racial Contract* (Ithaca: Cornell University Press, 1997), 67–8.

34. Bieber, "British Plantation Councils," 94–5; Cranston, *Locke: A Biography,* 153–5.

35. For Locke's involvement in Whig politics in the 1670s and early 1680s see Richard Ashcraft, *Revolutionary Politics and Locke's Two Treatises of Government* (Princeton, NJ: Princeton University Press, 1986).

36. Cranston, *Locke: A Biography,* 167.

37. Ashcraft, *Revolutionary Politics,* 327.

38. *Ibid*, 344–405.

39. On the composition date of the *Two Treatises*, see J. R. Milton, "Dating Locke's *Second Treatise*," *History of Political Thought* 16, no. 3 (1995): 356–90; Richard Tuck, *The Rights of War and Peace: Political Thought and the International Order from Grotius to Kant* (Oxford: Oxford University Press, 1999) 168; Armitage, "John Locke, Carolina."

40. Cranston, *Locke: A Biography*, 223–4.

41. Ashcraft, *Revolutionary Politics*, 403–5; Cranston, *Locke: A Biography*, 227–8.

42. Ashcraft, *Revolutionary Politics*, 406–11.

43. On Locke's friendships in Holland, see *Ibid*, 554–5.

44. Cranston, *Locke: A Biography*, 306–11.

45. *Ibid*, 312–3; David Armitage, "John Locke's International Thought" in *British International Thinkers from Hobbes to Namier*, eds. Ian Hall and Lisa Hill (New York, NY: Palgrave Macmillan, 2009), 34.

46. Patrick Hyde Kelly, ed., *Locke on Money, Volume 1* (Oxford, UK: Clarendon Press, 1991) and John Locke; Patrick Hyde Kelly, ed., *Locke on Money, Volume 2* (Oxford, UK: Clarendon Press, 1991).

47. See Peter Laslett, "John Locke, the Great Recoinage, and the Origins of the Board of Trade: 1695–1698," *The William and Mary Quarterly* 14, no. 3 (1957): 370–402.

48. GBPRO, *Calendar of State Papers Colonial: America and West Indies, Volume 15, 1696–1697*, ed. J. W. Fortescue (London, 1904), 1. Although promoting English trade and overseeing the colonies were the Board's primary duties, the Board's May 1696 commission from the King also lists additional duties such as developing plans for the employment of the poor in England and investigating England's fisheries, see CO 391/9, 1–6.

49. Stephen Saunders Webb, "William Blathwayt, Imperial Fixer: Muddling Through to Empire, 1689–1717," *The William and Mary Quarterly* 26, no. 3 (July 1969): 373–415.

50. *Ibid*, 398.

51. The removal of Fletcher is discussed in Chapter Three, and the removal of Edmund Andros in Chapter Four. Also see Webb, "William Blathwayt," 398.

52. See C. B. Macpherson, *The Political Theory of Possessive Individualism: Hobbes to Locke* (Don Mills, ON: Oxford University Press, 2011); Nancy J. Hirschmann, "Liberal Conservativism, Once and Again: Locke's 'Essay on the Poor Law' and Contemporary US Welfare Reform," *Constellations* 9, no. 3 (2002): 335–55.

53. Richard Ashcraft, "Political Theory and Political Reform: John Locke's Essay on Virginia," *Political Research Quarterly* 22 (1969): 742–58.

54. Alex Tuckness, "John Locke and Public Administration," *Administration and Society* 40, no. 3 (2008): 253–70.

55. Holly Brewer, "Slavery, Sovereignty, and 'Inheritable Blood': The Struggle over Locke's Virginia Plan of 1698 in the Wake of the Glorious Revolution" (unpublished working paper).

56. The business of the Board of Trade was recorded in a Journal that noted the attendees, discussion, and decisions at each meeting, and in collections of the correspondence that the Board received and sent. A quorum of Board members had to be present for formal decisions to be made, and the Board's records identified which members had approved that decision. If there was serious disagreement among Board members then they would fail to make a decision on an issue, defer the decision until a day when the dissenting members were not present, or the dissenting individual(s) could refuse to sign the recommendation approved by the others. For example, in the autumn of 1697 disagreement between the Board over the issue of poor law reform led to the Board deferring a decision until Locke left London for the winter, at which point the other Board members rejected his scheme, as I discuss in Chapter Four. Similarly, in 1698 Blathwayt demonstrated his disagreement with the Board's report on Virginia (of which Locke was the prime mover) by refusing to sign it, see Laslett, "John Locke, the Great Recoinage," 400; and Brewer, "Slavery, Sovereignty," 17.

57. John Locke, "Verses on the Dutch War" in *Locke: Political Essays*, 201–2. The poem was originally published in *Musarum Oxoniensium Helaiophoria* (Oxford, 1654), 94–5.

58. John Locke "Trade," 221–2; John Locke, "For a General Naturalisation" in *Locke: Political Essays*, 323–4.

59. Armitage, "John Locke's International Thought," 45.

60. See Arneil, *John Locke and America;* Tully, *Approach to Political Philosophy,* 137–76; and Parekh, "Liberalism and Colonialism." Many subsequent scholars have made related arguments about colonialism and Locke's political thought including Duncan Ivison, "Locke, Liberalism and Empire," in *The Philosophy of John Locke: New Perspectives,* ed. P. Anstey (London and New York: Routledge, 2003), 86–105; Armitage, "John Locke, Carolina"; and Buchan, "Empire of Political Thought."

61. On empire and colonialism in the history of Western political thought see Mills, *Racial Contract;* Uday Singh Mehta, *Liberalism and Empire: A Study in Nineteenth Century British Liberal Thought* (Chicago and London: University of Chicago Press, 1999); Sankar Muthu, *Enlightenment Against Empire* (Princeton, NJ: Princeton University Press, 2003); Jeanne Morefield, *Covenants Without Swords: Idealist Liberalism and the Spirit of Empire* (Princeton, NJ: Princeton University Press, 2005); Jennifer Pitts, *A Turn to Empire: The Rise of Liberal Imperialism in Britain and France* (Princeton and Oxford: Princeton University Press, 2005); Margaret Kohn and Daniel I. O'Neill, "A Tale of Two Indias: Burke and Mill on Empire and Slavery in the West Indies and America," *Political Theory* 34, no. 2 (2006): 192–228; Duncan Bell, *The Idea of Greater Britain: Empire and the Future of World Order, 1860–1900* (Princeton, NJ: Princeton University Press, 2007); Daniel I. O'Neill, "Rethinking Burke and India," *History of Political Thought* 30, no. 3 (2009): 492–52; Sankar Muthu, ed., *Empire and Modern Political Thought* (Cambridge: Cambridge University Press, 2012).

62. A rare discussion of the significance of the oceans in political theory is provided in Jonathan Scott, "Maritime Orientalism, of the Political Theory of Water," *History of Political Thought* 35, no. 1 (2014): 70–90.

63. Peter Laslett, "Introduction," in Locke, *Two Treatises,* 3–126; Ashcraft, *Revolutionary Politics;* Armitage, "John Locke: Theorist of Empire."

64. Arneil, *John Locke and America*; Armitage, "John Locke, Carolina."

65. At times Ashcraft also consults Locke's Board of Trade writing for indications of how he may have intended ideas in the *Two Treatises* to be applied, for example the discussion of the "Essay on Virginia" in Ashcraft, "Political Theory and Political Reform."

66. See Laslett, "Introduction," in Locke, *Two Treatises,* 29–31.

67. *Ibid,* 8–9.

68. See Nicholas Rogers, *The Press Gang: Naval Impressment and Its Opponents in Georgian Britain* (London and New York: Continuum Books, 2007); Denver Brunsman, *The Evil Necessity: British Naval Impressment in the Eighteenth-Century Atlantic World* (University of Virginia Press: Charlottesville and London, 2013).

69. See Carole Pateman, *The Sexual Contract* (Stanford, CA: Stanford University Press, 1988); Nancy J. Hirschmann and Kirstie M. McClure, eds., *Feminist Interpretations of John Locke* (University Park, PA: Pennsylvania State University Press, 2007); Torrey Shanks, *Authority Figures: Rhetoric and Experience in John Locke's Political Thought* (University Park, PA: Pennsylvania State University Press, 2014).

70. Locke, *Two Treatises,* II §30 289.

Chapter One

Who Owns the Oceans?

Locke's Theory of Property at Sea

In recent years a growing body of literature has developed about colonialism in Locke's political thought.[1] This scholarship shows how the *Two Treatises* provide a theoretical justification for the acquisition and control of land in the Americas, thereby legitimizing the territorial component of English imperialism. However, this literature largely overlooks Locke's views about another major component of English imperialism: the exercise of power at sea.[2] The oceans were a crucial and contested space in the early modern period, because European colonization of the Americas depended on ships using trade winds to sail across the Atlantic.[3] The success and expansion of European colonies then required the ongoing circulation of people, goods, capital, and ideas by sea.[4] Throughout the seventeenth and eighteenth centuries Europeans crossed the Atlantic to become settlers, Africans were carried across the Atlantic to become slave laborers, European manufactures were exported to colonial markets, and colonial products such as tobacco and sugar were shipped to Europe. This circulation was achieved by fleets of merchant and navy ships manned by a large maritime labor force of professional sailors. Conflict between European empires also occurred at sea, including through disputes between merchants, privateer and pirate raids, and naval warfare. From the fifteenth century onward, European political power in the Americas was both a territorial and maritime project that relied (to varying degrees) on navies and merchant ships as well as the acquisition and control of land.

Since European colonies in the Americas required both initial and ongoing use of the oceans, a theoretical justification was needed for oceanic travel, and this led to a "battle of the books" between competing conceptions

1

of maritime law. The central issue in early modern debates over maritime law is the right to use the world's oceans, and this turns on theories of property and state jurisdiction at sea. Simply put, who owns the oceans and who or what governs them? If oceans are privately owned then the owners may be entitled to restrict use of the ocean by others, for example by prohibiting travel through a given area. On the other hand, if oceans belong to all people collectively then all may be entitled to use them, but this raises questions about the ownership of extractable marine resources such as fish. Legitimate use of the oceans also turns on issues of state jurisdiction. If oceans are part of exclusive state jurisdiction then they can be regulated by national law, but if oceans are not part of exclusive state jurisdiction then what laws apply there? If no law existed at sea then there would be no prohibition of theft and violence, such as piracy. Alternately, if natural law applies at sea then what acts does it allow or prohibit, and how will it be enforced? As I will show, Locke's *Two Treatises* provides answers to these questions. In this chapter I examine Locke's conceptions of property and state jurisdiction on the oceans. In the next chapter I consider what activities are allowed or prohibited at sea under Locke's conception of natural law and discuss the enforcement of natural law at sea, with particular attention to the issue of piracy.

Understanding how the *Two Treatises* contributes to theories of natural law at sea requires attention both to what Locke argues and to how his theories diverge from earlier accounts of natural law and the seas. To show the distinctiveness of Locke's contribution to these debates I compare his arguments to two other influential theories of maritime law: Hugo Grotius's *Mare Liberum* and John Selden's *Mare Clausum*. As a proponent of free seas, Grotius argued that the oceans could not be owned by individuals or become part of the exclusive jurisdiction of a state and were therefore available to all for travel and fishing. In opposition, John Selden argued that states could establish exclusive ownership and jurisdiction over regions of seas and therefore had the right to exclude others from trading or fishing in those waters. Locke was familiar with the work of Grotius and Selden, so he responds to and cites their arguments in the *Two Treatises*. Locke shares Grotius's view that the seas are the common property of all humans, are governed by natural law, and are not part of the exclusive jurisdiction of a state, but he disagrees with Grotius's reasoning for these positions. Grotius argues that the oceans remained common property because private property was established through occupation and oceans had not been and could not be occupied, but Selden counters that oceans can be occupied and that many areas had been occupied and were therefore privately owned. Selden's challenge to Grotius had proved that the free seas perspective did not have an unshakeable theoretical foundation. In the *Two Treatises* Locke adds to this debate by providing a new justification for free seas through his innovative theory of property, and thereby contributes to theories of maritime law.

CLOSED OR OPEN SEAS

As Europeans began to establish colonies and trading relationships in other continents the seas became a contentious area of legal and political thought. Beginning in the late fifteenth century the Spanish and Portuguese authorities argued that papal grants had given them exclusive rights over regions of ocean and over non-European lands. In 1452 the Pope issued the first of a series of bulls granting Spain and Portugal sole rights to explore distant, non-Christian lands, claim the lands, and convert the occupants. To clearly distinguish the regions explored by each state, papal bulls in 1493 established a north-south Line of Demarcation in the Atlantic that ran a hundred leagues west of the Cape Verde Islands.[5] Spain was given rights to explore lands and seas west of this line, which encompassed most of the Americas, while Portugal was given the rights to lands and seas east of the line, which included Africa and Asia. The principle of a Line of Demarcation was confirmed the following year in the Treaty of Tordesillas between Spain and Portugal. In the Treaty, Portugal and Spain divided the Atlantic Ocean between them, claimed exclusive powers over their own region, and agreed that their ships would be prohibited from entering each other's region of the ocean except in order to reach their own possessions. Spanish ships were therefore entitled to sail through the eastern Atlantic in order to reach lands in the Americas, but were not entitled to explore or claim non-Christian lands west of the line. This Iberian closed seas perspective was soon challenged by other European states. By the mid sixteenth century the English and Dutch had established trade routes to Asia that lay within the area claimed by Portugal,[6] and in the 1580s the English began to challenge Spanish claims in the Americas. Under Elizabeth I England contested the Spanish claim to exclusive jurisdiction over the western Atlantic by arguing that the seas were not part of the jurisdiction of any state and were therefore free for all to navigate, and by supporting the creation of English colonies.[7] In March 1584 Elizabeth I granted Sir Walter Raleigh a patent to discover, acquire, and occupy lands in North America.[8] To build support for this enterprise, Raleigh asked Richard Hakluyt to write a justification of English colonialism in the Americas. Hakluyt's *Discourse of Western Planting* was presented to the Queen in October 1584, and it argues that English colonies in North America would provide a new source of import goods,[9] expand English exports,[10] solve domestic overpopulation and unemployment,[11] and achieve glory by converting savages to Protestantism and civilization.[12] The following year Raleigh dispatched seven ships to establish the colony, and they built a fort on Roanoke Island.[13] Raleigh also funded numerous privateer voyages, some of which combined raids on Spanish ships with attempts to found English settlements.[14]

While the Dutch authorities advocated free seas for much of the seventeenth century, the English stance on maritime law fluctuated depending on
the ruler's views about economics, foreign policy, and the nature of political
authority. Although England had advocated free seas under Elizabeth I, the
Stuart Kings took a closed seas perspective in relation to the waters surrounding the British Isles. In keeping with earlier Stuart policy in Scotland,
James I and his successors proclaimed exclusive English jurisdiction over
neighboring seas and ownership of local fishing grounds,[15] and they asked
the lawyer John Selden to defend this view in *Mare Clausum*.[16] After the
Glorious Revolution, the English government under William and Mary returned to advocating free seas and the expansion of international trade, which
paved the way for the eighteenth century British maritime empire.[17] Locke's
account of natural law at sea in the *Two Treatises* accords with these policies
of free seas, the promotion of maritime trade, and colonial expansion. This
correspondence between Locke's maritime political thought and English
government policies in the 1690s is not surprising given that Locke had a
good relationship with King William and was closely involved in England's
colonial and trade policy as a leading member of the Board of Trade.

The most famous justification of Dutch maritime activity is Grotius's
Mare Liberum, which was written to defend the seizure of a Portuguese ship.
In 1602 a Dutch East India Company vessel captained by Grotius's cousin
Jacob Van Heemskerck captured the Portuguese ship *Santa Catarina* in the
straights of Malacca and took it back to Amsterdam.[18] Van Heemskerck
argued that the seizure of the *Santa Catarina* was justified because the Portuguese had violently and unlawfully tried to prevent Dutch ships from trading
in the East Indies.[19] Seizures of foreign ships were sometimes legal under the
rules of privateering and reprisal, but many investors in the Dutch East India
Company (the Vereenigde Oost-Indische Compagnie, or VOC) criticized the
capture of the *Santa Catarina*.[20] If Van Heemskerck and his supporters could
persuade the Dutch authorities that their seizure of the *Santa Catarina* was
lawful then they could keep the ship and its cargo of silk, porcelain, and
bullion, worth three million guilders;[21] if not, they must relinquish the ship
and its contents. The potential gain was immense, but the VOC needed to
make a persuasive case that Portuguese actions in the East Indies were unlawful and hence that reprisals against the Portuguese were justified. In 1604
the Amsterdam Admiralty Board ruled that the ship was a lawful prize, but
the logic of their ruling was confusing,[22] so the VOC directors asked Grotius
to provide a clear justification for the *Santa Catarina*'s capture.[23]

Grotius's central argument is summarized in the full title of his work,
which translates as *The Freedom of the Seas, or the Right which belongs to
the Dutch to take part in the East Indian trade.* Grotius begins by arguing
that God created natural laws that underlie the authority of statute law,[24] and
that dictate the laws of the sea.[25] Next, Grotius outlines the status of colonial-

ism under natural law by arguing that ownership and sovereignty of land can be lawfully acquired by discovery, but only when the discovered land is initially unowned (*res nullius*),[26] and is then actually possessed and defended by the entity claiming to discover it. Since lands in the East Indies have their own rulers and laws, Grotius reasons that they are not *res nullius,* cannot be acquired by discovery, and thus the Portuguese are not owners or sovereigns of those lands.[27] While Grotius acknowledges the existence of papal bulls granting Portuguese jurisdiction in the East Indies, he argues that the pope lacks authority over temporal affairs and non-Christians so he "did not have the power"[28] to grant sovereignty or exclusive trading rights.

Grotius then turns to natural law about property. Here, he argues that all property was originally held in common, but that most property in land and goods became privately owned through possession: "Possession of movables implies seizure, and possession of immovables requires either the erection of buildings or some determination of boundaries, such as fencing in."[29] Since Grotius maintains that public ownership and sovereignty originate from the same basis as private ownership by individuals,[30] it follows that unoccupied and unbounded areas are not part of the jurisdiction of any state.[31] Grotius then applies this theory of property to the seas, and concludes that seas are "the common property of all and the private property of none."[32] Grotius presents two arguments to justify this account of the seas as a common outside state jurisdiction. Firstly, he contends that the seas are a space of navigation that cannot be occupied and thus cannot be privately owned: "that which cannot be occupied . . . cannot be the property of any one, because all property has arisen from occupation."[33] While the occupation of land turns common property into private property that becomes part of state jurisdiction, Grotius argues that the uninhabitable nature of the seas makes them incapable of possession by an individual or state. Secondly, Grotius develops a conception of non-rivalrous resources, which he explains as those that "although serving some one person it still suffices for the common use of all other persons."[34] Grotius argues that non-rivalrous resources cannot be privately owned, and that the seas are in this category because they are "adapted to the use of all, whether we consider it from the point of view of navigation or of fisheries."[35] To prevent any uncertainty about his conclusions, Grotius summarizes: "the sea is one of the things . . . which cannot become private property . . . no part of the sea can be considered as the territory of any people whatsoever."[36] Following from this, Grotius reasons that states have no right to impose their laws on foreigners who travel or fish in neighboring waters,[37] and that pirates are punished by "the common right which other free peoples also enjoy on the sea."[38]

Since the Portuguese do not own or have sovereignty over lands in the East Indies, do not rule the oceans, and are not harmed by the trading activity of Dutch ships, Grotius regards the Portuguese attempts to exclude Dutch ships from trading in the East Indies as "most outrageous."[39] If the seas are common property and free to all for navigation, as Grotius maintains, then Portuguese efforts to exclude non-Portuguese ships from any area of the oceans are unlawful. Further, Grotius argues that natural law includes a "freedom of trade"[40] that is also violated by Portuguese interference with Dutch traders in the East Indies. Given these violations of natural law Grotius believes that courts should rule against the Portuguese, but he argues that if justice cannot be promptly obtained from an independent judge then individuals have the right to enforce the law of nature by punishing offenders.[41] By impeding Dutch navigation and trade in the East Indies the Portuguese are breaking natural law, so Grotius maintains that reprisals against the Portuguese constitute a legal form of punishment, thereby justifying van Heemskerck's capture of the *Santa Catarina*. Grotius's argument that the world's seas are open to all under natural law therefore serves to legitimate both Dutch trade in the East Indies and punitive violence against those who seek to prevent free travel across the world's oceans.

Initially Grotius's arguments were only circulated among the VOC, but in 1607 Spanish negotiators for the truce of Antwerp asked the Dutch to relinquish their right to trade in the East Indies. Alarmed by this request, the VOC asked Grotius to publish the parts of his brief justifying the freedom of the seas, which appeared in 1609 as *Mare Liberum.*[42] Most of the central principles of *Mare Liberum* are also reiterated in Grotius's wider theory of international law, *De Jure Belli ac Pacis*, which was published in 1625.[43] Here, Grotius repeats that "the sea, either as a whole or in its principal divisions, cannot become subject to private ownership"[44] because it is unlimited and a non-rivalrous resource.[45] Again Grotius argues that there is a right of trade that means "no one . . . has the right to hinder any nation from carrying on commerce with any other nation at a distance."[46] If these laws of nature justifying international trade and free travel at sea are broken then Grotius advocates punishment of the offenders and argues that the victims can justifiably seek reparations for the harms they suffered. As in *Mare Liberum*, Grotius maintains that justice should be obtained from courts where possible, but that "in places where there are no courts, as, for example, on the sea" individuals have the right to enforce natural law by punishing offenders such as pirates.[47]

The free seas arguments that Grotius presented in *Mare Liberum* and *De Jure Belli ac Pacis* were soon read outside of the Dutch Republic, and provoked opposition in England. Under James I the English and Scottish Crown favored "a stringent version of maritime protectionism" that claimed ownership and state jurisdiction over the seas surrounding England and Scotland,[48] including the right to regulate and tax the large Dutch fishing fleet that operated each year off these coasts.[49] This policy was opposed by the Dutch and in direct contravention of the arguments expressed in *Mare Liberum,* so

James I sought a legal justification for his position. In 1619 James I asked the prominent lawyer John Selden to provide this justification and Selden promptly produced *Mare Clausum,* which rejected Grotius's free seas arguments and argued that the British Crown had exclusive rights to the seas around the British coastline. Although *Mare Clausum* was written in 1619 it was not published until 1635,[50] when Charles I persuaded Selden to revise it in support of his claim to ownership and jurisdiction over the North Sea.

In *Mare Clausum* Selden makes two central arguments: "That the Sea, by the Law of Nature or Nations, is not common to allmen, but capable of private Dominion or proprietie as well as the Land; *The other*, that the King of *Great Britain* is Lord of the Sea flowing about, as an inseperable and perpetual Appendant of the British Empire."[51] In Book 1 Selden seeks to establish that seas can be privately owned, including by providing a detailed rebuttal of Grotius's arguments in *Mare Liberum*. Selden begins by dividing property into two types: property held in common by all, and property that is privately owned by particular individuals or states who have the right to exclude others.[52] To determine how land, seas, animals, and goods were originally owned, Selden refers to the biblical grants of dominion in *Genesis*. Selden argues that in *Genesis 1:28* God gave Adam an exclusive property right over the world so that he became "Lord of the whole World, not without such a peculiar possession or proprietie to himself."[53] By contrast, Selden interprets the later grant of dominion in *Genesis 9:2* as establishing communal ownership between Noah and his sons,[54] which he takes as evidence that God gave the world to all men in common. To explain how this common property became privately owned Selden argues that after the flood mankind agreed to relinquish their rights to common ownership through "consent of the whole bodie or universalitie of mankinde (by the mediation of somthing like a compact, which might binde their posteritie)."[55] Common ownership of an area was then replaced by private ownership, and vacant land became open to appropriation by the first occupier.[56] In support of this argument that common land was abolished through consent and that vacant land can therefore be acquired through occupation, Selden quotes Grotius's arguments about common property in *De Jure Belli ac Pacis*.[57]

Selden then provides a detailed rejection of Grotius's argument that the seas cannot be privately owned. Whereas Grotius argues that seas cannot be privately appropriated, Selden counters that ownership at sea is established in the same way as on land: vacant areas were appropriated by the first occupier.[58] Ownership of an area of seas is therefore determined by first occupation, which establishes a right of use by the owner, a right to prohibit or permit use by others, and prohibits use without the owner's permission.[59] Whereas Grotius describes the seas as "so limitless,"[60] Selden retorts that "every Sea hath its Bounds on the Shore"[61] and that areas of the seas are distinguished by landmarks such as islands, and by lines of latitude and longitude.[62] Selden therefore maintains that the oceans are finite and that boundaries can be identified at sea as they are on land. Next, Selden challenges Grotius's argument that the seas cannot be privately owned because they are non-rivalrous. First, Selden observes that other non-rivalrous goods can be owned and that the fact that one "can receiv no dammage by other men's using it" is not seen as inconsistent with private ownership of candles or fires, which provide light and ignition to others without reducing their value to the owner.[63] Secondly, Selden argues that seas are not truly non-rivalrous because valuable marine resources such as fish, pearls, and coral become exhausted by over-exploitation and thus "wee often see, that the Sea it self, by reason of other men's Fishing, Navigation, and Commerce, becom's the wors for him that own's it."[64] Selden therefore rejects Grotius's characterization of the ocean as non-rivalrous due to Grotius's inaccurate assumptions about the plenitude of fish and other marine resources, but maintains that even if the ocean were non-rivalrous then this would not establish that it could not be privately owned.

In Book 2 Selden turns to the issue of state ownership and argues that "the Kings of Great Britain have had a peculiar Dominion or propiertie over the Sea flowing about it."[65] Here, Selden states that ownership of a region of seas is established by asserting exclusive authority through imposing laws, providing defense, admitting or excluding other ships, and using the marine resources:

> Arguments are not to bee derived altogether from a bare Occupation or Dominion of Countries, whose shores are washed by the Sea: But from such a private or peculiar use or enjoiment of the Sea, as consist's in a setting forth Ships to Sea, either to defend or make good the Dominion; in prescribing Rules of Navigation to such as pass through it; in receiving such Profits and Commodities as are peculiar to every kinde of Sea-Dominion whatsoever; and, which is the principal, either in admitting or excluding others at pleasure.[66]

Selden's criteria for state ownership of the seas combine features of private property ownership and powers associated with sovereignty. Based on these criteria, Selden argues that British rulers have historically owned and continue to own the seas on all British coasts, including the English Channel, North Sea, Irish Sea, and the eastern edge of the Atlantic. By asserting British ownership of these waters and the right to exclude others from sailing and fishing there Selden challenges both Grotius's free seas principles and the Dutch practice of fishing in the North Sea without authorization from the British Crown.

Although Selden's primary concern is British control of her coastal waters he briefly mentions English possessions in the Americas at the end of *Mare Clausum.*[67] Here, Selden claims that the English Crown owns a vast area of land and seas in North America because the English colony in St.

John established dominion over "the whole Sea as well as Land on every side, for the space of six hundred miles."[68] Selden seems aware that this assertion of ownership in the Americas is inconsistent with his earlier conditions for possession of the seas, such as excluding other ships and enforcing laws, because he introduces a new basis for ownership. While Selden earlier stipulated that one can only own the area that one occupies, he now argues that possession of an area by right of discovery does not require current occupation of the entire area but merely occupation of some part with an intent to occupy the rest.[69] Selden thereby maintains that the combination of a small English port in North America and an intent to occupy a larger area establish exclusive English ownership and jurisdiction across an area of land and seas spanning over a thousand miles. Whereas Selden provides extensive theoretical and empirical justification for British claims to seas around the British Isles he gives no empirical evidence and little theoretical justification for his claim of English dominion in North America. This discussion of English colonialism in the Americas therefore reads as a brief and underdeveloped afterthought to Selden's main thesis about British control of her coastal waters. For Selden and his royal sponsors defending the right to engage in transatlantic trade and colonialism was less important than establishing British control of waters and fishing grounds in Northern Europe.

Grotius and Selden both argue that God created a natural law that extends over the entire world, that all land and seas were at one point commonly owned, that common ownership of land was later replaced by private ownership, and that privatization of formerly common land was established through occupation. Where Grotius and Selden disagree is over the status of the oceans after the beginning of private ownership of land. Grotius argues that areas owned in common can only become privately owned if they are bounded and occupied, and since seas are unbounded and incapable of being occupied they cannot be privately owned. Further, Grotius argues that the seas are a non-rivalrous resource where use by one person does not reduce the resources available to others, and that the non-rivalrous nature of the seas prevents private ownership. In opposition, Selden argues that the seas are bounded by coastlines, and that occupation of a region of the seas is established through private use, regulation, and control of that area. By these criteria, Selden argues that the first occupier of a formerly common area of the seas established private ownership of the region through occupation. Selden counters Grotius's claim that oceans are non-rivalrous and therefore incapable of private ownership by pointing out that other non-rivalrous resources are privately owned, and that saltwater fisheries are a rivalrous resource. This disagreement between Grotius and Selden about whether the seas are rivalrous partly reflects the different activities that each seeks to defend: Grotius aimed to justify Dutch maritime trade, whereas Selden aimed to justify control of fisheries around the British coastline. It is therefore possible that both Grotius and Selden are right about the use of the seas for their intended purpose: oceans may be effectively non-rivalrous for the purposes of travel and trade, but rivalrous for fishing. If seas are non-rivalrous for travel but rivalrous for fishing then proclaiming the oceans to be common property with universal rights of access might enable trade while undermining the long-term productivity and existence of fisheries.

Grotius's work is now far more widely read and cited than Selden's, but this is not indicative of the relative quality or significance of their arguments. Like Grotius, Selden presents a theory of natural law at sea that addresses issues of ownership, use, and state jurisdiction, and that draws on statutory law, common law, and international customs and agreements.[70] More importantly, by providing reasons to believe that oceans are bounded, capable of being occupied, and rivalrous Selden provides powerful counter-arguments to each of Grotius's reasons for claiming that the oceans are commonly owned and that there are universal access rights. In short, *Mare Clausum* provides a compelling rebuttal to the free seas arguments of *Mare Liberum*. However, Selden makes a less persuasive case for his own closed seas position, because his account of British ownership and sovereignty over the seas surrounding the British Isles and British colonies in the Americas is weakened by the selective evidence that he presents and by his theoretical inconsistency about how to establish ownership of an area by occupation. *Mare Clausum* is therefore more successful at refuting Grotius's arguments for free seas than at making a persuasive case for closed seas. The challenge that *Mare Clausum* poses to proponents of free seas is to develop a strong argument for common ownership of the oceans that is based on a different and more convincing theory of property.

The Latin edition of *Mare Clausum* published in 1635 had a limited circulation, but in the run-up to the First Anglo-Dutch War the English government paid for it to be translated into English. The 1652 English translation was influential during the Interregnum and after the Restoration, because it provided arguments that supported England's claims to own its coastal seas and English claims to empire in the Americas.[71] Further attention was drawn to *Mare Clausum* by the prominent references to it in Sir Robert Filmer's justification of royal power, *Patriarcha*.[72] In *Patriarcha* Filmer argues that the King of England is monarch of the world and owner of the land and seas by divine authorization descended from Adam, and he challenges Selden's accounts of property and political authority. First, Filmer argues that in *Genesis 1:28* God gave Adam dominion and command over the entire world, including his children, thereby providing a divine basis for royal authority.[73] Next Filmer argues that this political authority over people, creatures, land, and seas was inherited by Adam's heirs: "by right descending from him the Patriarchs did enjoy, was as large and ample as the absolutest dominion of any monarch which hath been since the creation."[74] Filmer therefore suggests that political authority on land and at sea are the same: absolute patriarchal rule that was established through God's grant to Adam and transferred to his successors. In Chapter VIII of *Patriarcha* Filmer then turns to Grotius's and Selden's accounts of the origin of property.[75] Here, Filmer agrees with Selden that God gave Adam sole ownership of the world in *Genesis 1:28*, but rejects Selden's argument that *Genesis 9:2* established communal ownership between Noah and his sons. Instead, Filmer contends that *Genesis 9:2* granted Noah sole dominion and ownership after which Noah exercised his patriarchal power by choosing to divide his property among his three sons.[76] By rejecting Selden's interpretation of *Genesis 9:2* Filmer thereby rejects his claim that the world was owned by all humans in common after the flood, and instead argues that the world was always privately owned and ruled by the divinely authorized monarch or his appointed heirs. Filmer and Selden therefore agree that the seas can become the exclusive property of a monarch, but their explanations of the origin and scope of this right differ greatly: Filmer argues that the King of England is owner and monarch of the world by divine right, whereas Selden claims that the British Crown owns and governs its coastal waters because its history of occupation established possession under natural law.

By the 1680s *Patriarcha* had become the English Crown's favorite justification of monarchical power, which made it the focus of Whig attacks by Algernon Sidney, James Tyrrell, and Locke. The prominent references to *Mare Clausum* in *Patriarcha* therefore drew the attention of Whig thinkers to Selden's interpretation of Genesis and his theories of property.[77] Locke provides a detailed rebuttal of *Patriarcha* in the *First Treatise* so he clearly knew of *Mare Clausum* through Filmer, but he may also have known the text independently because Selden was a well-regarded scholar of history and law whose book *Titles of Honor* Locke recommended as general reading in "Some Thoughts Concerning Reading and Study for a Gentleman."[78] Although Selden argues in *Mare Clausum* that ownership and rule over British coastal waters belongs to the Crown, not Parliament, his account of maritime law had also appealed to Parliamentarians during the Interregnum. Moreover, as an MP in the 1630s and 1640s Selden was directly involved in challenging royal power and asserting the rights of Parliament, much like the Whigs in the 1670s and 1680s. When renewed conflict over natural law and royal power motivated Locke to write the *Two Treatises* it is therefore not entirely surprising that Locke referred to the earlier arguments developed by Filmer and by Selden.

LOCKE'S THEORY OF PROPERTY AND THE OCEANS

Although most analyses of Locke's theory of property focus on Chapter Five
of the *Second Treatise*, Locke's account of property actually begins in the
First Treatise. Filmer's argument for the divine right of Kings is based on his
interpretation of the Bible, and Filmer reads *Genesis 1:28* as God granting
Adam ownership and political authority over the entire world, including
mankind. Locke responds in the *First Treatise* by arguing that Filmer is mis-
reading *Genesis 1:28,* which Locke interprets as a grant of property ownership over fish, birds, and "irrational Creatures" on land. [79] Since Filmer's
reading of the Bible refers to Selden's interpretations in *Mare Clausum*,
Locke's response also engages with Selden's arguments. Quoting Selden,
Locke argues that *Genesis 1:28* established property ownership, but not
political authority: "for, as Mr *Selden* has properly worded it, *Adam was
made General Lord of all Things*, one may very clearly understand him, that
he means nothing to be granted to *Adam* here but Property, and therefore he
says not one word of *Adam's Monarchy.*" [80] Locke's approving reference to
Selden here does not indicate his agreement with Selden's reading of *Genesis
1:28,* because Selden interprets it as granting Adam private property while
Locke interprets it as a grant of communal property. Instead, Locke seeks to
undercut Filmer's claims by showing that the passages from *Mare Clausum*
that Filmer quotes in support of his view actually contradict his position.
Locke's own disagreement with Selden is outlined in the next paragraph,
where Locke argues that *Genesis 1:28* did not establish monarchy, patriarchal power, or private ownership by Adam, but instead created a property
"right in common with all Mankind." [81] Later in the *First Treatise* Locke
quotes a passage from *Patriarcha* in which Filmer discusses Selden's arguments about God's grant after the flood in *Genesis 9:2.* [82] Here, Selden argues
that God gave ownership of the world to Noah and his sons jointly, whereas
Filmer contends that God granted ownership of the world to Noah alone, and
Locke sides with Selden in interpreting the passage as a grant of communal
property right. [83] Locke therefore refers to Selden's arguments in *Mare
Clausum* both to support his interpretation of *Genesis 1:28* as a grant of
property right, not monarchy, and to support his interpretation of *Genesis 9:2*
as a grant of communal property right, not private property right.

In the *First Treatise* Locke treats the land and seas as alike insofar as God
granted mankind communal ownership of "all the Species of irrational Animals of the *Terraqueous Globe,*" [84] but in the *Second Treatise* he differentiates them. Locke begins Chapter Five of the *Second Treatise* by reiterating
his argument that God has given the earth to "Mankind in common" [85] and
therefore all land was originally the communal property of all. However,
Locke quickly adds that God also gave men reason so that they could use
their property "to the best advantage of Life, and convenience," [86] which he

claims requires private appropriation. Locke then argues that individuals acquire private property by mixing their labor with common property in the state of nature, so farming establishes a right of private property over land: "*As much Land* as a Man Tills, Plants, Improves, Cultivates, and can use the Product of, so much is his *Property.*"[87] Locke justifies this appropriation of common land by arguing that the land itself has very little value and that labor enormously increases its productivity,[88] which creates more goods for mankind. The appropriation of land through cultivation therefore greatly increases the overall supply of goods, improving standards of living, and Locke drives home this message by contrasting the standard of living in England to that of Native Americans:

> There cannot be a clearer demonstration of any thing, than several Nations of the *Americans* are of this, who are rich in Land, and poor in all the Comforts of Life . . . yet for want of improving it by labour, have not one hundreth part of the Conveniences we enjoy: And a King of a large and fruitful Territory there feeds, lodges, and is clad worse than a day Labourer in *England.*[89]

Locke's account of appropriation in the state of nature also contains two restrictions, often termed the sufficiency and spoilage provisos: the sufficiency proviso states that you must leave "enough, and as good"[90] common resources for others, while the spoilage proviso stipulates that legitimate private ownership requires exhaustive use of the resource, thus prohibiting waste.[91] These conditions initially prevent individuals from acquiring very large areas of land, but Locke argues that the restrictions are removed when people consent to the introduction of currency.[92]

Locke's explanation of how land becomes part of the territory of a state follows from this account of appropriation. In the state of nature, all are individually responsible for enforcing the laws of nature, including by punishing those who infringe on their property rights. When men in the state of nature consent to form political society they retain their individual property, but become a united body with a common process of enforcing law that includes "the Power to preserve the Property."[93] Incorporation into civil society means that the group is now responsible for punishing attacks on the life, liberty, or property of its members, but not for defending nonmembers or their property. By creating a collective power and responsibility for enforcing natural law over the land owned by group members, the transition into civil society therefore creates informal territorial jurisdiction. When the civil society agrees to form a commonwealth then the property owned by its members becomes part of this commonwealth: "By the same Act therefore, whereby any one unites his Person, which was before free, to any Commonwealth; by the same he unites his Possessions, which were before free, to it also."[94] Through the social contract the informal territorial jurisdiction of the civil society is transformed into the formal territory of the commonwealth,[95] so exclusive individual or group ownership of land co-exists with state jurisdiction over that land.[96]

Although much of the formerly common land has become both private property and part of state territory, Locke describes the oceans as "that great and still remaining Common of Mankind."[97] This description makes it clear that oceans are not owned by any individual, and by specifying that oceans are a "Common of Mankind" Locke also distinguishes their status from that of common land within a state, which he describes as "Common, in respect of some Men, it is not so to all Mankind; but is the joint property of this Country, or this Parish."[98] Whereas common land in England is collectively owned by a specific subset of mankind who are entitled to exclude others, the ocean is collectively owned by all humans and none are excluded. Locke identifies state territory as composed of individual property[99] and property that is common to a specific group,[100] so his description of the ocean as the common property of mankind indicates that the oceans are not part of the territory of a state. Moreover, when Locke discusses migration he argues that "Government has a direct Jurisdiction only over the Land"[101] thereby indicating that the oceans are outside this scope. The spatial restriction of civil society and direct state jurisdiction to particular areas of land leaves the oceans outside the boundaries of direct political authority, and therefore in a state of nature.

Locke's discussion of property clearly positions his view of the oceans in relation to those of Grotius and Selden.[102] By characterizing the oceans as a "Common of Mankind" Locke echoes both the substance and the phrasing of Grotius's description of the ocean as "inter communia omnium" or "among the things common to all mankind."[103] Locke therefore follows Grotius in characterizing the seas as a space that is not exclusively owned by individuals, groups, or states, but he disagrees with Grotius about the reason why the oceans are a common. Grotius argues that private ownership of an area is established through occupation, and that the seas are a common because they cannot be occupied. However, Selden uses Grotius's theory of appropriation through occupation to argue that many areas of the seas had been occupied and therefore became "possessed in a private manner, or so secluded both by Right and Occupation, that is ceaseth to bee common."[104] Since the Grotian theory of property had been used to justify both free seas and closed seas it did not provide a secure theoretical foundation for the view that the seas were common property. In response, Locke provides a new criterion for private ownership of a region: that appropriation requires the improvement of the area through labor. Regardless of whether regions of the oceans have historically been occupied or not, Locke argues that the oceans are a common of mankind because the land and seas were given by God to all mankind in common and the seas have not been improved through the mixture of human labor with the common waters. Locke therefore adopts aspects of both Grotius's and Selden's accounts of natural law and the oceans, and rejects aspects of both accounts. He adopts Grotius's view of the oceans as a common of mankind, but rejects Grotius's theory of property and thus his reasoning about why the oceans are a common. Conversely, Locke adopts Selden's view that mankind was granted communal ownership of the land and seas in *Genesis 9:2*, but rejects Selden's claim that many regions of the oceans later became private property.

Although Locke states that the oceans are currently a common[105] he does not explicitly stipulate that the oceans will remain common property in future. This creates some ambiguity about whether Locke believes that the oceans are a common that is capable of private appropriation through labor, like common land in America, or whether the oceans cannot be privately appropriated and will remain a common forever. To determine whether the oceans can be appropriated it is necessary to look beyond Locke's explicit statements and consider the logic of how his theory of property applies to the seas. This question about whether Locke's theory of property enables one to appropriate the ocean has been taken up by Robert Nozick, who asks: "If I own a can of tomato juice and spill it into the sea so that its molecules (made radioactive so that I can check this) mingle evenly throughout the sea, do I thereby come to own the sea, or I have I foolishly dissipated my tomato juice?"[106] Nozick's example is designed to show that Locke's theory of property does not merely consist of mixing something that one owns with something unowned, but also requires the creation of added value through labor. During his discussion of added value Nozick implicitly answers his own question: the spilled tomato juice does not entitle him to claim ownership of the ocean, because he has not added value to the ocean. Nozick's analysis shows that oceans cannot be privately owned under Locke's theory of property unless the mixture of private property or labor with the common ocean produces added value.

Locke's theory of property also contains an implicit requirement about the amount of added value that must be created in order to justify private appropriation of a common area. In Chapter Five of the *Second Treatise* Locke explains that farming an area justifies appropriation because "the improvement of *labour makes* the far greater part of *the value*."[107] Initially, Locke argues that cultivated land is ten times more productive than uncultivated common land,[108] but he amends this to suggest that the difference is "nearer an hundred to one,"[109] and later states that uncultivated land in America is less than one thousandth as productive as farmed land in England.[110] Although Locke does not require an increase in productivity of at least tenfold in order to appropriate an area of common land he repeatedly states that labor creates most of the value of land and that uncultivated land is of relatively little value: "'T'is *Labour* then which *puts the greatest part of*

Value upon Land, without which it would scarcely be worth any thing."[111] These passages suggest that the appropriation of formerly common land is legitimate because the added value created through labor is far greater than the value of the unimproved land. Simply put, private ownership of land is justified because human labor more than doubles the value and productivity of the land, which means that the majority of the value of the improved land is attributable to labor and only a small proportion derives from the natural resource alone. Since Locke estimates that cultivation characteristically increases the productivity of land by ten to a thousand times he assumes that farming land will easily create enough added value to justify appropriation. However, greatly increasing the value and productivity of a region through one's labor would be far more difficult to achieve at sea.

In principle, the logic of Locke's theory of property suggests that an area of the oceans could be privately appropriated if labor was mixed with the ocean in a way that at least doubled the value and productivity of those waters. Whether the oceans can be privately owned therefore depends on whether or not they can be "improved," and answering this requires an explanation of what value the oceans provide. In Locke's work the value of the oceans seems to be twofold: they are a source of extractable resources, and a space for travel and trade. In the *Second Treatise* Locke provides two examples of acquiring extractable resources from the ocean: catching fish, and collecting the valuable perfume ingredient ambergris.[112] Locke argues that the act of fishing involves mixing one's labor with the fish and thereby transforms "what Fish any one catches in the Ocean" into the private property of the fisherman.[113] Similarly, Locke maintains that the effort of collecting ambergris turns it into private property: "what Ambergriese any one takes up here, is *by* the *Labour* that removes it out of that common state Nature left it in, *made* his *Property*."[114] Fishing was an important economic activity in the seventeenth century, so it is also mentioned in Locke's unpublished papers. In his notes on the Carolina colony Locke provides detailed information about local fish stocks, including descriptions of the plentiful supplies of oysters, mussels, crabs, and mullet and the availability of whales, sturgeon, trout, and eels.[115] The economic significance of fishing is also emphasized in a 1679 paper in Locke's collection, which argues that the English Royal Fishery Company benefited the country by employing over a hundred thousand English people.[116]

In the *Two Treatises* Locke acknowledges the importance of maritime travel and trade, which he argues underpins the domestic economy such that even the production of a loaf of bread in England indirectly involves "Pitch, Tar, Masts, Ropes, and all the Materials made use of in the Ship, that brought the Commodities made use of by any of the Workmen, to any part of the Work."[117] The value of the ocean as a space for international trade is also a major theme in Locke's economic writings. In the 1674 paper "Trade" Locke defines trade as involving either domestic manufacture or "Carriage, i.e. navigation and merchandise,"[118] so the transportation of goods is acknowledged as an important economic activity. Locke argues that trade increases the prosperity and population of a state, and that wealth lies in the possibility of foreign exchange: "Riches consist in plenty of movables, that will yield a price to [a] foreigner . . . especially in plenty of gold and silver."[119] The policies that Locke recommends for promoting trade therefore include measures to encourage foreign exchange such as "freedom of trade" and "increase and encouragement of seamen."[120] This claim that maritime transportation is an important component of trade is repeated in Locke's 1693 paper "For a General Naturalisation" where he reiterates that the export of English goods benefits the economy,[121] and attributes the economic success of the Dutch to their prominent role in the global transportation of goods.[122]

In the *Two Treatises* Locke characterizes the world's oceans as a common despite acknowledging maritime trade, travel, and fishing, so he clearly does not regard sailing through or fishing in an area of the ocean as constituting improvement that would justify appropriation. However, might some other activity improve a region of the oceans in a way that would justify its appropriation under Locke's theory of property? For example, in the centuries since the *Two Treatises* people have introduced man-made navigational aids such as lighthouses and buoys to help ships travel safely.[123] If a lighthouse or buoys steer ships away from hazards then the resulting prevention of shipwrecks seems to constitute improvement of that region for navigational purposes. Does this added navigational value justify appropriation of the area? While the provision of lighthouses or buoys might create added navigational value in a region of the seas, it seems unlikely to create enough added value to justify appropriation. On land, Locke argues that appropriation of a common area is justified because labor increases the productivity of the area by tenfold or a thousandfold, which sets a very high bar for the degree of improvement required. If most of the navigational value of the seas for travel derives from the natural resource alone and only a small increase can be achieved through labor then Locke's theory of property would not justify appropriation of the seas. Moreover, lighthouses and buoys would only create added value in relatively small areas of dangerous and shallow water, so this means of improvement would not extend to the deep waters of the open ocean. Attempts to appropriate the oceans by improving their navigational value would therefore encounter two problems: the extreme difficulty of creating enough added value to justify appropriation under Locke's agriculturalist theory of property, and the small proportion of the world's oceans that could be improved by man-made navigational features.

Alternately, one might attempt to appropriate a region of the ocean by improving the production or value of extractable resources. If mixing your labor with an area of the ocean doubled the number of fish in that area, or even produced a tenfold or thousandfold increase in fish, then would this entitle you to appropriate those waters? It is doubtful if labor could produce such a large increase in the productivity of a fishery, but even if it did then problems would arise over enclosure. In Chapter Five of the *Second Treatise* Locke repeatedly describes the appropriation of land as a process of enclosure, stating that "Whatsoever he tilled and reaped, laid up and made use of, before it spoiled, that was his peculiar Right; whatsoever he enclosed, and could feed, and make use of, the Cattle and Product was also his."[124] Locke's description of appropriation as "inclosure"[125] indicates that he conceptualizes private ownership of a region as involving the right to exclude others from that area and the establishment of fixed boundaries, such as a fence or hedge.[126] Such literal enclosure of a region is possible on land and in some coastal bays and inlets,[127] but not on the open ocean. Without a visible boundary people might mistake private waters for common waters, and thereby unwittingly infringe on property rights. Moreover, the absence of fences would allow marine creatures to travel in and out of private waters, so the extra fish generated through one's labor could swim away. The impracticality of enclosing a region of the open seas means that even if someone improved an area by multiplying the fish population then it would be very difficult to enforce and benefit from the resulting property rights. Even if new technology made it possible to erect fences in the ocean then this would impede travel by ships, thereby damaging the overall productivity of the waters and potentially negating one's claim to have improved the region.

Although Locke does not explicitly state that oceans are incapable of private appropriation, his agriculturalist theory of property establishes stringent criteria that would make it practically impossible to appropriate the world's oceans. On land Locke argues that farming hugely increases the productivity of a region, thereby justifying its appropriation. At sea there is no equivalent way to boost the value or productivity of a region, so it would be difficult to create enough added value to justify appropriation. Even if one managed to improve an area enough to justify appropriating it, for example by building a lighthouse to boost the navigational value of dangerous waters, then this might be impossible to replicate in other regions. Similarly, on land the process of appropriation involves enclosing an area in order to communicate and protect one's property rights. At sea it is not possible to establish fences so it would be far more difficult to communicate or enforce maritime property rights. Overall, Locke's agriculturalist theory of property establishes criteria that are intended to be easy to meet on land, but impossible to meet at sea. Since Locke argues that all regions were originally owned in common and provides a theory of property under which only land can be justifiably appropriated, he is able to portray the oceans as "that great and still remaining Common of Mankind."[128] Moreover, Locke makes it clear that the status of the oceans as a common means that there are universal rights of access and use for travel, trade, and fishing.

While it is impractical to improve the oceans in the way that Locke believes agriculture improves land, it might be possible to prevent the value or productivity of an area of the ocean from becoming depleted and this could provide an alternate justification for private ownership. In *Mare Clausum* Selden argues that extractable marine resources are finite and that fish, pearls, and oysters will be depleted if we characterize the oceans as a common where all have rights of access. [129] From Selden's perspective, free seas are a recipe for destructive overfishing, whereas closed seas would enable regulation and conservation of fish stocks. Given that shortages of fish and whales were occurring in European seas by the late sixteenth century and worsened thereafter, [130] Selden's concerns about scarcity reflect a realistic assessment of European fisheries. The overuse of common resources is a major theme in recent environmental scholarship, and Garrett Hardin famously describes oceanic fishing as exemplifying the tragedy of the commons: "Professing to believe in the 'inexhaustible resources of the oceans,' they bring species after species of fish and whales closer to extinction." [131] To prevent the depletion of large common resources Hardin recommends either transferring the resource into private ownership, or state action to prevent overuse. [132] Both contemporary environmental scholarship and early modern debates about maritime law therefore show that questions of resource ownership are connected to questions about the scarcity of the resource and efficient ways of using it. Whereas Grotius's case for the common oceans rests on the claim that oceanic travel and fishing are non-rivalrous and effectively inexhaustible resources, Selden and Hardin justify private ownership of oceans or oceanic fisheries on the grounds that fish are finite and should be conserved.

Locke acknowledges in the *Two Treatises* that the ocean produces extractable resources such as fish and ambergris, but he does not recognize that these resources are finite and could be depleted through overextraction. Locke's inattention to the potential problems of resource scarcity is not confined to the oceans, because he argues that property in general was abundant before currency was introduced:

> No Mans Labor could subdue, or appropriate all: nor could his Enjoyment consume more than a small part; so that it was impossible for any Man, this way, to intrench upon the right of another, or acquire, to himself, a Property, to the Prejudice of his Neighbour. [133]

If fish are included in this account of "Property," then Locke seems to be following Grotius in assuming that fish are naturally plentiful. This assumption of natural abundance leads Grotius, and perhaps Locke, to overlook the risk of overfishing and the increased likelihood of overfishing if there are universal rights to fish in the world's oceans. If Locke saw fish as a scarce resource that is depleted by overuse, as Selden did, then perhaps this would have changed his view about access and ownership to fisheries and the world's oceans.

Efforts to conserve oceanic fisheries would be consistent with Locke's concern that the acquisition of private property by one person should not harm others, exemplified in the sufficiency proviso prior to the introduction of currency, but would conflict with other aspects of his theory of property. Arguments for fisheries conservation are based on the recognition that the productivity of a fishery stems largely from ecological factors, and that human access to the fishery is more likely to deplete the resource than to improve it. By contrast, Locke's theory of property begins from the premise that the potential productivity of natural resources derives mainly from the application of human labor, and not from the inherent value of the resource. This premise has led commentators to argue that Locke's theory of property greatly underestimates the value that ecosystems provide, over-estimates the contribution of human labor, and ignores the risk of resource depletion. [134] For example, Robert Markley argues that Locke overlooks the full value and scarcity of natural resources with the result that his theory rests on a "fiction of endless production" whereby "we can use nature's resources to raise our standard of living, but we can never use them up." [135] If the labor involved in fishing provides only a small proportion of the value of the fish then it undermines Locke's argument that acts of gathering, hunting, or fishing constitute grounds for private appropriation of extractable resources. Recognizing the true value and productive contribution of ecosystems could therefore call Locke's entire theory of property into question. In addition, resource conservation seems to conflict with Locke's account of the divinely intended human purpose, which involves being industrious [136] and avoiding waste. [137] These values lead Locke to criticize Native American practices of land use as leaving land "lyeing wast in common," [138] instead of using the land more productively. [139] This celebration of labor and prohibition of waste might lead Locke to reject sustainable fishing practices on the grounds that more work would lead to the extraction of more fish. Locke's conception of the seas as a common of mankind to which all have rights of access is therefore linked both to his nonrecognition of the value of ecosystems and the scarcity of fish, and to his normative convictions that the purpose of human life is to work hard and avoid waste.

Although commentators have largely overlooked the implications of Locke's natural law theory for the world's oceans, the *Two Treatises* nonetheless provide a systematic political theory of the seas. In the *First Treatise* Locke draws on Selden's arguments in *Mare Clausum* to argue that God gave ownership of the world's land, seas, and animals to all men in common, but did not grant Adam political authority over other humans. In the *Second Treatise* Locke builds on this to argue that the oceans are still a "Common of Mankind,"[140] but that labor entitles people to appropriate extractable resources from the ocean, for example by fishing. Locke's agriculturalist theory of property also makes it very difficult—perhaps impossible—for the oceans to be appropriated in future, because this would require people to "improve" a region of the ocean in a manner analogous to how agriculture increases the productivity of land. Even if one managed to create enough added value in an area of the seas to justify appropriating it then the impracticality of enclosing the area would hinder efforts to protect one's property rights. Further, Locke indicates that oceans are not part of the territory or direct jurisdiction of a state, which extends only over land that is privately owned or "the joint property of this Country, or this Parish."[141] Under Locke's theory of property the oceans therefore seem destined to remain the common property of all humans and to remain in the state of nature.

In the *Two Treatises* Locke contributes to debates about the legal status of the oceans that were central to early modern natural law theory and had direct practical significance for England's economic and foreign policy. Grotius had provided a theoretical justification for universal rights to peaceful travel and trade at sea, but his theory had been subjected to a compelling critique by Selden. Selden's closed seas arguments attracted considerable support in England from the 1630s to the 1680s, but by 1682 Locke was among the Whigs advocating an ideological sea-change in England and the replacement of the Stuart monarchy.[142] Locke responded to the ongoing debates over natural law by developing a new theory of property that enabled private ownership of land while portraying the world's oceans as a common that was free to all for travel, trade, and fishing. Locke's theory of property therefore justifies English political expansion not only by enabling the acquisition and control of land in the Americas, as scholars such as Tully and Arneil have argued, but also by justifying the maritime travel necessary to transport English colonists and goods. This legal justification of free seas legitimated the expansion of English merchants into seas in Africa, Asia, and South America where Spain and Portugal had asserted exclusive rights, and where the Dutch were trading profitably. Recognizing how the *Two Treatises* contributes to theories of natural law at sea therefore shows that the imperial themes in Locke's work extend not only to land and the Americas but also to the world's oceans and the activities of traders such as the Royal Africa Company and East India Company. By the 1690s Locke was directly involved in making policy about these colonies and merchants as a member of the Board of Trade, so he was able to implement some of his theoretical ideas about the nature and enforcement of natural law at sea.

NOTES

1. Tully, *Approach to Political Philosophy*; Parekh, "Liberalism and Colonialism"; Arneil, *John Locke and America*; Armitage, "John Locke, Carolina"; and Ivison, "Locke, Liberalism and Empire."

2. One exception is the brief account of Locke's views about the significance of the seas for trade in Arneil, *John Locke and America*, 103–7.

3. The prevailing oceanic currents and trade winds in the North Atlantic circulate in a roughly clockwise direction. To take advantage of the currents and trade winds European sailing ships traveling to North America would sail south to the Canary Islands, west across the North Atlantic to the Caribbean, and (depending on the destination) could then follow the trade winds north up the east coast of North America. To follow the trade winds from North America to Europe a ship would sail northeast up the east coast of North America and then northeast across the Atlantic.

4. See Rediker, *Between the Devil*; David Armitage and Michael J. Braddick, eds., *The British Atlantic World 1500–1800* (New York: Palgrave Macmillan, 2002); Jeremy Black, *The British Seaborne Empire* (New Haven, CT, and London: Yale University Press, 2004); Nicholas Canny and Philip Morgan, eds., *The Oxford Handbook of the Atlantic World, c. 1450–c. 1850* (New York and Oxford: Oxford University Press, 2011); Joseph C. Miller, ed., *The Princeton Companion to Atlantic History* (Princeton, NJ, and Oxford: Princeton University Press, 2015).

5. Philip E. Steinberg, *The Social Construction of the Ocean* (Cambridge: Cambridge University Press, 2001), 76.

6. *Ibid*, 89.

7. Tuck, *Rights of War and Peace*, 112.

8. Mark Nicholls and Penry Williams, *Sir Walter Raleigh in Life and Legend* (London and New York: Continuum Books, 2011), 48.

9. Richard Hakluyt, *A Particuler Discourse Concerning the Greate Necessitie and Manifolde Commodyties that are Like to Growe to This Realm of England By the Westerne Discoueries Lately Attempted*, eds. David B. Quinn and Alison M. Quinn (London: Hakluyt Society, 1993), 16–24.

10. *Ibid*, 31.

11. *Ibid*, 28.

12. *Ibid*, 8.

13. Nicholls and Williams, *Sir Walter Raleigh*, 55.

14. *Ibid*, 67.

15. David Armitage, *The Ideological Origins of the British Empire* (Cambridge: Cambridge University Press, 2000), 108–9.

16. John Selden, *Mare Clausum: The Right and Dominion of the Sea*, trans. Marchmont Nedham and ed. J. H. Grant (London, 1663).

17. Armitage, *Ideological Origins*, 167.

18. Tuck, *Rights of War and Peace*, 79; Hugo Grotius, *The Freedom of the Seas, or the Right Which Belongs to the Dutch to Take Part in the East Indian Trade*, trans. Ralph van Deman Magoffin (New York: Oxford University Press, 1916), vi.

19. Martine Julia van Ittersum, "Hugo Grotius in Context: Van Heemskerk's Capture of the *Santa Catarina* and Its Justification in *De Jure Praedae* (1604–1606)," *Asian Journal of Social Sciences* 31, no. 3 (2003): 511–48.

20. Grotius, *Freedom of the Seas*, vii.

21. Tuck, *Rights of War and Peace*, 79.

22. van Ittersum, "Hugo Grotius in Context," 521.

23. *Ibid*, 524.

24. Grotius, *Freedom of the Seas*, 2.

25. *Ibid*, 4–5.

26. *Ibid*, 13.

27. *Ibid*, 21.

28. *Ibid*, 66.

29. *Ibid*, 25.

30. *Ibid*, 26 and 30.

31. *Ibid*, 26.

32. *Ibid*, 28.

33. *Ibid*, 27.

34. *Ibid*, 27.

35. *Ibid*, 28.

36. *Ibid*, 34.

37. *Ibid*, 36.

38. *Ibid*, 35.

39. *Ibid*, 38.

40. *Ibid*, 63.

41. *Ibid*, 74–5. When Grotius refers to a right of free trade he means that no state has the right to restrict subjects of another state from engaging in trade with subjects of a third state. Grotius is not advocating free trade in the later sense of criticizing economic protectionism (i.e., regulations intended to benefit the state's own economy and trade at the expense of rival states).

42. *Ibid*, viii.

43. Martine Julia van Ittersum, *Profit and Principle: Hugo Grotius, Natural Rights Theories and the Rise of Dutch Power in the East Indies, 1595–1615* (Leiden and Boston: Brill Academic Publishers, 2006), 418–9.

44. Stephen C. Neff, ed. *Hugo Grotius: On the Law of War and Peace* (Cambridge: Cambridge University Press, 2010), 94.

45. *Ibid*, 94–5.

46. *Ibid*, 100.

47. *Ibid*, 274.

48. Tuck, *Rights of War and Peace*, 112–3.

49. *Ibid*, 114.

50. James I advised against publication in 1619 because he was worried that *Mare Clausum* would offend the Danish King, see Helen Thornton, "John Selden's Response to Hugo Grotius: The Argument for Closed Seas," *International Journal of Maritime History* 18, no. 2 (2006): 107.

51. Selden, *Mare Clausum*, e2.

52. *Ibid*, 16.

53. *Ibid*, 20.

54. *Ibid*, 19.

55. *Ibid*, 21.

56. *Ibid*, 22–3.

57. *Ibid*, 23. The passage that Selden quotes is from Grotius's *De Jure Belli ac Pacis* Book II Ch II §2, see Neff, ed. *Hugo Grotius: On the Law of War and Peace*, 94.

58. Selden, *Mare Clausum*, 24–5.

59. *Ibid*, 24.

60. Grotius, *Freedom of the Seas*, 28.

61. *Ibid*, 137.

62. *Ibid*, 137–8.

63. *Ibid*, 141.

64. *Ibid*, 141.

65. *Ibid*, 182.

66. *Ibid*, 188.

67. Selden's interest in the Americas was professional as well as theoretical, because in 1621 he was engaged by the Virginia Company to work on a legal dispute within the company about the allocation of coastal fishing rights, see Thornton, "John Selden's Response," 125.

68. Selden, *Mare Clausum*, 441.

69. *Ibid*, 441–2.

70. Thornton, "John Selden's Response," 126–7.

71. Armitage, *Ideological Origins*, 118–21.

72. Filmer wrote *Patriarcha* at some point between 1635 and 1642, see Robert Filmer, *Patriarcha and Other Political Works of Sir Robert Filmer,* ed. Peter Laslett (Oxford: Basil Blackwell, 1949), 3. Filmer also knew Selden personally, which may explain his references to Selden's work, *Ibid*, 4.

73. *Ibid*, 57–8.

74. *Ibid*, 58.

75. *Ibid*, 63–6.

76. *Ibid*, 58 and 64.

77. For example, Tyrrell refers to Selden's arguments in *Mare Clausum* several times in *Patriarcha Non Monarcha* in order to refute Filmer's claims about the grant of authority and property to Adam in *Genesis* and to re-interpret *Genesis 1:28* as establishing a common right for humans to use the plants and creatures of the earth for their sustenance, see James Tyrrell, *Patriarcha Non Monarcha. The Patriarch Unmonarch'd* (London, 1681) retrieved from http://oll.libertyfund.org/titles/2168.

78. John Locke, "Some Thoughts Concerning Reading and Study for a Gentleman" in *Locke: Political Essays*, 379.

79. Locke, *Two Treatises*, I §23 157.

80. *Ibid*, I §23 157. The phrase that Locke attributes to Selden seems to be an alternate translation of a passage from Book I, Chapter IV of the 1635 Latin edition. In the 1653 English translation of *Mare Clausum* the passage Locke refers to is translated as God granting Adam the status of "Lord of the whole World" which Selden immediately clarifies as a private property right, see Selden, *Mare Clausum*, 20.

81. Locke, *Two Treatises*, I §24 157.

82. *Ibid*, I §32 163.

83. *Ibid*, I §32 163.

84. *Ibid*, I §27 160.

85. *Ibid*, II §25 286.

86. *Ibid*, II §26 286.

87. *Ibid*, II §32 290.

88. *Ibid*, II §40 296.

89. *Ibid*, II §41 296–7.

90. *Ibid*, II §33 291.

91. *Ibid*, II §32 290.

92. *Ibid*, II §50 302.

93. *Ibid*, II §87 324.

94. *Ibid*, II §120 348.

95. Locke notes that some land in England is collectively owned, but he does not explain how that land could have become part of the territory of a state without first being individually owned, see *Ibid*, II §35 292.

96. *Ibid*, II §120 348.

97. *Ibid*, II §30 289.

98. *Ibid*, II §35 292.

99. *Ibid*, II §120 348.

100. *Ibid*, II §35 292.

101. *Ibid*, II §121 349.

102. For the references to Selden see Locke, *Two Treatises*, I §21 156, I §23 157, I §32 165. For the references to Grotius, see Locke, *Two Treatises*, I §18 154, I §50–51 177, I §76 196. Locke also owned texts by both authors, including seven legal and historical works by Selden and copies of both *Mare Liberum* and *De Jure Belli ac Pacis*, see John Harrison and Peter Laslett, *The Library of John Locke* (Oxford: Oxford University Press, 1965), 147 and 229.

103. Grotius, *Freedom of the Seas,* 28.

104. Selden, *Mare Clausum*, g.

105. Locke, *Two Treatises*, II §30 289.

106. Robert Nozick, *Anarchy, State, and Utopia* (Oxford: Blackwell, 1974), 175.

107. Locke, *Two Treatises*, II §40 296.

108. *Ibid*, II §37 294.

109. *Ibid*, II §37 294.
110. *Ibid*, II §43 298.
111. *Ibid*, II §43 298.
112. Ambergris is produced by sperm whales and is sometimes found floating on the surface of the ocean.
113. Locke, *Two Treatises*, II §30 289.
114. *Ibid*, II §30 289–90.
115. Locke MS c.30 fols 31–2, Bodleian Library, Oxford.
116. Locke MS c.30 fols 27–8, Bodleian Library, Oxford.
117. Locke, *Two Treatises*, II §43 298.
118. Locke "Trade," 222.
119. *Ibid*, 221–2.
120. *Ibid*, 222.
121. Locke, "For a General Naturalisation," 323–4.
122. *Ibid*, 325.
123. A few lighthouses and buoys existed around the English coast in the late seventeenth century, but they did not come into widespread use until centuries later, see Erik Lindberg, "From Private to Public Provision of Public Goods: English Lighthouses Between the Seventeenth and Nineteenth Centuries," *The Journal of Policy History* 25, no. 4 (2013): 545.
124. Locke, *Two Treatises*, II §38 295.
125. *Ibid*, II §33 291.
126. See the discussion of enclosure in Arneil, *John Locke and America*, 140.
127. Even Grotius, the exemplary free seas theorist, argues that private property rights can be established over inlets of the sea. In *Mare Liberum* Grotius notes that Romans established private saltwater fisheries in coastal inlets, and he argues that fencing off an inlet of the sea does turn it into private property, see Grotius, *Freedom of the Seas,* 32–3. Grotius therefore differentiates between coastal inlets and the open oceans: he argues that inlets are bounded and can be occupied, whereas the open ocean is unbounded and cannot be occupied. This practice of enclosing inlets to create private fisheries continues in the present day with saltwater fish farms, for example by farming salmon in Scottish lochs.
128. Locke, *Two Treatises*, II §30 289.
129. Selden, *Mare Clausum*, 142–3.
130. W. Jeffrey Bolster, "Putting the Ocean Back in Atlantic History: Maritime Communities and Marine Ecology in the Northwest Atlantic, 1500–1800," *The American Historical Review* 113, no.1 (2008): 28.
131. Garrett Hardin, "The Tragedy of the Commons," *Science* 162, no. 3859 (1968): 1245.
132. *Ibid*, 1247.
133. Locke, *Two Treatises*, II §36 292.
134. Brent M. Haddad, "Property Rights, Ecosystem Management, and John Locke's Labor Theory of Ownership," *Ecological Economics* 46, no. 1 (2003): 19–31.
135. Robert Markley, "'Land Enough in the World': Locke's Golden Age and the Infinite Extension of 'Use,'" *The South Atlantic Quarterly* 98, no. 4 (1999): 833 and 828.
136. Locke, *Two Treatises*, II §34 291.
137. *Ibid*, II §31 290.
138. *Ibid*, II §37 294.
139. For discussion of Locke's critique of Native American societies and land use, see Tully, *Approach to Political Philosophy,* 137–76; Parekh, "Liberalism and Colonialism"; Arneil, *John Locke and America,* 133–67; Mark Neocleous, "War on Waste: Law, Original Accumulation and the Violence of Capital," *Science and Society* 75, no. 4 (2011): 506–28.
140. Locke, *Two Treatises*, II §30 289.
141. *Ibid*, II §35 292.
142. See Armitage, "John Locke, Carolina," and Ashcraft, *Revolutionary Politics.*

Chapter Two

"Robbers and Pyrates"

Locke's Theory of Natural Law at Sea

In the previous chapter I considered how the theory of property in the *Two Treatises* applies to the oceans. According to Locke, the oceans are a "Common of Mankind"[1] that are owned collectively by all humans and are outside of state borders and jurisdiction, which means there are universal rights to use the oceans for travel and fishing. Although Locke does not explicitly state that the oceans will remain a common indefinitely, his agriculturalist theory of property imposes stringent criteria that would make it practically impossible to establish private ownership of the world's oceans. However, there are still limits to what people can lawfully do at sea, because Locke outlines natural laws and rights that exist both at sea and on land. This chapter continues the examination of Locke's maritime political thought by investigating his account of crime and law enforcement on the oceans. I begin by examining Locke's arguments in the *Two Treatises* about what activities are prohibited by natural law, what penalties are appropriate, and how natural law is enforced by individuals and states. Next, I consider an example of maritime crime and punishment by analyzing Locke's discussion of piracy in the *Two Treatises*. This analysis shows that Locke condemns pirates for infringing on victims' rights to life, liberty, and property, and that he compares pirates to several categories of criminals on land, including robbers, tyrants, and unlawful rebels. Locke suggests that pirates can be punished under natural law or under national legislation, and he argues that victims of piracy have the right to use violence in self-defense. Lastly, I briefly consider what a manuscript about piracy that Locke wrote for the Board of Trade in 1697 adds to our understanding of his views about piracy and the enforcement of maritime law.

NATURAL LAW ON LAND

At the beginning of the *Second Treatise* Locke argues that natural law governs human conduct in the state of nature, and that it prohibits attacks on "the Life, the Liberty, Health, Limb or Goods of another."[2] Locke maintains that people who use their reason will recognize the content of natural law and understand that everyone is obliged to follow it,[3] but if someone breaks natural law then he argues that they should be punished.[4] In the state of nature Locke contends that all individuals have the right to enforce natural law by judging and punishing other individuals: "the *Execution* of the Law of Nature is in that State, put into every Mans hands."[5] This right to punish criminals is important, because Locke recognizes that some people will not follow natural law and that the existence of laws is of little value unless there is a means of enforcement.[6] Locke's state of regulated and responsible freedom, which he describes as liberty from "restraint and violence from others,"[7] therefore depends on the right to punish criminals in the state of nature; otherwise, unchallenged crime would cause a descent into war and chaos. Within this power to enforce law against criminals Locke then identifies two distinct rights: the right to punish, and the right to receive reparations from a criminal whose crime harmed you. Everyone in the state of nature has the right to punish a criminal and Locke maintains that "Each Transgression may be *punished* to that *degree*, and with so much *Severity* as will suffice to make it an ill bargain to the Offender, give him cause to repent, and terrifie others from doing the like."[8] Further, Locke argues that victims have the right to receive reparation from the offender "so much as may make satisfaction for the harm he has suffr'd" and may receive help from others in gaining this reparation.[9] Law enforcement in the state of nature therefore involves both a general right to punish criminals, and a specific right for the victim(s) of a crime to receive compensation from the offender(s).

Although Locke argues that both punishment and reparation must be proportional to the offense he also condones very severe punishments, including death and slavery. Locke begins by claiming that death is a just and proportional punishment for murder[10] because murderers have "renounced Reason, the common Rule and Measure" and can therefore be "destroyed as a *Lyon* or *Tyger*, one of those wild Savage Beasts, with whom Men can have no Society nor Security."[11] By committing murder an offender shows himself to be irrational and an ongoing threat to the lives of other humans, so he forfeits his natural rights and full human status. Locke then extends this reasoning by arguing that individuals have the right to kill anyone who creates a state of war that "threatens me with Destruction."[12] Death is therefore an appropriate punishment for murderers and attempted murderers,[13] which includes those who use violence "to get another Man into his Absolute

Power . . . It being understood as a Declaration of a Design upon his Life."[14] By defining an attack on someone's liberty as an implicit attack on their life Locke reasons that it is just to kill any criminal who uses force to threaten one's freedom:

> This makes it Lawful for a Man to *kill a Thief*, who has not in the least hurt him, nor declared any design upon his Life, any farther then by the use of Force, so to get him in his Power, as to take away his Money, or what he pleases from him: because using force, where he has no Right, to get me into his Power, let his pretence be what it will, I have no reason to suppose, that he, who would *take away my Liberty*, would not when he had me in his Power, take away every thing else.[15]

Even if we accept Locke's claim that death is a proportionate punishment for murder, is it really a proportionate penalty for theft? Locke's answer depends on whether the theft involved violence or coercion. If the thief did not use violence or coercion then his actions would not threaten the liberty of the victim, so the thief should not be treated as a potential murderer and the victim is not automatically justified in killing him. If the thief did use violence or coercion then Locke argues that the victim's rights to both property and liberty have been violated, which he believes the victim should interpret as a threat to their life.[16] Since anyone who unlawfully threatens another individual's life or liberty has created a state of war between them, Locke argues that a victim of violence or coercion can justly use force to defend their life and liberty, including by killing the offender.[17] In the state of nature, the victim of a violent crime therefore has the right to kill their attacker in self-defense and the right to take reparations from the attacker in compensation for any harms they suffered. If the victim does not successfully resist the aggressor at the time of the offense then they retain the right to enforce the law of nature at a later date by imposing punishment and taking reparations. However, acts that are justifiable in self-defense during the crime may not be justifiable as punishment after the crime has been committed. If the thief used force to steal from the victim but did not attempt to enslave or kill the victim then it is clear after the fact that they were not an attempted murderer, so they should be punished for theft but not for attempted murder. As Dilts explains: "The problem is temporal: during the crime, the thief has yet to become only a thief. . . . The aggressor only becomes a 'thief' in retrospect, when it turns out that his design was not my death but merely the appropriation of my horse and coat."[18] Locke's theory of slavery builds on his claim that criminals can be justly killed by arguing that a victim who can justly kill an offender owns the offender's life and therefore has the right to enslave them,[19] as I discuss in Chapter Four.

Although the state of nature contains a basic system of criminal law and a means of enforcement, Locke identifies three major problems with criminal punishment in the state of nature. First, Locke notes that many criminals claim that the general principles of natural law do not apply to their own case and therefore deny that they have broken the law: "he who was so unjust as to do his Brother an injury, will scarce be so just as to condemn himself for it."[20] Secondly, Locke claims that people are biased in favor of themselves and that this leads them to seek disproportionate punishments for an offense: victims and their friends will favor punishments that are too severe, while offenders and their friends will favor punishments that are too lenient.[21] The fact that everyone in the state of nature has the right to enforce the laws of nature therefore leads to people judging their own cases and making biased decisions. Thirdly, Locke notes that criminals will violently resist justice, which makes punishing offenders "dangerous, and frequently destructive, to those who attempt it."[22] These three problems make the state of nature "very unsafe, very insecure,"[23] and Locke argues that the appropriate remedy is to leave the state of nature and create a civil society or a state.[24] The difficulty of enforcing natural law in the state of nature motivates people to create a commonwealth with "an *establish'd*, settled, known *Law*," "a *known and indifferent Judge*," and the power to effectively punish offenders.[25] Remedying the flaws of law enforcement in the state of nature therefore requires not only the creation of a state, but more specifically a state with the rule of law, an independent judiciary, and a formal penal system.

When individuals participate in the social contract they agree to give up their individual right to enforce natural law, so the power to punish criminals is transferred to the civil society or commonwealth.[26] Through the social contract the government therefore acquires the power and responsibility to make and enforce law over its members and over "the Territories belonging to any Government, to all parts whereof the force of its Law extends."[27] Although some of those present within a state's territory may be noncitizens who have not expressly consented to obey its laws, Locke argues that residents give tacit consent by owning land or enjoying the benefits of government.[28] The extension of a state's law is therefore determined both by citizenship and geography: the state has the right to make and enforce laws over citizens who have given express consent, and over the territory where it has exclusive jurisdiction. This dual nature of legal jurisdiction opens the possibility that an individual in a given area could be governed by two different sets of law. For example, an English citizen traveling in the areas of America that Locke describes as the state of nature might be obliged to follow both natural law, which applies in the state of nature, and English law, which they consented to follow through the social contract. Similarly, a Dutch citizen living in England might be obliged to follow Dutch laws because he explicitly consented to do so when he became a citizen, and to follow English law because he tacitly consented to do so as a result of his residence. The application of a state's laws to both citizens and those within the state's territory therefore creates the potential for two states to claim simultaneous legal jurisdiction over the same person, and for that person to be obliged to follow two sets of law at the same time.

The powers that states possess over their citizens and within their territorial jurisdiction include passing criminal laws, judging accused criminals, and imposing appropriate punishments. These responsibilities to make and enforce the law are constrained by the requirement for the state to act in the public good, and Locke argues that the state may mitigate punishments if it would promote the public good. However, Locke maintains that the state does not have the power to deny reparations to victims because "he who has suffered the damage has a Right to demand in his own name, and he alone can *remit*."[29] Whatever punishment the state imposes, the victim therefore retains a right to receive compensation for the harms that they suffered from the criminal.[30] Residents of a commonwealth also retain a right of self-defense against violent criminals at the moment of the attack, because Locke reasons that the delay involved in asking the state for justice against a violent criminal might lead to your death, which the state cannot later remedy. To prevent such irreparable harm Locke argues that individuals have the right to self-preservation in situations where it is not practical to appeal to the state for protection: "the aggressor allows not time to appeal to our common Judge, nor the decision of the Law, for remedy in a Case, where the mischief may be irreparable."[31] Victims therefore have the right to forcibly defend themselves while they are under threat from an aggressor, but once the crime has been committed the responsibility for punishing the criminal lies with the state.

Criminal punishment is central to Locke's conceptions of law and government in the *Two Treatises*, but he says little about its relationship to economic activity. Locke's silence about the economic significance of crime is somewhat surprising given that crime threatens private property and trade, both of which Locke advocates because they encourage people to work harder[32] and thereby promote higher standards of living.[33] This relationship between economics and crime has been discussed by later proponents of private ownership and trade, many of whom argue that functioning markets require state provision of effective criminal law and punishment. For example, the economist Milton Friedman famously advocates a small state that intervenes minimally in the economy, but also argues that free markets cannot exist without the state enforcing law: "the basic requisite is the maintenance of law and order to prevent physical coercion of one individual by another and to enforce contracts voluntarily entered into."[34] The libertarian Robert Nozick similarly argues that free markets require the state to act as a "night watchman" by enforcing contracts and laws about crime.[35] Both Friedman and Nozick view secure property rights and voluntary economic exchange as central to market economies, which means that involuntary economic exchanges such as theft must be prohibited and punished. Whether or not one accepts these conceptions of the relationship between the market and the state—and there may be good reasons not to do so, as scholars such as Bernhard Harcourt have argued[36]—the works of Friedman and Nozick emphasize that state provision of legal and penal systems underlies economic transactions. Nozick's insights make it clear that the legitimate economic activities described in Chapter Five of the *Second Treatise* all rely on the existence and enforcement of criminal law that prohibits theft and violence. Without the enforcement of such prohibitions Locke's system of lawful property ownership, production, and voluntary exchange would be undermined by involuntary exchanges based on violence or coercion. In short, both the political and economic systems that Locke advocates in the *Two Treatises* depend on the enforcement of natural law through punishing theft and violent crimes.

When individuals enter a social contract they leave the state of nature, but this does not mean that the state of nature ceases to exist. Although Locke initially portrays the state of nature as a pre-governmental stage of development he later explains that it exists wherever there is no centralized legal authority: *"Want of a common Judge with Authority, puts all Men in a State of Nature."*[37] This identification of the state of nature with an absence of centralized judicial authority means that the state of nature exists in the international realm: "since all *Princes* and Rulers of *Independent* Governments all through the World, are in a State of Nature, 'tis plain the World never was, nor ever will be, without Numbers of Men in that State."[38] The rulers of all sovereign states are therefore in the state of nature with respect to the rulers of other states. This international state of nature is not ended by the creation of international treaties, because Locke stipulates that it only ends when participants consent "together mutually to enter into one Community, and make one Body Politick."[39] Relationships in the international state of nature take place between states and Locke argues that each community is "one Body in the State of Nature, in respect of all other States or Persons out of its Community."[40] In the international context, the state of nature therefore refers to multiple, distinct political communities who are not part of a single overarching community with the power to make and enforce law. While Locke portrays the state of nature between individuals on land as temporary, he argues that the international state of nature will persist indefinitely.

In the international state of nature governments have the right to punish violations of natural law that harm their citizens, because Locke stipulates that a commonwealth has "the power to punish any Injury done unto any of its Members, by any one that is not of it, (which is the *power of War and Peace*;) and all this for the preservation of the property of all the Members of that Society."[41] If foreigners attack English citizens then the English state is therefore empowered to use its foreign policy to defend their rights, including by going to war against the state(s) of which those foreigners are members. However, Locke's position is less clear on the question of whether third-party states have the right to punish crimes by noncitizens if their own citizens were not harmed. If, for example, a Spanish citizen violently seizes the property of an English citizen then is the French state entitled to use its power in the international state of nature to punish Spain? Locke scholars provide conflicting interpretations on this issue of third-party punishment in the international state of nature. Richard Tuck and David Armitage read Locke as arguing that states have rights of international punishment analogous to those of individuals in the state of nature, which means that all states have the right to punish violations of natural law by any foreign state or people.[42] This reading suggests that states have the right to enforce the laws of nature and punish noncitizens even if their own citizens were not victimized, so in the example above France would have the right to punish Spain. In opposition, Alex Tuckness interprets Locke as arguing that each state's right to punish crimes by noncitizens is limited by its responsibility to its own citizenry, and that a state is not justified in punishing noncitizens if this will bring no benefit to its own citizens.[43] In the example above, Tuckness's interpretation of Locke would suggest that France only has the right to punish Spain for the theft of English property if doing so will benefit the people of France. If punishing Spain would bring no benefits to the French people then Tuckness argues that intervention by the French state would be a violation of its obligation to promote the common good of its own citizens. These differing interpretations of law enforcement in the international state of nature mean that there is also disagreement about the implications of Locke's theory for the enforcement of law at sea.

NATURAL LAW AT SEA

In the *Two Treatises* Locke makes it clear that there is a universal natural law prohibiting attacks on the life, liberty, and property of others, and that this extends to the oceans. Since the oceans are a "Common of Mankind"[44] outside the exclusive jurisdiction of a commonwealth or other centralized legal authority it follows that the region is in the state of nature. However, just as the protection of natural rights on land requires efforts to prevent and punish offenders, the protection of natural rights at sea requires efforts to punish criminals such as pirates. If the individual right to enforce the laws of nature applied at sea in the same way that it does on land then individuals would enforce the laws of nature themselves against maritime criminals. This system would enable the victims of maritime crime to resist their attackers and would mean that everyone at sea had the right to punish maritime criminals, for example by capturing and killing pirates. In addition, victims of crime possess "a particular Right to seek *Reparation* from him that has done it,"[45] so the victim of a pirate raid has the right to reclaim his goods or obtain reparations from the pirates as compensation for his losses.

The enforcement of natural law at sea by individuals might lead to the punishment of some maritime criminals, but the system seems even less reliable than the individual enforcement of natural law on land. Locke argues that the self-enforcement of natural law on land will not be very effective because criminals will deny that laws apply to their case, those enforcing the law will be biased, and criminals may violently resist punishment. All three of these problems seem likely to occur at sea, and further problems would arise from the scale and nature of the oceans. The vast scale of the oceans means that a ship under attack from a powerful aggressor often would not have other ships nearby to whom they could appeal for help in defending themselves and punishing the aggressor. Moreover, the boundlessness and fluidity of the oceans make it possible for maritime criminals to escape punishment by sailing away to a different region. In combination, these problems mean that self-enforcement of natural law at sea would not be very effective and maritime criminals might often go unpunished. On land, Locke argues that the difficulty of individually enforcing natural law motivates people to leave the state of nature and create a commonwealth, but this solution does not seem practicable at sea. Locke's theory of property makes it practically impossible to appropriate an area of sea and Locke provides no explanation of how a region could become part of a civil society or state without first being privately appropriated. As a result, the oceans seem condemned to remain outside the exclusive territorial jurisdiction of any political community or state. However, the fact that the oceans are outside the exclusive territorial jurisdiction of states does not mean that states have no legal powers there. Instead, states have the right to enforce natural law in the international domain, and when citizens of different states meet on the common oceans their interactions take place in the international state of nature.

The lack of central legal authority in the international realm means that states are in the state of nature with respect to each other. Since natural law is universal everyone is required to follow it, and states can enforce natural law internationally by punishing other states if they violate it. Each state in the international state of nature is "one Body in the State of Nature, in respect of all other States or Persons out of its Community,"[46] so conflict between an English ship and a Spanish ship on the ocean is conflict between England and Spain. If an English ship at sea violently attacked a Spanish ship and seized its cargo then the Spanish would have the right to punish the English through international war.[47] By conceptualizing the population of each state as a unified entity in the international domain Locke turns an incident of maritime crime between citizens of different states into potential grounds for international war. The powers that states possess to enforce natural law at sea then depend on how one interprets Locke's view of third-party punishment. If states only possess the right to enforce law in the international context for the sake of benefiting their citizens, as Tuckness suggests, then states would only be justified in enforcing natural law at sea for their own national interest. It seems likely that the punishment of offenders' states by victims' states would suffer from problems of bias, because the rulers of the victims' state might seek a disproportionately severe punishment[48] and the rulers of the offenders' state might resist punishment of their citizens.[49] A prohibition on altruistic punishment by states might therefore reproduce the problems of law enforcement encountered by individuals in the state of nature. Alternatively, if Tuck and Armitage are correct that states in the international state of nature have the right to punish any violation of natural law by noncitizens, then third party states would have the right to punish crimes committed at sea. This would mean that if an English ship attacked a Spanish ship in the vicinity of a French naval vessel then the French could arrest, try, and punish the offenders even if this did not benefit French citizens. Punishment by third party states might produce more effective enforcement of natural law, because third party states are likely to be more impartial than the states of the criminals and victims, and it would enable interstate cooperation to punish maritime crimes committed by citizens of powerful states. However, even if states have a right of altruistic third-party punishment then there is little incentive for them to act on it. Locke acknowledges this lack of incentive to punish crimes against third parties as a problem in the state of nature between individuals, arguing that "negligence, and unconcernedness" is liable to make people "too remiss" in punishing offenses against others.[50] Whether or not we interpret Locke as arguing that states possess a right to engage in altruistic punishment in the international realm, it seems unlikely that states would often expend the resources of their citizens in punishing crimes by noncitizens unless they expected their people to benefit.

In addition to using their foreign policy to act in the international state of nature, states also have the power to pass national laws governing the conduct of their own citizens at sea. Locke argues that commonwealths have the right to legislate about the conduct of their citizens,[51] so the English state could pass laws prohibiting its citizens from engaging in aggressive violence or theft anywhere in the world, which would create a statutory basis for the English state to try English citizens for crimes committed at sea. This would mean that if an English citizen committed murder aboard a ship in the mid Atlantic then the English state could try the offender under domestic laws and then punish him with the English penal system. In Locke's view, this law enforcement by the state largely resolves the problems encountered with the enforcement of natural law by individuals. Where the citizen of one state commits a crime against the citizen of the same state at sea then the enforcement of national laws should be able to produce just and effective punishment. In practice, English ships in the seventeenth century were governed by English statutory and common law at sea, which provided the legal basis to try and punish crimes between people on English ships. English national law also regulated the behavior of English ships toward one another, for example by prohibiting English pirates from attacking English merchants.

This system of states enforcing their national laws over their own citizens at sea becomes more complicated when citizens commit crimes against non-citizens. If English law prohibited English citizens from engaging in aggressive violence and theft anywhere in the world then an Englishman who stole from a Spaniard at sea would be violating both English law and natural law. The English state would therefore be justified in trying and punishing its citizen under national law, but the Spanish would also have the right to punish the violation of natural law by using its foreign policy against England. In this situation the English state might have conflicting responsibilities: on the one hand it is responsible for upholding the law and punishing criminals, but on the other hand it is responsible for promoting the public good of its citizens. The English state might punish its citizen for this theft and provide reparations to the Spaniard, in which case the Spanish would have received justice without needing to threaten or use warfare. Alternatively, the English state might decide that the public good would be best served by not punishing or minimally punishing the theft, in which case Spain could use its foreign policy against the English. The punishment of maritime crime through interstate warfare would therefore be necessary only when that crime was not adequately punished and reparations provided by states' enforcement of national law. Locke's description of the citizens of each state as part of "one Body"[52] in the international state of nature reflects the fact that states can legally regulate the conduct of their own citizens and are therefore indirectly responsible for their citizens' actions, and for punishing those actions if necessary.

If the oceans are governed both by national laws and by natural law in the international state of nature then maritime crimes can be punished after the fact by a state enforcing its national law over its own citizens, or by a state enforcing the laws of nature in the international realm. However, victims of maritime crime still retain two important rights: the right to self-defense at the time of the crime, and the right to receive reparations. The Spaniards attacked by English pirates would therefore have the right to defend themselves against the pirates at the time of the crime, but not to punish the pirates after the fact. The Spaniards would also have the right to receive reparations for the harms caused by the English pirates, and could seek to enforce this right by appealing to English courts and/or to the Spanish state. The English courts might justly award reparations to the victims, but if they did not then the Spanish state could pursue the cause through its foreign policy against England. However, the Spanish state might decide that pursuing England for reparations would not be in the national interest, in which case the victims could remain uncompensated. Law enforcement in the international state of nature therefore depends on judgments of national interest and the public good, which might lead a state to refuse compensation to foreign victims of crimes committed by its citizens, or to decline to use foreign policy to obtain just reparations for citizens victimized by foreigners at sea. To remedy this problem, Grotius argues in *Mare Liberum* and *De Jure Belli ac Pacis* that in the absence of courts who justly enforce natural law individuals have the right to enforce it themselves, including by seizing foreign ships in reparation for their harms.[53] By contrast, Locke stipulates that citizens of a commonwealth have the right to receive reparations for their losses and that their state cannot waive this right, but he does not give victims the right to bypass the judicial process by directly seizing goods from the offender as reparation for their harm.

By categorizing the oceans as "that great and still remaining Common of Mankind"[54] Locke ensures that the seas are governed by natural law and indirectly by the statute law of commonwealths whose citizens travel at sea. This creates a complex legal situation whereby multiple entities have different rights to act in response to crimes committed at sea. If the victims are citizens of a state then they have the right to defend themselves while the crime is in process, the right to receive reparations after the fact, and can appeal to their state to punish the violation of natural law and obtain reparations. The offenders' state would also have the right to punish its citizens if they broke its national law, as occurred when English citizens violated English piracy law. Third party states might also have rights to punish the offenders: Tuckness would argue that third party states can only enforce natural law at sea if it benefits their citizens, whereas scholars who interpret Locke as advocating an unlimited right of third-party punishment would argue that any state can punish any crime committed at sea. The system for punishing maritime crime therefore depends on the citizenship (or lack thereof) of both the offenders and the victims, on the existence and content of national laws governing their citizens' conduct at sea, and on how one interprets Locke's account of the rights of states to impose punishment internationally. This system of law enforcement at sea is far from perfect and would suffer from bias due to competing national interests and from difficulties in punishing offenders who are citizens of powerful states. Judging by Locke's comments about enforcing natural law on land, he would expect the lack of established law, impartial judges, and a centralized enforcement power to limit the effectiveness of natural law enforcement at sea and to generate international conflict.

PIRACY IN THE *TWO TREATISES*

The system of law enforcement at sea that Locke proposes in the *Two Treatises* is complex and potentially confusing, so it may be helpful to consider how it applies to a specific form of maritime crime. Helpfully, Locke mentions maritime crime several times in the *Two Treatises* and his discussion centers on the archetypal maritime crime of piracy. Locke initially mentions piracy in the *First Treatise* during his critique of Robert Filmer's account of the divine right of Kings. Here, Locke observes that the claim that the descendant of Adam holds divinely authorized authority is inadequate because it is not clear who this descendant is and therefore who holds the authority. Locke scornfully rejects the notion that combining an existing King with belief in the principle of divinely authorized authority provides any reason to regard that King as divinely authorized, arguing "If this were not so, there would be no distinction between Pirates and Lawful Princes, he that has Force is without any more ado to be obey'd, and Crowns and Scepters would become the inheritance only of Violence and Rapine."[55] In this passage Locke uses pirates to provide a reductio ad absurdum of the claim that combining a general theoretical defense of the right to rule with de facto power constitutes political legitimacy or grounds for obedience.[56] By comparing pirates to unlawful rulers Locke draws attention to how piracy infringes on individual rights to life and liberty, as opposed to its threat to property.

Locke's identification of piracy with the attempt to assert illegitimate power by using force recurs in the *Second Treatise*. During his discussion of conquest Locke argues that aggressive violence cannot establish legitimate political authority, and he drives home this point by using the example of pirates:

> That the *Aggressor*, who puts himself into the state of War with another, and *unjustly invades* another Man's right, *can*, by such an unjust War, *never* come to *have a right over the Conquered*, will be easily agreed by all Men, who will not think, that Robbers and Pyrates have a Right of Empire over whomsoever they have Force enough to master; or that Men are bound by promises, which unlawful Force extorts from them.[57]

This reference to "Robbers and Pyrates" establishes a clear parallel between violent theft on land and violent theft at sea, and Locke makes it clear that both actions violate natural law in the same way. Moreover, Locke makes two significant arguments about the relationship between piracy and political authority. First, Locke argues that political authority cannot be established through illegal conquest and supports this claim by asserting that rulers who seek to establish authority over a people through aggressive violence are no different than violent criminals such as pirates. The similarity that Locke identifies between pirates and those who wage unjust wars is that both have broken the laws of nature by attacking the liberty, and perhaps the life and property, of other people. Moreover, piracy is a crime that ordinarily occurs in the international state of nature, so by analogizing unjust conquest to piracy Locke seeks to establish that unjust conquest is also a crime because it violates natural law in the international state of nature. Secondly, Locke maintains that agreements made under threat of illegal violence are not legally or morally binding, so coerced agreement does not count as true consent. If a person under duress agreed to obey the commands of a pirate or an unlawful conqueror then their coerced agreement is void, so neither piracy nor unlawful conquest can provide the basis for a voluntary contract.

Locke's arguments about the parallels between piracy and unlawful conquest clearly support his wider theory about natural law and the social contract, but they also have implications for seventeenth-century maritime practices. Throughout the seventeenth century European sailors (and some unlucky residents of coastal towns) were captured and enslaved by Barbary corsairs originating from the coastal cities of Morocco and the Ottoman empire.[58] The Barbary corsairs were infamous in England, and their capture of thousands of English people during the 1630s added to the controversy over Ship Money that contributed to the English Civil War. Prisoners captured by the corsairs were enslaved or ransomed, which may explain why Locke condemns piracy primarily on the grounds that it infringes on freedom. The widespread condemnation of the Barbary corsairs in England may be what Locke has in mind in this passage when he argues that the illegitimacy of pirates and robbers will be "easily agreed by all men."[59] However, the corsairs were not alone in using force to curtail the liberty of seventeenth-century English sailors, because in wartime the English navy seized thousands of unwilling sailors and forced them into naval service through impressment,[60] as I discuss in Chapter Five. The fact that maritime coercion was widely used both by foreign slavers and by the English state may be why Locke objects only to promises extracted through "unlawful Force"[61] and not to all promises extracted by force. If impressment was defined as legal and promises extracted by legal force were valid then the coerced agreement of a pressed man could be portrayed as voluntary and binding.

By comparing pirates to unlawful governments Locke makes it clear that his condemnation of power based on violence applies to individuals and states, thereby calling into question coercive state practices. To drive home this point, Locke argues explicitly that the same normative standards apply to both individuals and rulers:

> The Injury and the Crime is equal, whether committed by the wearer of a Crown, or some petty Villain. The Title of the Offender, and the Number of his Followers make no difference in the Offence, unless it be to aggravate it. The

only difference is, Great Robbers punish little ones, to keep them in their
Obedience, but the great ones are rewarded with Laurels and Triumphs, because they are too big for the weak hands of Justice in this World, and have the
power in their own possession, which should punish Offenders. [62]

In this passage Locke explicitly recognizes the practical difficulty of obtain-
ing punishment for rulers who violate natural law, which shows that he does
not expect law enforcement to be easy or particularly effective in the international state of nature. Locke also claims that kings who break natural law
should be condemned as much or more than petty criminals—an argument
that is radical, but not unprecedented. In *City of God* Augustine makes a very
similar argument that unjust governments are akin to violent thieves, asking
"Justice being taken away, then, what are kingdoms but great robberies? For
what are robberies themselves, but little kingdoms?"[63] Augustine develops
this point by using the example of pirates and identifying several parallels
between pirates and states: both are communities with the authority of a
leader, a cooperative pact, and agreed division of the spoils. For emphasis,
Augustine recounts an exchange between Alexander the Great and a pirate
who observes that the difference between himself and Alexander's empire is
only a matter of scale. Locke may have been unaware of Augustine's discussion of pirates,[64] but the tale of Alexander and the pirate also appears in
Cicero's *De Re Publica*[65] and Locke was certainly familiar with Cicero's
work.[66] Whether or not Locke's echo of Cicero and Augustine is deliberate,
his use of pirates to exemplify illegitimate political power based on violence
is part of a longer history of pirates being condemned as illegitimate authority figures within European political thought.

Locke makes a further reference to piracy in his discussion of the dissolution of government. Here, Locke argues that an unjust government breaks the
social contract and thereby begins "*a state of War*, which is that of Force
without Authority"[67] between the ruler and the people. Efforts to resist or
remove that illegitimate government are therefore acts of justifiable self-
defense against an aggressor. To emphasize his argument that the people can
lawfully resist illegitimate rulers, Locke uses the example of pirates:

But if they, who say it *lays a foundation for Rebellion*, mean that it may
occasion Civil Wars, or Intestine Broils, to tell the People that they are ab-
solved from Obedience, when illegal attempts are made upon their Liberties or
Properties, and may oppose the unlawful violence of those, who were their
Magistrates . . . They may as well say upon the same ground, that honest Men
may not oppose Robbers or Pirates, because this may occasion disorder or
bloodshed. If any *mischief* come in such Cases, it is not *to be charged* upon
him, who defends his own right, but *on him*, that *invades* his Neighbours. [68]

Here, Locke makes it clear that resistance against both pirates and unlawful governments is justifiable even though these actions may lead to violence and political instability. Locke therefore acknowledges that refusing to obey an illegitimate ruler may have some negative consequences, but argues that the responsibility for these consequences lies with the aggressor: if resisting the unlawful demands of a pirate leads to bloodshed then the fault lies with the pirates for their unlawful aggression, and not with the victim for resisting it.[69] Moreover, Locke argues that resisting such unlawful authority is more beneficial than acceding to it, because otherwise aggressors will dominate or destroy their victims.[70] Locke's implicit comparison between the benefits of resisting pirates and unlawful rulers is revealing, because opposing pirates may benefit an individual ship by enabling it to protect its cargo, but also conveys a broader social benefit by discouraging piracy and thus indirectly making other ships safer.[71] By analogizing unlawful rulers to pirates Locke therefore suggests that resistance to unjust governments is not only legitimate, but also serves the public good.

While Locke defends those who resist an illegitimate government he argues that there is no right to resist or remove a lawful government, and condemns rebels against legitimate governments as "the common Enemy and Pest of Mankind."[72] This denunciation of unlawful rebels echoes the Roman categorization of pirates as *hostis humani generi*, or the enemy of mankind. Roman law labeled pirates as *hostis humani generi* on the reasoning that the seas were open to all and therefore predation by pirates threatened the shipping of every state.[73] By describing rebels against legitimate governments as the enemy of mankind Locke similarly suggests that those who rebel against a lawful government threaten not only the specific government that they seek to remove, but all lawful governments everywhere in the world. Further, Locke argues that unlawful rebels commit similar crimes to pirates, because their destruction of the legitimate constitution will cause: "Blood, Rapine, and Desolation."[74] Initially this link between pirates and rebellion seems contrary to Locke's account of pirates elsewhere in the *Two Treatises*, where they are consistently equated with tyranny, but this tension can be resolved by closer consideration of the practice of piracy. It is logical for Locke to regard pirates as rebellious because pirate crews often formed through mutiny against their former captain, which is why the 1700 Piracy Act defined mutineers as pirates.[75] Pirates are therefore unlawful rebels insofar as the founding of a pirate crew involves rebellion against their legitimate captain. However, pirates are also tyrants insofar as they use unlawful force and coercion to remove the liberty of their victims and to steal from them. Locke therefore suggests that piracy involves two distinct crimes: the illegal overthrow of a legitimate ruler that takes place when would-be pirates mutiny against their legitimate captain, and the illegal attacks on victims that occur when the pirates raid other ships.

Locke refers to pirates repeatedly in the *Two Treatises* and in each case compares them to other criminal figures, including robbers, illegitimate rulers, and unlawful rebels. By repeatedly comparing crimes at sea to crimes on land Locke makes it clear that natural law extends across the world's oceans and that the same punishments are appropriate for maritime and terrestrial criminals. These passages also indicate that pirates are guilty of breaking natural law in multiple ways: their theft violates natural law about property, but their use of force also violates the victims' rights to liberty, health, and life. By creating a state of war pirates pose a simultaneous threat to all the natural rights of their victims, so the victims have the right to use violence in self-defense, including by killing the pirates. When comparing pirates to illegitimate rulers Locke argues that the combination of a general theoretical justification of the right to rule and a de facto ruler does not establish that the ruler is legitimate: just as pirates may have seized control of the ship from the legitimate captain, a tyrant may have seized control of the state from the lawful king. Locke develops this point by arguing that force can never establish legitimate political authority, and that aggression by rulers is at least as blameworthy as that by pirates. By equating the crimes committed by pirates to those committed by rulers who attempt to establish political power through conquest Locke thereby suggests that punishment is appropriate both for pirates and for unjust governments that use force. Further, Locke adds that promises extracted by threats of illegal force carry no legal or moral weight, so neither rulers nor pirates can use violence or intimidation to establish a contract with their victims. In relation to the right of resistance, Locke argues that the victims of both pirates and unlawful rulers have the right to resist unjust force and should not be discouraged by the risk of violence and political disorder. Throughout the *Two Treatises* Locke identifies piracy with illegitimate power, violence, and theft by force.

The passages about piracy in the *Two Treatises* leave no doubt that natural law applies at sea, that pirates are guilty of violating natural law, and that victims of piracy can legitimately use violence to resist and defend themselves against the pirates. Locke's condemnation of pirates in the *Two Treatises* is consistent with his position in the unpublished paper "Pyracy 97," which I will discuss in more detail in the next chapter. In "Pyracy 97" Locke argues that piracy seriously threatens trade and damages the international reputation of Christians, so he advocates the punishment of pirates throughout the world. [76] To enable the more effective punishment of pirates Locke calls for the major European maritime states to make a treaty agreeing to pass laws against piracy, punish citizens who commit piracy, and agree that if they apprehend any noncitizen pirates then they will either punish them or send them to their country of citizenship for punishment. [77] In "Pyracy 97" Locke therefore implies that states have the right to pass national laws prohibiting piracy and to enforce these laws over their own citizens, and that it would be beneficial for states to do so. Moreover, Locke's proposals in "Pyracy 97" imply that states can legally use their national laws to try noncitizens for piracy and punish them accordingly, an act with the potential to cause international conflict between the pirates' state and the state imposing the punishment. Although "Pyracy 97" suggests that states can and should prohibit and punish piracy Locke does not explain the moral and legal principles underlying this position in the text; instead, Locke presents his normative principles around piracy in the *Two Treatises* and his specific policy proposals in "Pyracy 97."

Locke's discussions of piracy in the *Two Treatises* and "Pyracy 97" reflect the fact that maritime crime was a serious and growing problem in the late seventeenth century, as Locke knew from his colonial and economic work. Locke was an acknowledged expert on international trade and twice held a national office relating to trade policy: he was Secretary and Treasurer to the Board of Trade and Plantations from October 1673 to December 1674,[78] and from June 1696 to June 1700 he was the most prominent member of the renamed Board of Trade. The Council of Trade and Foreign Plantations was responsible for advising colonial governors and approving laws passed in Jamaica, Barbados, the Leeward Islands, and Virginia, and maritime theft by pirates and privateers was common in these areas. One of Locke's first tasks for the Council was to write advice about how to recapture New York from a fleet of Dutch navy ships and privateers, and this document from November 1673 bears his signature in the margin.[79] Issues of privateering and piracy[80] recurred throughout Locke's appointment when the Council received complaints about raids on British traders by Spanish and Dutch ships.[81] Moreover, it is likely that Locke considered the issue of piracy while managing his colonial investments and those of Anthony Ashley Cooper, later the Earl of Shaftesbury. Piracy in the seventeenth century was concentrated in the Red Sea, Caribbean, Africa, and the east coast of the Americas. This geographical distribution of piracy coincides with Locke's areas of financial interest, because he personally owned stakes in the Bahamas Company and the Royal African Company, and he managed the affairs of the Carolinas as part of his work for Shaftesbury. Locke's references to pirates in the *Two Treatises* should therefore be understood in the context of his existing knowledge about piracy and the problems that it caused for English colonies and trade.

While the social contract improves law enforcement on land, Locke's *Two Treatises* portray the seas as a permanent common that is outside exclusive state jurisdiction, which makes law enforcement on the oceans highly complex. Since states have the right to pass laws regulating the conduct of their citizens they can prohibit their citizens from engaging in certain activities at sea, and punish those who do so. In addition, citizens of one state who encounter citizens of another state at sea are in the international state of nature with respect to each other, so any violation of natural law can be resolved by foreign policy between their respective states. However, if people who are not part of a state or civil society travel on the seas then they are individuals in the state of nature and each have individual rights to enforce natural law. Conduct at sea is therefore restricted both by natural law and by the national legislation of multiple states, which may not always agree. Depending on the situation, criminals at sea may be punished under natural law or national laws, and the right to punish maritime criminals may lie with the individual victims, the state of whom the victims are citizens, or the state of whom the offenders are citizens. Nonetheless, maritime crime might not be effectively punished, because offenders might evade punishment by fleeing to other parts of the globe and/or states might decide that it was not in their national interest to punish offenders. Since Locke argues that effective punishment reduces crime through deterrence and incapacitation,[82] non-punishment or under-punishment of maritime crimes would presumably increase crime rates at sea, which could threaten maritime trade. This lack of reliable law enforcement at sea is problematic given that Locke favors the expansion of international trade,[83] which requires efforts to uphold lawful ownership and exchange. This tension between Locke's commitment to trade and the lack of effective law enforcement at sea was not only a theoretical problem. By 1697 the negative impact of piracy on English trade motivated Locke to propose an international treaty between the major European states that would prohibit and severely punish pirates throughout the world.

NOTES

1. Locke, *Two Treatises*, II §30 289.
2. *Ibid*, II §6 271.
3. *Ibid*, II §6 271.
4. *Ibid*, II §11 274.
5. *Ibid*, II §7 271.
6. *Ibid*, II §7 271.
7. *Ibid*, II §57 306.
8. *Ibid*, II §12 275.
9. *Ibid*, II §10 273.
10. *Ibid*, II §11 274.
11. *Ibid*, II §11 274.
12. *Ibid*, II §16 278.
13. *Ibid*, II §16 279.
14. *Ibid*, II §17 279.
15. *Ibid*, II §18 279–80.
16. Andrew Dilts, "To Kill a Thief: Punishment, Proportionality, and Criminal Subjectivity in Locke's *Second Treatise*," *Political Theory* 40, no. 1 (2012): 63.
17. Locke, *Two Treatises*, II §19 280.
18. Dilts, "To Kill a Thief," 65.
19. Locke, *Two Treatises*, II §123 284.
20. *Ibid*, II §13 276.
21. *Ibid*, II §125 351.

22. *Ibid*, II §126 351.
23. *Ibid*, II §123 350.
24. *Ibid*, II §13 276.
25. *Ibid*, II §124–6 351.
26. *Ibid*, II §130 353.
27. *Ibid*, II §122 349.
28. *Ibid*, II §9 273 and §122 349.
29. *Ibid*, II §11 274.
30. The existence of these two distinct rights to punish criminals and to receive reparations is also described in "Atlantis," which Locke wrote in the late 1670s. In "Atlantis" Locke outlines principles for a potential colony, including the proposal that criminals be required to pay monetary reparations as well as receiving a proportionate punishment: "If afterwards he shall commit any fault that is criminal he shall not only be punished proportionately to the crime but his sureties shall make reparation for it, viz. if he has robbed he shall be hanged and his sureties make good to the robbed both their loss and the charge of prosecution." See John Locke, "Atlantis" in *Locke: Political Essays*, 252.
31. Locke, *Two Treatises*, II §19 280–1.
32. *Ibid*, II §48 301. Locke also presents arguments about the importance of engaging in work in "Atlantis" and his "Essay on the Poor Law," see Locke, "Atlantis," 252–9; John Locke, "An Essay on the Poor Law," in *Locke: Political Essays*, 182–98.
33. Locke, *Two Treatises*, II §41 296–7.
34. Milton Friedman, *Capitalism and Freedom: Fortieth Anniversary Edition* (Chicago: University of Chicago Press, 2002), 14.
35. Nozick, *Anarchy, State, and Utopia*, 24.
36. Bernhard Harcourt, *The Illusion of Free Markets: Punishment and the Myth of Natural Order* (Cambridge, MA: Harvard University Press, 2011).
37. Locke, *Two Treatises*, II §19 281.
38. *Ibid*, II §14 276.
39. *Ibid*, II §14 277.
40. *Ibid*, II §145 365.
41. *Ibid*, II §88 324.
42. Tuck, *Rights of War and Peace*, 177; Armitage, "John Locke's International Thought," 39.
43. Alex Tuckness, "Punishment, Property, and the Limits of Altruism: Locke's International Asymmetry," *The American Political Science Review* 102, no. 4 (2008): 472.
44. Locke, *Two Treatises*, II §30 289.
45. *Ibid*, II §10 273.
46. *Ibid*, II §145 365.
47. *Ibid*, II §88 324.
48. *Ibid*, II §125 351.
49. *Ibid*, II §124 351 and §126 351.
50. *Ibid*, II §125 351.
51. *Ibid*, II §129 352.
52. *Ibid*, II §145 365.
53. Grotius, *Freedom of the Seas*, 74–5; Neff, *Hugo Grotius*, 274.
54. Locke, *Two Treatises*, II §30 289.
55. *Ibid*, I §81 203.
56. Several decades later Hume uses the example of pirates to make the same point in equally scathing terms: "Nor has the greatest and most lawful prince any more reason, upon that account, to plead a peculiar sacredness or inviolable authority, than an inferior magistrate, or even an usurper, or even a robber and a pirate," see David Hume "Of the Original Contract," in *Social Contract: Essays by Locke, Hume, and Rousseau*, ed. Ernest Barker (London: Oxford University Press, 1947), 210–1.
57. Locke, *Two Treatises*, II §176 385.
58. Nabil Matar, "The Barbary Corsairs, King Charles I and the Civil War," *The Seventeenth Century* 16, no. 2 (2001): 239–58.

59. Locke, *Two Treatises*, II §176 385.

60. Again, Hume makes a related point with his example of how a man carried on board a ship while asleep is faced with the choice of remaining on board, or drowning. This example is both a critique of Locke's argument that residents of a state tacitly consent to obey its laws, and an apparent criticism of the practice of impressment, see Hume "Of the Original Contract," 222.

61. Locke, *Two Treatises*, II §176 385.

62. *Ibid*, II §176 385–6.

63. Augustin, *St. Augustin's City of God and Christian Doctrine*, trans. Philip Schaf (Grand Rapids, MI: Christian Classics Ethereal Library, 1890), 104.

64. Locke does not cite *City of God* and his library did not include work by Augustine, see Harrison and Laslett, *Library of John Locke*.

65. Cicero, *De Re Publica & De Legibus*, trans. Clinton Walker Keyes (Cambridge, MA: Harvard University Press, 1928) III: xv, 205.

66. Locke owned many texts by Cicero and recommended Cicero's work both to his students at Oxford and in "Some Thoughts Concerning Reading and study for a Gentleman," see Harrison and Laslett, *Library of John Locke*, 108–9; Woolhouse, *Locke: A Biography* (New York: Cambridge University Press, 2007), 47; and Locke, "Some Thoughts," 376.

67. Locke, *Two Treatises*, II §227 416.

68. *Ibid*, II §228 416–7.

69. *Ibid*, II §228 417.

70. *Ibid*, II §228 417.

71. To encourage crews to oppose pirates and thus discourage piracy, the 1700 Piracy Act provided rewards for crews that repelled pirate attacks. For discussion of the Act and Locke's involvement in drafting it, see Chapter Three.

72. Locke, *Two Treatises*, II §230 418.

73. Daniel Heller-Roazen, *The Enemy of All: Piracy and the Law of Nations* (New York: Zone Books, 2009).

74. Locke, *Two Treatises*, II §230 418.

75. Piracy was defined to include "any seaman or mariner, [who] shall in any place where the admiral hath jurisdiction, betray his trust, and turn pirate, enemy, or rebel, and piratically and feloniously run away with his or their ship or ships," An Act for the More Effectuall Suppressions of Piracy (Piracy Act), 1698, 11 Will. 3, c. 7.

76. MS Locke c. 30, fol. 62, Bodleian Library, Oxford.

77. *Ibid*, fol. 62.

78. Bieber, "British Plantation Councils."

79. GBPRO, *Calendar of State Papers Colonial*, vol. 7, 530–1.

80. There is a significant legal distinction between pirates and privateers. Privateers had a letter of marque issued by a government that gave them a legal right to attack and steal from ships belonging to hostile nations. In principle, privateers were therefore legal from the perspective of their home state, although in practice the situation was often messier. By contrast, pirates had no government-issued letter of marque, so their activity lacked a legal justification. Despite this legal distinction, the behavior of privateers and pirates was often quite similar, see Peter Hayes, "Pirates, Privateers and the Contract Theories of Hobbes and Locke," *History of Political Thought*, 29, no. 3 (2008): 461–84.

81. In late February 1674 the Council discussed privateers in response to a petition by merchants, and proposed the capture and recall of two English Captains who were privateering for Spain, GBPRO, *Calendar of State Papers Colonial*, vol. 7, 558–9. Then in March 1674 the Council received a letter from the governor of the Leeward Islands complaining about Dutch privateers attacking merchants, *Ibid*, 561.

82. Locke, *Two Treatises*, II §7 271.

83. John Locke, "Trade," 221–2.

Chapter Three

Locke's War on Piracy

In the previous two chapters I outlined the legal status of the seas in the *Two Treatises*, where Locke conceptualizes the oceans as belonging in common to all humans, existing outside state borders, and governed by natural law. Natural law prohibits attacks on the life, property, and freedom of any individual, so violence and theft by pirates breaks natural law. Locke argues that it is both legitimate and beneficial for victims to resist pirate attacks, and victims of piracy also have a right to receive reparations for the harms they suffered. However, the system for enforcing law at sea is complex and appropriate punishment may be difficult to achieve. Since the oceans are jointly owned by all humans they are outside the direct territorial jurisdiction of any state and are directly governed only by natural law. When citizens of different states meet on the oceans then their interactions take place in the international state of nature, so an attack at sea by English citizens upon Indian citizens is a violation of natural law by England for which the Indian authorities have the right to seek punishment and reparations. States also have the right to pass and enforce laws over their citizens, so when the citizens of a state travel on the oceans then the reach of that state's law is indirectly extended across the oceans. If the domestic laws of a state prohibit violent theft then according to Locke's theory any citizens of that state who commit violent theft at sea are breaking its domestic law, as well as breaking the laws of nature. If English laws prohibit piracy then English citizens who commit piracy can be tried for the crime in English courts and punished by the English penal system. Multiple entities therefore have different and sometimes overlapping rights to punish pirates, including the victims, the state of which the victims are citizens, and the state of which the offenders are citizens.

Although Locke makes it clear that pirates can legitimately be punished under natural law he also suggests that enforcing natural law is challenging, because criminals will deny that the law applies to them and resist punishment, and those imposing punishment may make biased decisions.[1] On land the "Inconveniences"[2] of enforcing natural law in the state of nature are temporary, because people respond by forming commonwealths. At sea the lack of a *"common Judge with Authority"*[3] over international crime and conflict means that the international state of nature and difficulties in enforcing law over maritime criminals will persist. The theory of maritime law that Locke presents in the *Two Treatises* therefore suggests that there will be serious and continuing difficulties in punishing maritime criminals such as pirates, and that maritime crime between the citizens of different states will be a source of international conflict. Although Locke does not resolve the problem of how to effectively enforce law at sea in the *Two Treatises*, he returned to the question as part of his work for the Board of Trade in the 1690s. In this chapter I examine Locke's Board of Trade work on piracy, including the proposals outlined in his unpublished "Pyracy 97" document. While Locke's Board of Trade writings and activity on piracy were consistent with his vision of law in the *Two Treatises*, they also had significant implications for English naval policy and the system of governance in England's Caribbean and American colonies.

PIRACY IN THE SEVENTEENTH CENTURY

Maritime theft was common throughout the seventeenth century, but the legal status of this activity depended on whether the culprits were privateers or pirates. Privateers had a letter of marque issued by a government or sovereign that proclaimed their legal right to attack and steal from ships belonging to hostile nations, which often meant English or Dutch privateers attacking Spanish or Portuguese ships. The proceeds of privateer raids were supposed to be declared to the authorities at a prize court and then shared between the sovereign, ship's owners, captain, and crew. The owners of privateer ships sought to protect their financial investment by appointing a powerful captain to command the crew, so privateer ships characteristically had inegalitarian pay and systems of governance.[4] By contrast, pirates had no letter of marque, so they were not held to its legal restrictions and could steal from ships without concern about the vessel's country of origin. Pirates did not declare their captures at prize courts, pay investors, or pay a proportion of their prize to a sovereign. Instead, pirates distributed their gains solely among the crew, which enabled an egalitarian pay structure and a more democratic model of governance on pirate ships.[5] In practice, this distinction between privateers and pirates was often less clear, because privateers frequently broke the terms of their letters of marque, colonial governors issued letters of marque that conflicted with national policy, and victims frequently could not differentiate privateers from pirates. Moreover, the perceived legality of privateers often depended on the nationality of the observer, so what the English regarded as lawful privateering was often seen as piracy by the Spanish.

English privateers had targeted Spanish ships and ports since the 1570s, and it was not uncommon for their actions to exceed authorized behavior and turn into piracy. One famous privateer-turned-pirate was Henry Morgan, who repeatedly raided the Spanish from the 1660s until his death in 1688. In 1668 Morgan caused a diplomatic incident when he attacked Santiago Castle in Portobello, ransomed the hostages he captured, and took away over 250,000 pesos, even though England was at peace with Spain at the time.[6] In return Morgan was sent back to England and imprisoned, but Charles II later relented and gave him a knighthood and the post of lieutenant governor of Jamaica. Morgan's career shows the high stakes and liminal status of privateers, who could be celebrated as national heroes for bringing England bullion and inconveniencing its enemies, or condemned as violent criminals whose actions risked international war. This uncertainty about how the English state would respond to privateers who acted outside the terms of their letter of marque reflects the unsettled nature of maritime law in the seventeenth century, ever-changing foreign policy, and the mixture of risks and rewards that officially sanctioned maritime theft offered the state. The common practice of privateering, complaints by victims, and sporadic piracy trials provide the context for Locke's colonial work and his discussion of pirates in the *Two Treatises of Government*.

Locke first became involved in English maritime policy during his appointment as Secretary and Treasurer of the Council of Trade and Foreign Plantations in 1673. The Council was responsible for promoting England's foreign trade, advising colonial governors, and approving laws passed in the Crown colonies of Jamaica, Barbados, the Leeward Islands, and Virginia.[7] In July 1673 the Dutch had retaken control of New York from the English by attacking with a fleet of Dutch vessels and privateers,[8] and the Council repeatedly discussed this during late 1673.[9] As Secretary, Locke was given the task of composing the Council's advice to the King about recapturing New York, which recommended sending four English navy ships and armed merchant vessels.[10] Five days later the Council approved the document, which bears Locke's signature.[11] Soon afterwards the issue of privateer attacks recurred. In February 1674 the Council discussed a petition by a group of West Indies merchants about the seizure of their ships by the Spanish, and issued a proclamation forbidding two English Captains from privateering for Spain.[12] Then in March 1674 the Council received a letter from the governor of the Leeward Islands complaining about attacks on merchants by Dutch privateers, [13] and a petition about Dutch privateers from the representatives of St. Christopher's, Nevis, Montserrat, and Antigua. [14] Maritime crime was therefore a recurring issue in Locke's work for the Council until the dissolution of the Council of Trade and Foreign Plantations in late December 1674.

By 1696 pressure from Parliament led King William to reintroduce a body with powers similar to the previous Council of Trade and Foreign Plantations, which was termed the Commissioners of Trade and is now commonly referred to as the Board of Trade. [15] The Board was constituted in May 1696 and made responsible for "promoting the trade of the Kingdom and for inspecting and improving the Plantations." [16] Locke served on the Board from its creation until June 1700 and was the most influential Whig member, [17] but his views clashed with those of the influential Tory Board member, William Blathwayt. [18] Although Board decisions were collective, Board members refused to sign documents that they seriously disagreed with [19] and their individual perspectives are also expressed in their personal documents and letters. In practice, Locke and Blathwayt rarely coincided at meetings because each attended seasonally: Locke was present from around June to November each year, whereas Blathwayt attended in winter and spring. [20] Locke was engaged in Board affairs even when he was not able to attend meetings, and received both letters and Board minutes from the Board's Secretary, William Popple, who was Locke's own former Secretary. [21]

Ships from England's American and Caribbean colonies had been raiding vessels in the Red Sea since the early 1690s, when the governor of Jamaica reported that "pirates . . . have found their way into the Red Sea, where they have committed unheard of piracies, murders and barbarities. These are now returned with vast wealth to most of the northern plantations in America." [22] This Red Sea piracy did not create major problems for English colonial governance until August 1695, when English pirates led by Captain Avery [23] and Captain Tew attacked an Indian pilgrim fleet containing a ship owned by Aurangzeb, the Emperor of India. The Indian authorities held the East India Company responsible for the behavior of English ships, including the pirates, and responded by arresting East India Company staff and suspending their trade. It took months for news of the piracy and Indian response to reach England, [24] but on July 25, 1696, the Board of Trade was informed that sixty pirates from the Red Sea had arrived in the American colonies with treasure worth "£1,000 to £1,500 a man." [25] This information was soon confirmed by the senior customs official Edward Randolph who stated that Captain Tew originated from Rhode Island and accused the governors of the Bahamas, Carolina, Pennsylvania, and Rhode Island of harboring pirates. [26] By September 1696 the Board began to receive letters about Red Sea piracy from colonial governors and merchants, [27] including the governor of Jamaica who described the recent arrival of a pirate crew at the Bahamas with "great wealth, up to £300,000." [28] Locke attended discussions about piracy at the

Board meetings until mid November, when ill health forced him to leave London for the winter.[29]

The Board of Trade was evidently concerned by these reports of piracy, but initially told the King that the problem was due to "the encouragement offered to piracy by the entertainment of pirates by the Proprietary Colonies."[30] On December 3, 1696, the King responded by ordering that the Proprietors be required to "take care that such entertainment shall cease in future, under the severest penalties."[31] This first reaction of blaming the proprietary colonies[32] for piracy reflected a broader belief that the governance structure of these colonies made them more resistant to English laws and more likely to engage in illegal activity.[33] By holding proprietary colonies responsible for piracy, the English authorities created a justification for imposing greater Crown and Parliamentary control over those colonies. However, this initial explanation of piracy was quickly proved to be inadequate, because in late December 1696 the Board of Trade received papers from the East India Company proving that people in Crown colonies such as New York were also involved in piracy.[34] These documents made it clear that the Board of Trade would need to take further action, so in January and February 1697 the Board issued letters to colonial proprietors and governors informing them of the reports about piracy in their colonies and passing on the King's orders to suppress pirates.[35]

After issuing these letters the Board took no further action on piracy until the summer of 1697 when the Secretary, William Popple, exchanged letters with the new governor of New Jersey, Jeremiah Basse.[36] On July 26 Basse sent Popple a detailed account of piracy in the American colonies, reporting that "In all I am told that there are gone from Boston, New York, Pennsylvania, Carolina and Barbados, from each one ship and from Rhode Island two."[37] Basse also told the Board that pirates could not currently be tried in the colonies, because piracy trials could only occur in Admiralty courts and the colonies lacked Admiralty jurisdiction.[38] To remedy this, Basse proposed that the King authorize the creation of Admiralty courts in each colony. The Board read this letter on July 30 and responded by asking Basse for more information and proposing a new law to extend the existing English piracy law to the American and Caribbean colonies:

> Ordered, that Mr Bass be asked what Instances he can give of the Entertainment of Pyrats in Rhode-Island, New-Yorke, Carolina and Providence; which places he names in his letter; And that he be desired to name also the Pirats that he says are gon from Boston, Rhode-Island, New-York, Pensilvania, Carolina and Barbadoes; And also to give directions how the Mate of the Nassau whom he quotes for some Intelligence about Pirates may be spoke withall. Ordered also, that Enquiry be made of all the Plantations, what Laws they have in force for the Tryall of Pirates; And that when their Lordships shall be ready to make any report upon the Subject of Pirates it be remembered to

lay before the King, that the intent of the Statute of 28: Hen 8vi: Cap: 15 may
by proper Clauses in a New Act of Parliament here be extended to the Plantations.[39]

These instructions from the Board on July 30 are strikingly similar to the list
of questions and suggestions on the third page of Locke's undated "Pyracy
97" papers.

LOCKE'S PROPOSALS IN "PYRACY 97"

Locke's suggestions about how to respond to piracy are presented in an
unpublished manuscript labeled "Pyracy 97," held in the Bodleian Library.
The manuscript has three pages: the first two pages are on small sheets of
paper and make up a single document about piracy, which is written in
complete paragraphs and includes a short crossed-out passage.[40] Locke addresses "your Excellencys" the Lords Justices of England twice, suggesting
that the text was directed to them, but it is unclear if a copy of the document
was sent or received.[41] The third page is written on a larger sheet of paper
and contains a list of rough questions.[42] All three sheets are undated, but on
the first sheet Locke refers to the "Christian princes & states now assembled
by their ministers in Holland,"[43] indicating that it was composed during
negotiations for the Treaty of Ryswick. A more precise composition date can
be inferred by comparing "Pyracy 97" to the Board Journal and Basse's letter
of July 26. On the third page of "Pyracy 97" Locke lists known instances of
piracy from the colonies identical to those described in Basse's letter, and the
content and sequence of questions match those recorded in the Board of
Trade Journal:

> Q Rhode Island New Yorke Carolina & Providence Q what instances
> Gon from Boston 1. Rode Island 2. N Yorke 1. Pensylvania 1. Carolina 1.
> Barbados 1. Q their names
> Q the Mate of the Nassaw. Capt Say owner of the Nassaw
> Q Whether we should not give instructions to the Plantations to secure the
> pyrates
> Q Whether we should not the next Pt move for enlargring the Act for the tryal
> of Pyrates in the Plantations.[44]

This overlap suggests that either Locke's "Pyracy 97" paper was based on
the July 30, 1697, Board decision, or the Board decision was based on
Locke's paper.[45] The content of the first two pages of "Pyracy 97" also
suggests that they were written after reading Basse's July 26 letter, because
Locke proposes extending England's existing piracy law to the colonies,
which remedies the lack of Admiralty jurisdiction in the colonies that Basse
identified. It is therefore likely that "Pyracy 97" was written for discussion

by the Board at some point between receipt of Basse's letter on July 26, 1697, and the signing of the Treaty of Ryswick on September 20, 1697.[46]

Locke's serious concern about piracy is immediately apparent in "Pyracy 97," which opens with a strongly worded claim about the threat posed to Europe by pirates:

> Since there is noe thing can be more prejudicial to trade in General Than piracie & the Great collection of European pirates th is now gathered together in or about the Red Sea seems to threaten the whole trade of Europe as well as render the Christian name Odious through the whole world.[47]

Here, Locke makes both the general claim that piracy is the greatest risk to trade and the specific claim that current piracy in the Red Sea is highly damaging to Europe. Next, Locke expresses concern that the threat posed by piracy may increase, suggesting that it "may prove of fatal consequence if they should yr imbody and setle together upon any place where they might have a secure retreat."[48] This passage implies that Locke was aware of reports that pirates used a port in Madagascar,[49] and favors swift action to prevent them from developing settlements there. Locke then makes a series of proposals about how both Europe and England should tackle piracy. First, he suggests that all the states "now assembled by their ministers in Holland" introduce a six-month period of amnesty for their subjects who have engaged in piracy, provided that former pirates return their ship to its country of origin and apply for a legal pardon in their own country.[50] For pirates who do not apply for a pardon as stipulated or who commit future acts of piracy Locke proposes apprehension, trial, and punishment: "by the joynt force of all the said princes & their allies be prosecuted to the utmost parts of the world & whenever taken have the severitie of the law paste upon them without pardon or relaxation."[51] Further, Locke calls for an agreement between all the states assembled in Holland that they will not harbor pirates and that if any pirates arrive in their jurisdiction then they will either try and punish them or send the pirates to "their respective countries to receive there the sentence due."[52] Since English, French, Spanish, and Dutch representatives were all present at the Treaty negotiations, Locke is effectively proposing a formal international agreement about piracy between Europe's leading maritime and colonial states. The agreement that Locke recommends would have introduced a coordinated European response involving harsh punishment for all future piracy.

Next, Locke acknowledges that many of the pirates active in the Red Sea originated from English colonies in North America and "are apt to be too favorably rec'd in some of the English plantations there."[53] Given this, Locke suggests two amendments to English piracy laws: the explicit extension of these piracy laws to the American colonies, and revisions to ensure "the surer punishment of pirates, & effectuall restraint of piracie."[54] Locke therefore repeats the Board of Trade's July 30 recommendation that existing English laws on piracy should be extended to the colonies, but adds to it. Whereas the Board of Trade did not suggest that existing English laws on piracy were inadequate, Locke proposes changes to make it more certain that pirates will be punished and to more effectively prevent future acts of piracy. While Locke does not specify how piracy would be prevented, he argues in the *Second Treatise* that punishments for violating natural law should be severe enough to deter potential criminals and prevent dangerous people from re-offending.[55] If English piracy laws imposed punishments that did not deter piracy or stop recidivism then the logic of Locke's argument in the *Second Treatise* suggests that more severe punishment should be used, such as enslavement or death. Locke's suggestion that the law should better prevent piracy may therefore be a call for the introduction of more severe penalties for convicted pirates, potentially including the death penalty.

On a separate sheet Locke poses a series of questions about piracy originating in English colonies, and lists seven known instances of piracy from five American colonies and one Caribbean colony,[56] which match the list provided by Basse. Locke also suggests two policy responses for piracy: "Q. whether we should not give instructions to the plantations to secure the pyrates Q. whether we should not the next Pt move for enlarging the Act for Tryal of Pyrates in the plantations."[57] Locke's question about ordering the colonies to secure the pirates implies that he saw the colonial authorities as liable not to arrest the pirates unless they received an explicit order to do so, which might enable the pirates to escape justice. The final question about the extension of English piracy laws suggests that Locke favors a uniform piracy law for all English jurisdictions, which would be created by the English Parliament. Whereas Basse suggested giving Admiralty jurisdiction to the colonies, which would empower each colony to create its own piracy law and courts, Locke's proposal involves the imposition of uniform piracy laws from London. These questions suggest that Locke did not have confidence that colonial authorities would arrest pirates or pass appropriate legislation against piracy, and that he favored a uniform and centralized approach to combatting piracy in the English colonies.

Overall, the "Pyracy 97" document shows Locke's detailed knowledge about piracy and his focus on developing effective policies that would ensure the capture, trial, and severe punishment of pirates throughout the world. While some of Locke's proposals overlap with the suggestions developed by the Board of Trade, "Pyracy 97" goes far beyond the Board suggestions by proposing to include an agreement about piracy in the Treaty of Ryswick and to amend English piracy law to enable more certain punishment and more effective prevention of piracy. The originality and comprehensiveness of Locke's proposals is evident when they are compared to the suggestions developed by the East India Company, which was the English body most adversely affected by piracy in the Red Sea. In the period between Avery's raid in August 1695 and the Treaty of Ryswick in late September 1697 the East India Company officials in England proposed only two remedies for piracy in the Indian Ocean. First, the East India Company pushed for the capture, trial, and punishment of the pirates, including by offering large rewards for the seizure of Avery and his crew.[58] Then in February 1697 the Company unsuccessfully petitioned the King and the Admiralty for commissions enabling them to seize pirates in the Indian Ocean.[59] It was not until October 1697 that the East India Company began to focus on the prevention of future piracy and suggested that the governor of New York be told to apprehend pirates[60]—an instruction that Locke had already proposed and the Board of Trade had already issued.[61]

The most original and ambitious part of Locke's proposal is his suggestion that the participants in the Treaty of Ryswick should reach a formal agreement about piracy. The problem that Locke left unresolved in the *Second Treatise* is how to effectively enforce natural law at sea given that the ocean is a common. In "Pyracy 97," Locke suggests that the solution to maritime law enforcement is for Europe's major maritime states to make a formal agreement that if any pirates arrive in their jurisdiction then they will arrest, try, and punish the pirates, or transfer the pirates to another state for trial and punishment. This proposal to create an international piracy agreement is an example of what Locke describes in the *Second Treatise* as federative power: "the Power of War and Peace, Leagues and Alliances, and all the Transactions, with all Persons and Communities outside the Commonwealth."[62] Locke's proposed piracy treaty would have created a coordinated approach to piracy among Europe's major maritime and colonial powers, whose laws governed a high proportion of Europe's shipping. The policies that Locke proposes would be far more effective if used by multiple states, because it is difficult for any one state to police vast oceans and because pirates can easily relocate to ports in sympathetic jurisdictions. Moreover, efforts by one state to extend its piracy law across the world's oceans might be perceived as an unjustified claim to control the common seas, whereas a piracy policy created by a multilateral treaty would create a form of international law. While a treaty on piracy between England, France, Spain, and Holland would not bind other European states, it might create a norm that would exert pressure for non-signatories to punish pirates. Lastly, Locke's concern that piracy was damaging the reputation of Christendom suggests that he may have believed that a treaty would improve the perception of Europe among people in Asia. Both in practical and symbolic terms, a common policy about piracy created by treaty between England, France, Spain, and the Dutch would be greater than the sum of its parts.

Locke also suggested that the English Parliament amend the existing law to create a single, common piracy law within all of England's realms. The problem that Basse's letter identified was that piracy fell under Admiralty law and the colonies lacked Admiralty jurisdiction, so colonies were unable to pass laws against piracy or to hold piracy trials. Basse proposed to solve this problem by giving the colonies Admiralty jurisdiction, which would have enabled authorities in each colony to pass laws on piracy and try pirates, thereby combining a response to piracy with significant political autonomy for the colonies. By contrast, Locke proposes that the English Parliament at Westminster should extend England's piracy law to the colonies, which would prevent colonial proprietors, governors, and legislatures from exercising autonomy on the issue of piracy. Locke's proposal therefore involves strengthening the control that the metropole exercised over England's American and Caribbean colonies. While American colonists objected to the imposition of piracy law from London,[63] Locke's proposal is an effort to resolve the clash of interests between those in England's American colonies and those trading or traveling in the Red Sea, which included the East India Company. In the 1690s, ships originating from English colonies in America were sailing to the Red Sea, committing piracy, and returning to the American colonies to spend their fortunes. This practice benefited the economies of American colonies that harbored pirates, but seriously threatened the East India Company and other merchants whose ships risked being stolen or whose crews rebelled to become pirates, as occurred on the Royal African Company ship *Hannibal.*[64] The Indian government had responded to the pirate attacks by retaliating against the East India Company, who in turn appealed to the English government for help,[65] so the authorities in London felt compelled to adjudicate between the competing interests of different English colonies and merchants, and responded by adopting a more centralized model of colonial rule.

SUPPRESSING PIRACY IN ENGLISH COLONIES

It is unclear how effective the policy that Locke proposes in "Pyracy 97" would have been, because the participants in the Treaty of Ryswick did not make a formal agreement about piracy. Locke's suggestions to extend English piracy law to the colonies and amend it by introducing more certain punishment and better prevention of piracy were followed, but not until a new crisis over piracy developed in early 1700. In the meantime, the Admiralty Judge Sir Charles Hedges confirmed that English piracy laws did not apply in the colonies and recommended instructing the colonies to pass severe local laws against piracy modeled on the Jamaica Act,[66] which created local Admiralty Courts to try pirates and imposed the death penalty on those convicted. The Board took Hedges's advice and advised the King that:

The most effectual remedy would, we think, be a law enacted here to extend uniformly through all your Plantations by which the methods of trying pirates might be directed, and the punishment of that crime made capital. Till such an Act shall be made we propose that you direct that copies of the Act of Jamaica, for restraining and punishing privateers and pirates, be sent to the Governors of all your Colonies, the Proprieties and Charter Governments included, with orders to each of them to use their utmost endeavours with their Assemblies to pass an Act to the same effect.[67]

The King approved this proposal, and in early 1698 the Board sent the Jamaica Act to the colonies with instructions to pass it into law.[68] Some colonies cooperated, but others passed an amended law with lesser penalties for pirates,[69] and both New York and Rhode Island refused to pass the Act.[70] Whether or not the local piracy laws were changed, many colonial officials were unwilling to arrest pirates and some received bribes to ignore piracy. To end piracy in the American colonies Locke and the Board therefore needed to provide an alternate system for the apprehension of pirates, and to remove colonial governors and officials who harbored pirates.

Given that many colonial authorities were reluctant to arrest pirates and that those who wished to do so lacked the warships necessary to seize the pirates at sea, the Board turned to the English navy. In January 1698 the Board wrote to the King recommending that three warships be sent to intercept the pirates at Madagascar and the Red Sea.[71] In February the King ordered that the three warships be dispatched as the Board had suggested, and asked the Board to issue instructions for their commanders.[72] When this attempt to catch the pirates did not succeed, the Board called for more warships. In July 1698 Locke was among the Board members who recommended to the King that another warship be sent to the East Indies to fight pirates.[73] In January 1699 the Board then asked the King to send four warships to the American colonies to pursue pirates and suppress illegal trade.[74] In March 1699 the Royal African Company sent the Board proposals for suppressing piracy by sending warships to the Cape Verde Islands, Cape Coast Castle, and Barbados,[75] and the Board wrote to the King supporting these suggestions.[76] In November 1699 Locke and the other Board members called for more warships again, this time telling the King that the rise in pirate attacks off the coast of the American colonies required a fleet of warships:

The sum of our advices import that the pirates hovering upon those coasts do not only surprise ships coming into or sailing out of their ports and sometimes sink and destroy them, but enter into their very bays and harbours, plundering such ships as they can surprize . . . increasing thus their strength to such a degree that the apprehensions of future mischief may not only be from single ships but squadrons, and the corruption already spread and still further spreading by this means amongst our seamen may in the end prove too universal, that we humbly conceive the consequences are greatly to be dreaded. For the

remedy, therefore, the Governors having complained to us of the insufficiency
of the ships of war appointed to attend their respective governments, we offer
that such a sufficient force of well sailing ships as may be thought necessary
and proper to clear those seas from pirates be appointed for that service. [77]

The King immediately referred this proposal to the Admiralty, [78] but it is
unclear if they sent any extra ships. By calling for English warships to be sent
to fight pirates in the Red Sea, the coast of West Africa, the Caribbean, and
North America Locke and the other members of the Board contributed to the
growing influence and global extension of the English navy.

Locke's letters and papers for the Board provide two examples of his
efforts to ensure effective law enforcement against piracy in the colonies: his
efforts to reform colonial administration in Virginia, and his support for Lord
Bellomont as a colonial governor. The "Essay on Virginia" was composed
during the Board's discussion of piracy in 1697, was handwritten by Locke's
amanuensis, and may have had input from James Blair in addition to
Locke. [79] In the Essay, Locke argues that the excessive powers of the govern-
or of Virginia have led to widespread corruption and enabled people to
"cheat the King." [80] Instead of a system of independent institutions and mutu-
al oversight, Locke explains that the Virginian governor dominates the Council and that the members of the Council are also the judges, customs officers,
and naval officers. [81] To resolve this excessive concentration of political power and the potential conflict of interests, Locke calls for the appointment of
independent and qualified judges, [82] and for requirements that the Collector
and Naval Officer are different people and are not members of the Council. [83]
Locke does not explicitly mention pirates in the "Essay on Virginia," but
piracy is included in the problems of corruption and illegal trade that he
identifies and seeks to resolve. The changes that Locke recommends to enable better enforcement of the Navigation Acts, such as the appointment of
diligent, local customs collectors and naval officers to inspect and record
ships, would go a long way toward identifying and deterring pirates.

An even clearer example of Locke's efforts to ensure effective law en-
forcement for maritime crime in the colonies is provided by his support for
Lord Bellomont, a former Whig MP who was appointed governor of New
York, Massachusetts, and New England. [84] The former governor of New
York, Benjamin Fletcher, was an associate of the Tory Board member
William Blathwayt, but in Blathwayt's absence the Whig members of the
Board arranged to have Fletcher removed for corruption. [85] Bellomont was
appointed to replace Fletcher and was determined to suppress piracy, but
Blathwayt opposed his appointment and seemed likely to use his influence
on the Board to undermine Bellomont's position. [86] Given this Tory opposition, Bellomont sought assistance from Locke. In May 1697 Bellomont wrote
to Locke requesting support in "the steps I make towards my departure for

America"[87] and presumably received a positive reply because his second letter a few days later thanks Locke for his kind words.[88] As Bellomont was preparing to sail in August 1697, Locke signed a letter from the Board instructing Bellomont to "use all your endeavours to repress piracy and bring pirates to punishment."[89] When Bellomont arrived in New York he began working hard to suppress piracy, identify officials who had supported pirates and remove them from office, and collect evidence about Fletcher's corruption and support for pirates.[90] Bellomont immediately met resistance from local merchants, customs collectors, judges, and members of the Council of New York[91] and he soon became unpopular. In June 1698 Bellomont ordered the customs officers in New York to seize illegal East India goods at one home, but reported that "a tumult was raised by the merchants who came to the house, and by their advice the officers were locked up, and kept imprisoned for three hours before I had any notice of it, when my intelligence was that they were in danger of being murdered."[92] Bellomont also pressured other colonial governors to arrest pirates, and was sent to investigate accusations of piracy in Rhode Island.[93] By early 1700 Bellomont's efforts to suppress piracy had made the New Yorkers so furious that a group of them complained to the House of Commons that he was acting unlawfully and "calumniates the people of New York of being pirates and favourers of piracy and breaking the Acts of Navigation."[94]

As Bellomont struggled in North America, Locke continued to assist him. When Bellomont sought permission to pardon two pirates who confessed and gave evidence,[95] Locke signed the Board's recommendation that the Lords Justices approve the request.[96] In October 1698 Locke signed two letters to the Lords Justices in support of Bellomont, the first of which prevented his salary from being reduced.[97] In the second letter, the Board praised Bellomont's actions to oppose piracy and collect evidence against the former Governor Fletcher, and concluded that "unless Lord Bellomont's authority be strongly supported he will be able to do nothing."[98] The timing of these letters suggests that Locke used his influence to officially proclaim the Board's support for Bellomont and criticism of Fletcher before he left London for the winter, when Blathwayt would resume attendance. Locke's central role in these decisions is conveyed by a personal letter from Bellomont expressing his thanks:

> Mr. Popple writes me word in his Letter of the 21. of October Last . . . that you were so very kind as to direct the forming of the Representation that was made to the Lords Justices of England upon the memorials and evidences I transmitted to your Lordships against Colonel Fletcher; and he writes you were pleas'd to Charge him to make me a Complement from you. which favours I acknowledge with all the thankfulnesse Imaginable; and will make it my Care and Study to deserve the Continuance of them.[99]

A letter from Popple to Locke on October 31, 1698, also confirms Locke's particular attention to issues involving Bellomont, because Popple describes the receipt of more letters from Bellomont and states "I am sure your assistance will be wanted: But I am far from desiring it, at the price I know it must cost."[100] The clear implication of Popple's letter is that Locke might wish to attend the Board meetings about the letters, even though London air in winter made him unwell.[101] In September 1699 Bellomont wrote to Locke again describing his ongoing problems with pirates, expressing hope that Locke had been present at the Board meetings about his work, and asking Locke to "make use of that great and generall Influence you have on all the Ministers, to excite them to support and assist me vigorously and effectually."[102] In November 1699 Bellomont wrote to Popple asking him to "assure Mr. Locke of my humble service."[103] He then wrote to Locke that "I must refer you to the Letters I write to your Board, for accounts of all that passes here; of which I hope Mr Popple takes Care to inform you particularly" even though "this season of the year obliges you to your Country retreat."[104] These letters show that Bellomont both asked for and received close attention and support from Locke. Moreover, the letters prove that Bellomont knew when Locke was likely to attend meetings, which raises the possibility that he timed some of his requests to reach the Board when Locke would be present.[105]

By the end of 1699 Bellomont needed supporters in London more than ever, because his actions over piracy had inadvertently created a political crisis for the Whigs. In 1695 Bellomont had befriended a former privateer named William Kidd and they hatched a plan for Kidd to captain a privateer voyage to hunt pirates while Bellomont would act as an investor. Bellomont lobbied hard on Kidd's behalf and in December 1695 Kidd was granted a privateering commission, followed by royal sponsorship and a patent to hunt pirates.[106] Unfortunately for Bellomont, Kidd did not capture any pirates and soon committed piracy himself by attacking and capturing a trade ship called the *Quedah Merchant*.[107] In November 1698 the Lords Justices ordered Bellomont to arrest "Kidd with his ship and associates."[108] When Kidd reached Boston in the summer of 1699 he probably expected a warm welcome from his former sponsor, but instead Bellomont arrested Kidd and seized his goods.[109] Since Bellomont did not have confidence that Kidd would receive a fair trial and appropriate punishment in the colonies, he collected evidence about Kidd's piracy and then asked the authorities in London to provide a navy ship to carry the pirates and the evidence to London. In London, the Tories seized on Kidd's piracy as an opportunity to attack the Whigs. On December 6, 1699, the House of Commons held a long and heated debate on a motion stating that Kidd's privateering commission was illegal and had dishonored the King. The Whigs eventually defeated the motion, but the MP Edward Clarke wrote to Locke expressing his concern at the events.[110] Despite this political turmoil, Locke continued to support Bel-

lomont and wrote to Edward Clarke in February 1700 "that my Lord Bellomont ought to be supported by all those who would not abandon the Plantations I think I need not tell you."[111]

By March 1700 the Board of Trade was convinced that tackling piracy in
the American colonies required the English Parliament to pass a new piracy
law. In early March the House of Commons ordered the Board of Trade to
provide "an account of what advances they have made towards the improvement of the Trade of England,"[112] and the Board's response pointedly observes that piracy could not be eradicated until Parliament passed the law that
the Board had proposed to it in 1698:

> Being informed by many instances of the great countenance given to pirates in
> some of the Plantations, and chiefly in the Proprieties and Charter Govern-
> ments, by fitting out their ships from thence and furnishing them with all sorts
> of provisions and ammunition, and receiving them with their plunder at their
> return, and acquitting them upon feigned trials, we did make several represen-
> tations and proposed the enacting of laws there for the trial and punishment of
> pirates in conformity to a law heretofore passed in Jamaica to that effect,
> which having been refused in the Proprieties, we proposed as the only remedy
> for so great an evil the offering a Bill in Parliament for that purpose, wherein
> we consulted Sir Charles Hedges, Judge of H.M. High Court of Admiralty, by
> whose great care and assistance such a Bill has been prepared and is now lying
> before this honourable House.[113]

Locke's health prevented him from attending the Board's meeting in January, so he did not sign the representation to Parliament, but there is a copy in
his personal papers.[114] The combination of the Board's rebuke and the ongoing scandal over Kidd's piracy finally motivated Parliament to act, and within days the Act for the More Effectual Suppression of Piracy was debated
and approved by both Houses of Parliament.[115] This law empowered Admiralty courts to try "all Piracies Felonies and Robberies committed in or upon
the Sea" and to conduct investigations and trials "in any of His Majesties
Islands Plantations Colonies Dominions Forts of Factories."[116] This provision effectively extended the geographical scope of English piracy laws to all
English territory and the world's oceans. The Act also stipulated that senior
naval officers and anyone appointed for the purpose by the King had the
power to arrest pirates, issue warrants, summon and question witnesses, and
"assemble a Court of Admiralty on Shipboard or upon the Land."[117] By
enabling trials to occur at sea, this empowered the English navy to act as both
police and judges on the oceans.

Admiralty Courts assembled under the 1700 Piracy Act required seven
people, composed of senior naval officers and those appointed for the purpose by the King. If seven such people could not be easily assembled, then
the Act authorized three of them including a governor or naval Commander

to appoint judges from among junior naval officers and "knowne Merchants Factors or Planters."[118] This provision made it easier to assemble Admiralty Courts outside England while attempting to ensure that the Courts would be composed of reputable men. The Admiralty Courts were explicitly given the power to impose severe punishments upon convicted pirates, including "Sentence and Judgment of Death."[119] To further deter piracy, the Act defined "aiding abetting receiving and concealeing" pirates or their goods as the crime of accessory to piracy, for which the death penalty could also be imposed.[120] Whereas previously only pirates themselves could be punished, this provision criminalized those who funded pirate expeditions, received stolen pirate goods, or helped pirates to escape arrest, which would have included many of the corrupt merchants and local officials that Bellomont had encountered in New York. Further, the Act stipulated that if any colonial governor or "Persons in Authority" refused to obey the Act then this would "be a Forfeiture of all and every the Charters granted for the Government or Propriety of such Plantation."[121] This last provision specifically threatens Charter colonies by specifying that if they refuse to obey the new piracy law then the legal basis of the colony will cease to exist. Overall, the Act does all three of the things Locke suggested: it extends English piracy laws to the American colonies, enables more certain punishment of pirates through the Admiralty Courts outlined, and seeks to prevent piracy through the imposition of severe penalties for pirates and accessories to piracy.

In early April 1700, Kidd and his crew arrived in England and the Admiralty began an investigation that caused further embarrassment to the Whigs when the Admiralty opened and read Bellomont's private letters, which included indiscreet remarks about people in London.[122] In May 1700 the Board of Trade began work on the commissions needed to arrest and try pirates under the new Piracy Act,[123] and on June 5 the Board's representation to the King about it was signed by both Locke and Blathwayt.[124] The King promptly approved their recommendations and ordered the Commissions to be prepared.[125] The Board discussed piracy several more times before Locke tendered his resignation on June 28 on the grounds of ill health.[126] Although Locke was clearly elderly, unwell, and had been ill repeatedly during his time on the Board, it is noteworthy that he resigned shortly after the Piracy Act was finally passed and the Board had issued its suggestions about who would be commissioned to enforce it. Locke's resignation from the Board therefore coincides with the apparent resolution of the long-standing problem of piracy in the American colonies through the introduction of a law that Locke had advocated in 1697. It is also notable that the Board of Trade's approach to the colonies changed after Locke's resignation, when it began advocating for Blathwayt's favored policy of revoking the colonial charters.[127] While Locke had worked to introduce a uniform law on piracy and to strengthen the Board's control of the colonies by removing corrupt governors and officials, he did not challenge colonial charters. Lastly, it is notable that Locke's resignation follows the end of the Whig dominance in Parliament and the fall of Lord Somers, the former Attorney General, whose involvement in Kidd's privateer commission led him to be charged with treason.[128] Somers was one of Locke's associates and correspondents, had worked closely with him on the issue of recoinage, and discouraged Locke from resigning from the Board due to ill health in December 1696.[129] By supporting Bellomont's efforts to fight piracy in New York Locke had inadvertently contributed to the piracy scandal that ended the political careers of Somers and several other Whigs, and ushered in a period of Tory dominance in Parliament. While there is no evidence that Locke regretted his support for Bellomont, it seems likely that the declining political fortunes of Somers and the Whigs in the spring of 1700 contributed to his decision to resign from the Board.[130]

THE WAR ON PIRACY AND THE RISE OF BRITISH EMPIRE

In order to prevent English colonies in the Americas from harboring pirates, Locke and the Board of Trade amended colonial governance in a way that contributed to English empire both on land and at sea. First, Locke called for a multilateral agreement between Europe's major maritime powers to introduce severe punishment for pirates and prosecute them "to the utmost parts of the world."[131] Since the Treaty of Ryswick did not include an agreement about pirates, English piracy policy did not take the multilateral form that Locke initially recommended. However, the 1700 Piracy Act extended English piracy law across the world's oceans and empowered the Royal Navy to arrest and try pirates at sea, thereby enabling Locke's goal of pursuing pirates anywhere on the ocean. This extension of English maritime law and courts was combined with naval expansion and patrols against pirates in the Atlantic, Caribbean, and Indian Ocean, thereby contributing to the development of the eighteenth-century model of British empire as "Protestant, commercial, maritime, and free."[132] On land, Locke and the Board introduced greater control of the American colonies from London. Instead of a system of colonies with their own piracy laws, or lack thereof, Locke advocated for the English Parliament to impose a uniform piracy law across all English jurisdictions that was enforced by the navy and applied by Admiralty Courts appointed from London. Ending the practice of piracy in the American colonies also required the Board to introduce closer oversight of colonial authorities, including the removal of corrupt governors, councilors, and officials. Locke contributed to this process of closer oversight through his work to counter corruption in Virginia, and his support for Lord Bellomont, whose arrests of pirates and removal of corrupt officials led him to be attacked by

New Yorkers who had benefited from piracy under the former governor. Overall, the Board's war on piracy led to greater centralization of English colonial governance and less local autonomy for colonial governors, legislatures, and courts, thereby helping to transform a disjointed system of Crown and proprietary colonies into a more unified empire. The role of the Board's piracy policy in developing English empire has been acknowledged by historians,[133] and has provoked some to argue that piracy was an "excuse . . . to extend further control over the American colonies"[134] and a "problem whose roots lay more in the perceived threat to the English empire *qua* empire."[135]

In his Board of Trade work Locke contributed to a more centralized and legally uniform model of English empire, but this centralized imperial governance conflicted with his advocacy of government by consent in the *Two Treatises.* Moreover, Locke's letters show that he was aware of the tensions between English imperial governance and the *Two Treatises,* because the point was forcefully made by his friend William Molyneux, a philosopher and MP representing Dublin. In March 1698 Molyneux wrote to Locke that the English Parliament "bear very hard upon us in Ireland" and asked "How justly they can bind us without our Consent and Representatives, I leave the Author of the *Two Treatises of Government* to consider."[136] A month later Molyneux wrote again to say that his further thinking on the subject had motivated him to write a pamphlet titled *The Case of Ireland's being Bound by Acts of Parliament in England Stated*, which he enclosed. [137] Locke refused to be drawn into a written debate over the political theory of empire,[138] but he offered to discuss the issue verbally and tried to protect Molyneux from censure for his anticolonial pamphlet.[139] These letters show that Locke knew some residents of English colonies saw a tension between the principle of government by consent and the practice of England imposing laws and policies on unwilling colonies. Further, Molyneux's efforts to engage Locke in debate over the normative legitimacy of English imperial rule took place at the same time that Locke was considering responses to piracy in the American colonies.

If Locke's Board of Trade work on piracy conflicted with his advocacy of government by consent in the *Two Treatises* then how are we to understand the relationship between his theoretical views and his contribution to policy-making? While it is possible that Locke's actions simply diverged from his theoretical principles, as Waldron has suggested on the issue of slavery,[140] it is important to recognize that there are consistent theoretical principles underlying Locke's activity on the issue of piracy and that these are compatible with his account of natural law and piracy in the *Two Treatises.* While Tories such as Blathwayt may have favored empire for the sake of empire, Locke was a Whig who vehemently opposed excessive executive power and argued vigorously for the rule of law in the *Two Treatises* and in Board of Trade writings such as the "Essay on Virginia." This theme of law is similarly evident in "Pyracy 97" where Locke calls for states to arrest, try, and severely punish all future pirates. The theoretical basis for Locke's interventions against piracy therefore lies in the philosophy articulated in the *Second Treatise*: the principles of natural law, the translation of natural law into statute law in a commonwealth, and the effective enforcement of this law by impartial judges.

Locke regards natural law as pre-existing and universal, so if people break natural law by committing piracy then Locke argues repeatedly in the *Two Treatises* that they should be punished. In "Pyracy 97" Locke develops specific proposals for enforcing natural law at sea, which involve a coordinated legal framework to seize, try, and severely punish pirates. Locke therefore seeks to ensure that as many jurisdictions as possible enforce natural law against pirates, and that they do so through the rule of law. Further, Locke argues in the *Second Treatise* that states do not have the right to create statute law that conflicts with natural law because "the *Municipal Laws* of Countries, which are only so far right, as they are founded on the Law of Nature, by which they are to be regulated and interpreted."[141] American colonists who objected to the imposition of piracy policies from England received little sympathy from Locke because piracy violated his conception of natural law, and their approval for piracy did not change the fact that it was unlawful. In Locke's view, popular support for piracy in the American colonies did not legitimate piracy, but merely showed that the colonists were unwilling to obey or enforce natural law, which raised questions about their rationality and fitness for self-government. To ensure that natural law prohibiting piracy would be enforced Locke advocated the imposition of a uniform piracy law and the replacement of pro-piracy colonial governors and officials with those who would oppose and prosecute pirates. Locke therefore knowingly contributed to a more centralized and imperial mode of rule, but did this in the name of upholding natural law and the natural right to "liberty."[142] Since freedom of navigation and trade required the suppression of piracy, Locke supported the extension of English law and naval power across the world's oceans. This same motivation to defend liberty and prevent unlawful "license" motivated Locke to support Bellomont as governor of New York and advocate reform of the corrupt system in Virginia. In short, when faced by piracy in the 1690s, Locke's commitment to law led him to successfully argue for the extension of English naval power, for less colonial autonomy, and for greater control of the American colonies by London. In waging a war on piracy, Locke's universalistic conception of natural law provided a justification for changes in maritime law and colonial governance that contributed to the development of the eighteenth-century British empire.

NOTES

1. Locke, *Two Treatises*, II §124–6 351.
2. *Ibid*, II §13 276.
3. *Ibid*, II §19 281.
4. Peter T. Leeson, *The Invisible Hook: The Hidden Economics of Pirates* (Princeton, NJ: Princeton University Press, 2009), 38–40.
5. Marcus Rediker, *Villains of All Nations—Atlantic Pirates in the Golden Age* (London: Verso Books, 2004), 64–94; Leeson, *Invisible Hook*, 23–44.
6. David Cordingly, *Under the Black Flag: The Romance and the Reality of Life Among the Pirates* (New York: Random House, 1995), 46.
7. Bieber, "British Plantation Councils."
8. GBPRO, *Calendar of State Papers Colonial*, vol. 7, xiv.
9. Library of Congress MSS76737 Phillipps No. 8539, vol. 1, fol. 47.
10. The Council's Journal for November 8, 1673, states, "Ordered, that ye Secry draw up ye Humble Representation & Addresse of their Councill to His Majy that it is their Opinion that His Majy should send one 3d. Rate & one 4th Rate two 5th Rate frygates & 3: merchants ships each whereof should carry upwards of 40 Gunns & 3 Fire Ships & 600 foot soldiers for ye rescuing New Yorke." See *Ibid*, vol. 1, fol. 54.
11. Library of Congress MSS76737 Phillipps No. 8539, vol. 1, fol. 56; GBPRO, *Calendar of State Papers Colonial*, vol. 7, 530–1.
12. GBPRO, *Calendar of State Papers Colonial*, vol. 7, 558–9.
13. *Ibid*, 561.
14. *Ibid*, 572–3.
15. Cranston, *Locke: A Biography*, 400–4.
16. GBPRO, *Calendar of State Papers Colonial*, vol. 15, 1. Although promoting English trade and overseeing the colonies were the Board's primary duties, the Board's May 1696 commission from the King also lists additional duties such as developing plans for the employment of the poor in England and investigating England's fisheries, see CO 391/9, 1–6.
17. Laslett, "John Locke, the Great Recoinage."
18. Saunders Webb, "William Blathwayt."
19. For example, Blathwayt refused to sign the Board's highly critical report about colonial administration in Virginia, of which Locke was the primary mover, see Laslett, "John Locke, the Great Recoinage," 400; Brewer, "Slavery, Sovereignty," 17.
20. I. K. Steele, "The Board of Trade, the Quakers, and Resumption of Colonial Charters, 1699–1702," *The William and Mary Quarterly* 23, no. 4 (1966): 599. These attendance patterns are also recorded in the Board's Journals, which list the attendees at each meeting, see The National Archive CO 391/9 to CO 391/13.
21. Woolhouse, *Locke: A Biography*, 420.
22. GBPRO, *Calendar of State Papers Colonial: America and West Indies, Volume 14, 1693–1696*, ed. J. W. Fortescue (London, 1903), 114.
23. An alternate spelling in some sources is "Captain Every."
24. IOR B/41, June 19, 1696, 149 and June 24, 1696, 150.
25. GBPRO, *Calendar of State Papers Colonial*, vol. 14, 519.
26. GBPRO, *Calendar of State Papers Colonial*, vol. 15, 58, and 71–5.
27. The Board read the letter from Governor Fletcher of New York on September 1, see GBPRO, *Calendar of State Papers Colonial*, vol. 15, 7, and 91. On October 16 the board received further information from the Jamaica merchants, which they described in their journal as "many complaints of arbitrary pressing and about the encouragement of piracy in North America," see GBPRO, *Calendar of State Papers Colonial*, vol. 15, 179.
28. The Board read the letter from Beeston on November 5, see GBPRO, *Calendar of State Papers Colonial*, vol. 15, 20 and The National Archives, CO 391/9, 207–11 (original numbering).
29. Woolhouse, *Locke: A Biography*, 369.
30. GBPRO, *Calendar of State Papers Colonial*, vol. 15, 236.

31. *Ibid*, 236. The Board read the King's order on December 16, 1696, and decided to write to the respective colonies to convey this order, see National Archive, CO 391/9, 284 (original numbering).

32. As mentioned in the Introduction, there were three categories of English colonies: proprietary colonies governed by Lord Proprietors, such as Carolina; charter colonies whose legal basis lay in a charter granted by the English Crown, such as Rhode Island; and Crown colonies that were under the direct authority of the English Crown and ruled by a governor appointed by the monarch, such as Jamaica.

33. Douglas R. Burgess Jr., "A Crisis of Charter and Right: Piracy and Colonial Resistance in Seventeenth-Century Rhode Island," *Journal of Social History* 45, no. 3 (2012): 607.

34. The National Archives, CO 323/2, A35 109; The National Archives, CO 391/9, 309–312 (original numbering); GBPRO, *Calendar of State Papers Colonial*, vol. 15, 259–264.

35. GBPRO, *Calendar of State Papers Colonial*, vol. 15, 312, 342, 344, 356, 357, 362, and 363.

36. Basse wrote to the Board's Secretary William Popple mentioning pirates on July 18, 1697, GBPRO, *Calendar of State Papers Colonial*, vol. 15, 557–558. Popple replied on July 22nd questioning Basse about his knowledge of pirates, their treatment in the colonies, and his advice for suppressing them, GBPRO, *Calendar of State Papers Colonial*, vol. 15, 561. Basse replied on July 26, GBPRO, *Calendar of State Papers Colonial*, vol. 15, 563–5.

37. GBPRO, *Calendar of State Papers Colonial*, vol. 15, 563.

38. *Ibid*, 564.

39. The National Archives, CO 391/10, 177–8 (original numbering).

40. MS Locke c. 30, fol. 62, Bodleian Library, Oxford.

41. The Lords Justices administered William's kingdom while the King was away on military campaigns. The *Calendar of State Papers Domestic* contains no record of a document about piracy being received from Locke at any point in 1697, although they do record the receipt of other documents from the Board of Trade, including a report about linen and the trade with Ireland on September 2nd, see GBPRO, *Calendar of State Papers Domestic William III 1697*, 345.

42. MS Locke c. 30, fol. 63, Bodleian Library, Oxford.

43. *Ibid*, fol. 62.

44. *Ibid*, fol. 63.

45. The Board Journal records that Basse's July 26 letter was read on July 30. If Locke learned of the letter's contents in the July 30 meeting then he may have written the third page of "Pyracy 97" during the meeting, which would explain the abbreviated style. Alternatively, it is possible that Popple notified Locke about Basse's July 26 letter prior to the meeting and that Locke's questions were written in preparation for the Board discussion. Either way, it is very likely that the third page of "Pyracy 97" was written after Locke learned of the contents of Basse's July 26 letter.

46. Locke wrote several policy papers for discussion by the Board during the autumn of 1697, including the "Essay on the Poor Law" and "Essay on Virginia," see The National Archives, CO 391/10, 263–355.

47. MS Locke c. 30, fol. 62, Bodleian Library, Oxford.

48. *Ibid*, fol. 62.

49. The pirate base in Madagascar was mentioned in the documents forwarded by the East India Company in December 1696, see GBPRO, *Calendar of State Papers Colonial*, vol. 15, 259–64, and in Basse's letter of July 26, 1697, see GBPRO, *Calendar of State Papers Colonial*, vol. 15, 563–5.

50. MS Locke c. 30, fol. 62, Bodleian Library, Oxford.

51. *Ibid*, fol. 62.

52. *Ibid*, fol. 62.

53. *Ibid*, fol. 62.

54. *Ibid*, fol. 62.

55. Locke, *Two Treatises*, II §7 271 and §8 272. Also see Dilts, "To Kill a Thief."

56. MS Locke c. 30, fol. 63, Bodleian Library, Oxford.

57. *Ibid*, fol. 63.

58. The Company offered five hundred pounds and four thousand rupees for Avery's capture, and fifty pounds for capturing any of his crew, see IOR B/41, 155–6, 163, and 169.

59. *Ibid*, 295 and 301.

60. *Ibid*, 403.

61. The letter from the Board of Trade to Bellomont is dated August 26, 1697, see GBPRO, *Calendar of State Papers Colonial*, vol. 15, 587–8.

62. Locke, *Two Treatises*, II §146 365.

63. See Burgess, "Crisis of Charter."

64. IOR B/41, 355 and IOR H/26 291–5.

65. IOR B/41, 155, 169, 295, 302, and 400.

66. GBPRO, *Calendar of State Papers Colonial: America and West Indies, Volume 16, 1697–1698*, ed. J. W. Fortescue (London, 1905), 31, and The National Archives, CO 391/10, 352–4 (original numbering).

67. GBPRO, *Calendar of State Papers Colonial*, vol. 16, 60.

68. *Ibid*, 140–1.

69. For example, the Pennsylvania legislature passed a far weaker law against piracy, see GBPRO, *Calendar of State Papers Colonial*, vol. 17, 274–5.

70. Nutting, "Madagascar Connection," 211; Burgess, "Crisis of Charter," 609.

71. GBPRO, *Calendar of State Papers Colonial*, vol. 16, 88.

72. *Ibid*, 122.

73. *Ibid*, 354 and CO 391/11 151–3 (original numbering).

74. GBPRO, *Calendar of State Papers Colonial: America and West Indies, Volume 17, 1699 and Addenda*, ed. J. W. Fortescue (London, 1908), 15–7.

75. *Ibid*, 121–2.

76. *Ibid*, 169.

77. *Ibid*, 514.

78. *Ibid*, 515.

79. The relative roles of Locke and Blair as authors are disputed: Kammen attributes primary authorship to Blair, Laslett argues that both Locke and Blair contributed to it, and Ashcraft and Brewer attribute authorship to Locke. See James Blair, John Locke, and Michael Kammen, ed., "Virginia at the Close of the Seventeenth Century: An Appraisal by James Blair and John Locke," *The Virginia Magazine of History and Biography* 74, no. 2 (1966): 147–8; Laslett, "John Locke and the Great Recoinage," 400; Ashcraft, "Political Theory and Political Reform"; Brewer, "Slavery, Sovereignty."

80. Kammen, "Virginia at the Close," 160.

81. *Ibid*, 160.

82. *Ibid*, 162.

83. *Ibid*, 169.

84. Ritchie, *Captain Kidd*, 47.

85. *Ibid*, 50.

86. Webb, "William Blathwayt," 395 and 402.

87. E. S. De Beer, ed., *The Correspondence of John Locke, Volume 6* (Oxford: Clarendon, 1981), 131–2, No. 2268, May 25, 1697.

88. *Ibid*, 135, No. 2270, May 29, 1697.

89. GBPRO, *Calendar of State Papers Colonial*, vol. 15, 587–88.

90. Nutting, "Madagascar Connection," 210; Hanna, *Pirate Nests*, 259–73.

91. GBPRO, *Calendar of State Papers Colonial* vol. 16, 203–4, 224–9, 240–4, 279–89, and 314–6. Also see Ritchie, *Captain Kidd*, 170.

92. GBPRO, *Calendar of State Papers Colonial*, vol. 16, 279–89.

93. Burgess, "Crisis of Charter," 616.

94. GBPRO, Great Britain Public Record Office, *Calendar of State Papers Colonial, America and West Indies, Volume 18, 1700*, ed. Cecil Headlam (London, 1910), 115–9.

95. GBPRO, *Calendar of State Papers Colonial*, vol. 16, 225.

96. *Ibid*, 354.

97. *Ibid*, 479.

98. *Ibid*, 480–2.

99. De Beer, *Correspondence of John Locke*, vol. 6, 622–3, No. 2587, May 12, 1699.

100. *Ibid*, vol. 6, 500–1, No. 2503, October 31, 1698.

101. See Woolhouse, *Locke: A Biography*, 348, 375, and 400.

102. De Beer, *Correspondence of John Locke*, vol. 6, 622–3, No. 2587, May 12, 1699.

103. GBPRO, *Calendar of State Papers Colonial*, vol. 17, *1699 and Addenda*, ed. J. W. Fortescue (London, 1908), 509–10.

104. De Beer, *Correspondence of John Locke*, vol. 6, 736, No. 2636, November 29, 1699.

105. The seasonal pattern of Locke and Blathwayt's attendance meant that Board members were strategic about the timing of key decisions. In September 1696 and September 1697 the Whig members took advantage of Blathwayt's absence to attack his friend Governor Andros of Virginia, which led to Andros's resignation, see Webb, "William Blathwayt," 399–400.

106. Ritchie, *Captain Kidd*, 50–4.

107. *Ibid*, 108.

108. GBPRO, *Calendar of State Papers Domestic: William III 1698*, 418.

109. GBPRO, *Calendar of State Papers Colonial*, vol. 17, 366–79.

110. De Beer, *Correspondence of John Locke*, vol. 6, 754–6, No. 2646, December 7, 1699.

111. E. S. De Beer, ed., *The Correspondence of John Locke*, vol. 7 (Oxford, Clarendon Press, 1982) 20, No. 2268, February 26, 1700.

112. GBPRO, *Calendar of State Papers Colonial*, vol. 18, 109.

113. *Ibid*, 131–3.

114. MS Locke c. 30, fol. 119–124, Bodleian Library, Oxford.

115. Her Majesty's Stationery Office, *Journal of the House of Lords*, Volume 16, 1696–1701 (London, 1767–1830), 557–8, 562, and 564.

116. William III, 1698–9: An Act for the More Effectuall Suppressions of Piracy. [Chapter VII. Rot. Parl. 11 Gul. III. p. 2. n. 5.]', in Statutes of the Realm: Volume 7, 1695–1701, ed. John Raithby (s.l, 1820), pp. 590–594, section 1.

117. *Ibid*, section 1.

118. *Ibid*, section 3.

119. *Ibid*, section 4.

120. *Ibid*, section 9.

121. *Ibid*, section 15.

122. Ritchie, *Captain Kidd*, 195. Bellomont had written to both the Board of Trade and to Locke, so Popple visited the Admiralty to collect the letters and wrote to Locke about it, see De Beer, *Correspondence of John Locke*, vol. 7, 55–6, No. 2708, April 12, 1700, and 63–4, No. 2714, April 19, 1700.

123. GBPRO, *Calendar of State Papers Colonial*, vol. 18, 227, 230, 236, and 247.

124. GBPRO, *Calendar of State Papers Colonial*, vol. 18, 297–8.

125. *Ibid*, 303.

126. *Ibid*, 386.

127. Steele, "The Board of Trade," 603–8.

128. Her Majesty's Stationery Office, *Journal of the House of Lords*, vol. 16, 688–95.

129. Woolhouse, *Locke: A Biography*, 335, 356–7, and 374–5.

130. Patrick Kelly goes further, suggesting that the fall of Somers determined the timing of Locke's resignation from the Board of Trade, see Patrick Hyde Kelly, "General Introduction: Locke on Money" in Kelly, ed., *Locke on Money, Volume 1*, 14.

131. MS Locke c. 30, fol. 62, Bodleian Library, Oxford.

132. Armitage, *Ideological Origins*, 8.

133. See Hanna, *Pirate Nests*, 18 and 418–9.

134. Philip J. Stern, "British Asia and British Atlantic: Comparisons and Connections," *William and Mary Quarterly* 63, no. 4 (2006): 710.

135. Burgess, "A Crisis of Charter," 617.

136. De Beer, *Correspondence of John Locke*, vol. 6, 349, No. 2407, March 15, 1698. Molyneux's remarks were probably prompted by a much-resented law passed in early 1698 that imposed duties on the import of Irish wool to England, thereby aiding the English wool industry but providing no corresponding economic benefit to Ireland, see Fox Bourne, *Life of John Locke*, vol. 2, 464–467.

137. De Beer, *Correspondence of John Locke*, vol. 6, 376–7, No. 2422, April 19, 1698, and No. 2471, July 9, 1698.

138. *Ibid*, vol. 6, 368, No. 2414, April 6, 1698.

139. The English House of Commons expressed outrage over the arguments in Molyneux's pamphlet and urged King William to punish its author, see Fox Bourne, *Life of John Locke*, vol. 2, 466.

140. Jeremy Waldron, *God, Locke and Equality: Christian Foundations of John Locke's Political Thought* (Cambridge and New York: Cambridge University Press, 2002), 206.

141. Locke, *Two Treatises*, II §13 275.

142. *Ibid*, II §6 270.

Chapter Four

Locke's Theory of Penal Slavery

In the last chapter I outlined how Locke's Board of Trade work about piracy led him to successfully advocate the expansion of English legal and naval power at sea, and a reduction in political autonomy for the American colonies. Locke's contribution to English piracy policy was consistent with his account of natural rights and the rule of law in the *Two Treatises*, but it also meant that he was involved in imposing English laws and rulers on unwilling colonies. As Molyneux observed to Locke, the principle of government by consent outlined in the *Two Treatises* seemed to be in tension with the reality of English imperial rule. Other tensions between liberty and empire arose over seventeenth-century practices of forced labor and forced migration, as I discuss in this chapter and the next. This chapter considers Locke's writing and activity about the practice of forced migration and forced labor for English convicts, prisoners of war, and the poor. The following chapter examines Locke's views about forced labor in the context of military service, and specifically about the practice of compelling English sailors to serve in the English navy. Examining Locke's thought and actions about these contemporary practices of forced labor and forced migration helps us to better understand his views about the scope of individual freedom and the justifications for coercing English citizens. Moreover, analyzing Locke's theoretical writing about freedom and coercion alongside his practical writing and actions provides insights about how Locke applied, amended, or deviated from his theoretical ideas when he was engaged in policymaking as a member of the Board of Trade.

This chapter begins with a textual and philosophical analysis of Locke's theory of slavery in the *Two Treatises of Government*. In the *Second Treatise* Locke justifies the enslavement of those who break natural law by using aggressive violence, and he explicitly states that this applies to individual criminals and to members of an army engaged in an unjust war. By examining Locke's discussion of slavery in the *First Treatise* and *Second Treatise* I show that Locke's account of slavery includes a right for slaveowners to forcibly transport and sell their slaves. Next, I situate Locke's theory of slavery in historical context by explaining how his arguments compare to the practices of forced migration and forced labor used in English colonies during the late seventeenth century. Here, I briefly describe how the English state authorized the forced migration of English convicts, prisoners of war, and the poor to the colonies for sale into forced labor as indentured servants. Applying Locke's theory of slavery to each of these seventeenth-century practices shows that his theory justifies the forced migration and forced labor of English convicts and prisoners of war, but prohibits forced migration and forced labor for law-abiding English people. Next, I examine Locke's writing and activity about penal slavery and convict transportation as a member of the Board of Trade. This analysis shows that Locke advocated the forced transportation of English criminals to the colonies as forced laborers in two papers for the Board: the "Essay on the Poor Law" and "Essay on Virginia." Locke was also involved in arranging the forced migration of English convicts to the colonies, including by signing the Board's 1697 recommendation that fifty women convicts be transported to the Leeward Islands.[1] Reading the *Two Treatises* alongside Locke's Board of Trade work shows that Locke supported penal slavery in theory and in practice. Given the close correspondence between the theory of slavery in the *Second Treatise* and Locke's advocacy of penal slavery on the Board of Trade I suggest that his theory of slavery was intended to justify penal slavery, including for English convicts. Lastly I consider Locke's advocacy of forced labor and forced migration for the English poor in his writing for the Board, and discuss the relationship between this coercion of the poor and the theory of inalienable natural rights articulated in the *Two Treatises*.

PENAL SLAVERY IN THE *TWO TREATISES*

In the *Second Treatise* the topic of slavery is introduced as an extension of Locke's account of conflict in the state of nature. Locke explains that the state of nature is governed by natural law that includes individual rights to life, freedom, and property, and that prohibits attacks on the "Life, Health, Liberty, or Possessions" of others.[2] Those who break natural law forfeit these rights, and Locke argues that they should be punished in a way that is proportionate to the offense, deters further crimes, and provides reparation to the victim,[3] which he interprets as requiring severe penalties including "a Power to kill a Murderer."[4] Next, Locke argues that attacking someone's liberty is equivalent to attempted murder,[5] which makes it appropriate for a victim to kill an attacker who uses violence or coercion.[6] However, an alternate punishment is also available because Locke reasons that violent criminals have forfeited their right to life and can be justly enslaved:

> having, by his fault, forfeited his own Life, by some Act that deserves Death; he, to whom he has forfeited it, may (when he has him in his Power) delay to take it, and make use of him to his own Service, and he does him no injury by it.[7]

Crime therefore does not destroy the criminal's right to life but instead transfers that right from the offender to the punisher, which empowers the punisher to either execute or enslave the offender. The right to punish those who break natural law is, by extension, the right to become a potential enslaver of criminals.[8] In the state of nature all individuals have the right to enforce natural law, but through the social contract this power is transferred to the civil society or commonwealth. Victims of crime within a commonwealth retain a right of self-defense during an attack and this gives victims a temporary right to kill or enslave their aggressor. Once a crime has taken place then the state alone has the right to punish the offender, which gives the state rights to enslave criminals and to ongoing ownership of the slaves. This enslavement of offenders by the state could provide a means to compensate victims, because the state could require slaves to provide services to victims, or sell the slaves and use the proceeds to pay reparations to victims. Alternately, the state could use the slave's labor for the public good, for example by using slaves to build roads, or selling slaves to recoup the costs of law enforcement. The use of penal slavery in a commonwealth thus has the potential to benefit victims of crime and the citizenry as a whole.

Later in the *Second Treatise* Locke extends his discussion of slavery to address wars between armies, arguing that participants in an unjust war have broken natural law and can be legitimately killed or enslaved because their opponents possess "an Absolute Power over the Lives of those, who by an Unjust War have forfeited them."[9] A commonwealth that is attacked and defeats its aggressors therefore has the right to enslave the attacking army.[10] However, this right is restricted to punishing those who "assisted, concurr'd, or consented to that unjust force,"[11] so victors in a just war do not acquire rights over the peaceful families or neighbors of the enslaved.[12] Here, Locke provides two reasons for rejecting the intergenerational transfer of slave status: that children are not responsible for their parents' behavior and thus have not broken natural law, and that parents do not own and hence cannot forfeit the rights of their children.[13] The family of an enslaved aggressor thus retain their rights to life and liberty, and Locke extends this reasoning to argue that children of an aggressor have the right to inherit their parent's property because otherwise the children might die.[14] This inheritance provision means that there are two conflicting rights over the property of a justly enslaved parent: the victor in a just war has a right to take the aggressor's goods in reparations,[15] while the slave's children have a right to "their shares in the Estate he possessed."[16] In the attempt to balance these claims Locke argues that the lawful victor can take the aggressor's property in reparation, but that if taking full reparations from the aggressor's estate would endanger their family then the victor "must remit something of his full Satisfaction, and give way to the pressing and preferable Title of those, who are in danger to perish without it."[17] These conflicting rights of inheritance and reparations mean that just conquerors may not be permitted to take full compensation in goods for the cost and harm involved in the war. However, Locke suggests that the aggressor's family and children have no such claim over the aggressor's future labor, so there is no constraint on the right of the lawful victor to exploit the aggressor's labor. By advocating a right of inheritance for the children of those who participate in unjust wars Locke makes it less likely that victors will be able to take full reparations from the estates of the aggressors and more likely that the victors will need to enslave the aggressors in order to receive full reparations.

In the course of his theory of slavery Locke explains the differences between slaves and servants. Locke argues that slavery involves a complete and permanent transfer of an individual's rights to life and liberty, so an owner possesses "Absolute, Arbitrary Power" over their slave and has the right to kill the slave at any time.[18] Under the laws of nature, law-abiding individuals have inalienable rights to life and liberty, and an obligation of self-preservation. Locke argues that slavery is an inherent threat to one's life and liberty that violates the obligation to self-preservation, and consequently people cannot consent to become slaves.[19] By contrast, Locke states that the relationship between a master and servant involves only "a Temporary Power over him, and no greater, than what is contained in the *Contract* between 'em."[20] The incomplete and temporary loss of liberty involved in servitude does not pose an inherent threat to the servant's life, so people can consent to become servants without violating the obligation to self-preservation. Locke's distinction between a servant and a slave therefore centers on the issues of duration and the right to life. A slave forfeited their right to life, which now belongs to their master, whereas a servant cannot contractually give up their right to life due to the obligation of self-preservation. This distinction means that a master has the right to kill or maim a slave, but not to kill or maim a servant.[21] Moreover, slavery is indefinite and presumptively lifelong, whereas a servant is subordinate to an employer only for a temporary and specified period of time. The temporariness of servitude also prohibits violence by employers, because killing a servant would prevent them from regaining their liberty at the end of the contractual term and thereby violate the temporal aspect of the contract. To summarize, Locke argues that slavery is nonconsensual, lifelong, involves absolute power, and inherently threatens one's life, but that servitude is consensual, temporary, involves only partial subordination, and does not inherently threaten one's life.

Locke makes it clear that seventeenth-century England is a commonwealth,[22] so the English state has the responsibility to enforce law and punish criminals. The *Second Treatise* therefore provides clear criteria against which to assess penal slavery in England: an offender can be legitimately enslaved by the state if they violated the law in a manner that deserves death. Locke maintains that attacks on one's life or liberty deserve death, so penal slavery could be used to punish murder, attempted murder, physical assault, violent theft, and offenses against one's liberty, such as kidnapping or unlawful enslavement. However, Locke's argument that penalties should be severe enough to deter crime[23] suggests that the just use of penal slavery may extend even further. If whipping would deter people from committing nonviolent theft then it would presumably be disproportionate to impose the death penalty for that offense. If, on the other hand, a death sentence is required to deter people from committing nonviolent theft then it becomes legitimate to execute nonviolent thieves. By arguing that enslavement is a legitimate alternate penalty for any crime that would have justified a death sentence,[24] Locke ensures that death or enslavement are appropriate penalties for any offense that a non-capital penalty will not deter people from committing. Moreover, Locke argues that enslavement is an appropriate penalty for those actively involved in unjust wars. This provision would give victors of a just war the right to enslave prisoners of war who had participated in unlawful aggression either in a civil war or against a foreign state.

At first glance many readers assume that Locke's theory of slavery refers to the racialized enslavement of Africans, but Locke's theory fits poorly with this practice because he argues that slavery is justified only when the slave forfeited their rights by breaking the law, and he prohibits the intergenerational transfer of slave status.[25] Locke was well informed about the governance and economies of English colonies due to his work on the Carolinas and the Council of Trade and Foreign Plantations, so he would have known that the theory of slavery in the *Two Treatises* conflicted with practices of African slavery in North America and the Caribbean.[26] This tension between Locke's arguments in the *Two Treatises*, the reality of slavery in English colonies, and Locke's personal implication in slavery through his investment in the Royal African Company have led to debates about the intended referents of Locke's theory of slavery and its consistency with his other actions and writings. One way that scholars have sought to resolve the apparent tension in Locke's stance on slavery is by interpreting the theory of slavery in the *Two Treatises* in a manner that is consistent with Locke's acquiescence with African slavery through his investments and colonial work. This approach is taken by Peter Laslett, who argues that Locke believed enslaved

Africans to be criminals or captives taken in a just war and therefore viewed the slave-trading activities of the Royal African Company as legitimate.[27] Jennifer Welchman follows Laslett in arguing that Locke saw Africans captured in war as legitimate slaves, and argues that the *Two Treatises* allow hereditary slavery if the child was born after their parent was enslaved.[28] In response, many other scholars insist that the theory of slavery in the *Two Treatises* conflicts with the practice of African slavery. John Dunn argues that the theory of slavery in the *Second Treatise* clearly does not justify the activities of the Royal African Company or hereditary African slavery, and he suggests that Locke's lack of explicit discussion of these practices indicates his "immoral evasion" over slavery.[29] Similarly, Jeremy Waldron maintains that the theory of slavery in the *Two Treatises* is incompatible with African slavery, but concludes that there is an uneasy contradiction between the *Two Treatises* and Locke's own implication in African slavery.[30] Others seek to reconcile this tension between the reality of African slavery and Locke's theory by arguing that the theory of slavery in the *Two Treatises* was not intended to refer to Africans. James Farr argues that the discussion of slavery in the *Two Treatises* was intended to refer to the risk of political tyranny in England, and not to literal slaves.[31] Alternatively, James Tully and Brad Hinshelwood suggest that the theory of slavery in the *Two Treatises* was intended to justify the enslavement of Native Americans who infringed on the rights of colonists.[32] Locke's theory of slavery has therefore been variously interpreted as justifying the enslavement of Africans, prohibiting many features of the enslavement of Africans, justifying the enslavement of Native Americans, and condemning political tyranny in England.

Despite the large volume of literature about the theory of slavery in the *Two Treatises*, few commentators have considered the possibility that Locke's theory was intended to justify the enslavement of English convicts.[33] However, the fact that Locke justified slavery only as a punishment for breaking natural law means that the theory of slavery in the *Two Treatises* is specifically a theory of penal slavery. By committing unlawful acts an offender forfeits their rights to liberty and life, so they can be justly executed or enslaved. Lawful slave ownership is therefore an extension of the right to punish criminals with death or imprisonment. In Locke's view, the status of violent criminals is effectively the same as that of an army engaged in an unjust war: both have unlawfully created a state of war with their victims and have thereby forfeited their natural rights. Since both violent criminals and participants in aggressive wars have violated the laws of nature in a way that deserves death, both groups can be justly enslaved. However, those who begin the state of war forfeit only their own rights to life and liberty, so their wives, children, and countrymen cannot be lawfully enslaved. The theory of slavery in the *Two Treatises* therefore identifies two groups that can be justly enslaved for their involvement in illegal activity: criminals, and active participants in unjust wars. These groups directly correspond to two of the groups in seventeenth-century England that were legally subject to forced transportation and sale into forced labor: felons and prisoners of war.

FORCED MIGRATION AND FORCED LABOR IN ENGLISH COLONIES

In the early modern period the claimed "freedom" of English subjects coexisted with multiple practices of forced labor and forced migration, and these form the historical backdrop to Locke's theory of slavery. Between 1600 and 1800 over a million Europeans migrated to British colonies in the Americas and Caribbean, of whom up to three-quarters made the journey as transported convicts or indentured servants.[34] The practice of indentured servitude, also known as bond slavery, developed in response to the high cost of sailing across the Atlantic. Wealthy people could pay for a transatlantic voyage in advance, but the less affluent were unable to pay their travel costs upfront. Contracts of indentured servitude provided a way for the poor to finance a voyage to the Americas by paying the debt incurred during their journey through working for a specified period upon arrival. Demand for indentured servants existed in the colonies because tobacco and sugar were labor intensive to grow, and indentured servants provided a reliable long-term labor force that cost far less than free workers. The system of indentured servitude therefore made it possible for plantation owners in England's Caribbean and American colonies to farm their newly acquired land more productively and more profitably. Some people became indentured servants by choice, but during the late seventeenth century thousands of English, Scottish, and Irish people were forcibly transported to English colonies and sold involuntarily into indentured servitude. The ubiquity of forced migration and its major role in enabling European colonization of the Americas during the modern era has led some historians to describe forced transatlantic migration as "the structuring link between expropriation in one geographic setting and exploitation in another."[35] In addition, one hundred and fifty thousand British citizens were subjected to forced labor through naval impressment during the long eighteenth century,[36] as I discuss in the next chapter. The development of English empire therefore involved the coercion of Native Americans and Africans, and the selective coercion of English convicts, prisoners of war, sailors, and the poor for the purposes of populating, cultivating, and defending English colonies.

Indentured servants in English colonies usually served contractual terms of between four and seven years, and during this period they could not vote, could be legally whipped, were prohibited from marrying without their master's consent, and were not entitled to engage in trade.[37] Barbados was a common destination for indentured servants in the seventeenth century, and servants there were prohibited from leaving their master's plantation without permission.[38] Servants had the right to bring lawsuits about breaches of contract or extremely severe treatment, but magistrates often sided with the masters and could sentence the complainants to be whipped as a way to discourage legal challenges.[39] In practice, many indentured servants were badly treated, with long hours of hard labor, inadequate food, punitive violence,[40] and living conditions that have been described as "indistinguishable in practice from slavery."[41] Some indentured servants died before completing their term and others had their servitude extended as a punishment for offenses such as attempting to escape or becoming pregnant. At the end of their term indentured servants became free citizens, and were supposed to receive freedom dues in the form of land or sugar.[42] Although indentured servants were not free laborers their status was clearly preferable to that of African slaves. Unlike African slaves, the status of indentured servants was temporary so those who survived their servitude gained political and economic rights. Whereas the children of African slaves inherited slave status, most colonies did not deem indentured servitude heritable, so the children of indentured servants usually became free subjects.[43] Also unlike slaves, many indentured servants were protected by the terms of their indenture contracts, which were enforceable in court. Slaves consistently had fewer rights than indentured servants because they lacked the protection of an indenture contract, were often excluded from giving evidence in court, and could usually be lawfully killed by their owner.[44] Nonetheless, both slaves and indentured servants were treated as a form of property that could be bought, sold, inherited, or gambled away.[45] Locke's acceptance of the practice of indentured servitude is indicated by the passages in the *Second Treatise* where he defends voluntary contracts to enter a temporary and limited form of subordination, which he describes as *Drudgery* and the status of a servant.[46]

Many English people voluntarily traveled to the colonies to become indentured servants, but others were compelled to do so. During the seventeenth century the English state forcibly transported three groups to English colonies for sale as indentured servants: felons, prisoners of war, and the very poor. The idea of transporting English criminals to the colonies to serve a period of forced labor accompanied the beginning of English colonization in the Americas, and was proposed to Elizabeth I in Richard Hakluyt's *Discourse of Western Planting*.[47] In 1615 the Privy Council began transporting English felons to the colonies for sale as indentured servants, and this was intended to reduce overcrowding in English prisons and provide cheap labor to colonists.[48] Widespread poverty and crime in the seventeenth century led the English state to impose harsh penalties, including use of the death penalty for many nonviolent offenses. Convict transportation became popular in this context because it was seen as less severe than the death penalty and offered a way to prevent a criminal from re-offending in England without the expense of long-term imprisonment or Poor Relief.[49] Most transported English felons were sent to colonies that demanded plentiful cheap labor, such as the tobacco plantations of Virginia or the Caribbean sugar plantations, and they were sought after by employers because they often served longer terms of servitude than non-convicts.[50] From 1660 to 1699 the number of English convicts sentenced to transportation each year averaged between seventy-five and one hundred and fifty,[51] and the practice expanded further in the eighteenth century. Convicts were also used for forced labor by other European states in this period, including France, Spain, and Portugal.[52]

The practice of forcibly transporting prisoners of war to the colonies and selling them into forced labor as indentured servants was introduced after the English Civil War. Oliver Cromwell repeatedly ordered that prisoners of war be transported to Barbados to provide forced labor, including Scots captured at the battles of Dunbar and Worcester,[53] Irish troops captured at Drogheda,[54] and royalists from the 1655 Penruddock rising.[55] The scale of forced transportation during the Interregnum led to complaints from the Barbados planters, who claimed that by 1655 the island had received over ten thousand transportees.[56] This practice of transporting political opponents continued after the Restoration, when Charles II ordered the arrest and transportation to Barbados of hundreds of dissenters who refused to comply with the 1662 Act of Settlement.[57] After the Monmouth Rebellion in 1685 James II sentenced around nine hundred people to transportation to the Caribbean with orders that they should serve ten-year terms of indentured servitude.[58] Conditions for the transported men were often poor, and John Coad recalled that after Monmouth's rebellion twenty-two of the ninety-nine captives on his ship died during the voyage to Jamaica.[59] Successive governments in late seventeenth-century England therefore used forced migration and sale into forced labor as a punishment for opponents who had engaged in political resistance or violence within the British Isles.

Locke's support for forced labor for convicts and prisoners of war is indicated in the *Second Treatise* where he argues that it is legitimate to enslave criminals and participants in illegal warfare who could justly have been killed. The question of whether these slaves can be legitimately sold or forcibly transported is not explicitly addressed in the *Second Treatise*, but Locke's answer is implicit in his account of slavery. Locke specifies that masters have "Absolute, Arbitrary Power"[60] over slaves that is "purely Despotical,"[61] and for the power of a slaveowner to be as unrestricted as Locke describes it would need to include the right to dictate the slave's location and to transfer ownership of the slave.[62] Slaves might not wish to be sold or transported abroad, but they had no lawful grounds to object because they had forfeited their natural rights to life and liberty when they broke natural law. Further, Locke's account of government imposes no restriction on a

commonwealth's ability to forcibly transport or sell enslaved criminals provided that this serves the *"publick good* of the Society."[63] Locke states that
the legislative is empowered to determine who executes laws[64] and can des-
ignate the execution of specific laws to specific bodies "by positive Grant,
and Commission, delegated to them."[65] This power to delegate law enforcement to other entities means that the legislative are entitled to delegate the
task of executing criminals to an executioner, to delegate the imprisonment
of criminals to a jailer, and to transfer ownership of penal slaves to Barbados
planters.

Further support for the right to transport and sell penal slaves is provided
in the *First Treatise* where Locke describes the power that a Caribbean
plantation owner has over "Slaves bought with Money" and argues that a
master's power "over Slaves or Horses, was only from his purchase."[66]
While Drescher reads this passage as meaning that a master can lawfully own
any slave they buy, whether or not the slave forfeited their rights by breaking
natural law,[67] this interpretation plainly conflicts with the theories of slavery
and natural rights in the *Second Treatise*. A more plausible interpretation of
the passage is provided by Waldron, who suggests that "a slave *may* legitimately be sold on Locke's account" provided that the slave was justly acquired before the sale.[68] Locke's statement that the right of the purchaser
over the slave is established "by Bargain and Money"[69] therefore only explains why *this* master has power over the slave and not how the slave
became a slave. The slave's status as a slave was established when they
alienated their natural rights by beginning a state of war, which is Locke's
theory of just acquisition of slaves. The planter's status as owner of the slave
was established later when the slave was purchased from their previous legal
master, which is an example of the just transfer of property. This right to buy
and sell justly acquired slaves also implies the right to transport slaves without their consent, for example by taking slaves from a ship to their new
owner's plantation. Both Locke's account of the absolute power masters
have over slaves in the *Second Treatise* and his discussion of the sale of
slaves in the *First Treatise* therefore suggest that he saw it as legitimate to
transport a lawfully enslaved English criminal to the Caribbean and sell them
to a plantation owner.

There is a striking correspondence between the English state's practices
of forced labor for English convicts and prisoners of war, and Locke's justification for enslaving criminals and those engaged in unjust wars, but the
penalties differ in name and duration. In the *Two Treatises* Locke justifies the
permanent involuntary subordination of criminals and prisoners of war as
slaves, whereas seventeenth-century English convicts and prisoners of war
were sent to the colonies and sold into temporary involuntary subordination
as indentured servants. Despite these apparent differences, the forced migration and forced labor of English convicts and prisoners of war is inconsistent

with Locke's account of servant status and is justifiable only under his theory of slavery. Locke stipulates that servants have not forfeited their rights to life and liberty, so they can become subordinates only by consent. Forcing law-abiding English people to travel to the colonies and become indentured servants would be unlawful and would justify the punishment—indeed the enslavement—of those responsible. The involuntary nature of transportation and indentured servitude for convicts is therefore incompatible with servant status as defined in the *Two Treatises*. Instead, the *Two Treatises* specify that forced labor and forced migration are justified only for those who have been enslaved because they forfeited their natural rights by breaking natural law. For involuntary subordination to be legitimate under Locke's theory the individuals concerned needed to be classified as slaves, even if in practice this enslavement was temporary. Given that Locke justifies *permanent* enslavement for those who begin a state of war, the English state's practice of transporting English convicts and prisoners of war for sale into *temporary* subordination can be seen as a comparatively mild penalty. If the more severe punishment of permanent enslavement is legitimate then there can be no doubt that Locke's theory justifies the temporary enslavement of law-breakers by carrying them to English colonies and selling them into forced labor.

The third group targeted by the English state for forced migration and labor was the very poor. The practice of sending the poor to English colonies was introduced by a 1597 law legalizing the transportation of beggars,[70] which enabled thousands of English people to be sent to Virginia.[71] By 1620 the principle of forced migration for the poor was sufficiently well established that the City of London authorized the capture of a hundred poor children and their transportation to Virginia, with instructions to punish any who resisted.[72] Further grounds for forcibly transporting the poor was provided in the 1662 Poor Relief Act, which specified that "Vagabonds idle and disorderly persons and study Beggars" could legally be seized and either sent to workhouses or transported to English colonies.[73] This created a legal avenue for the forced migration of poor English men, women, and children provided that approval was given by a Justice of the Peace. The English Poor Laws therefore created a means to coerce the very poor into unpaid labor, which in turn was used to justify sending them to English colonies for sale into indentured servitude. Locke's account of natural rights in the *Two Treatises* suggests that it is a violation of natural law to infringe on the freedom of people who had not committed crimes, which would seemingly prohibit forced transportation and forced labor for the law-abiding poor. However, in the "Essay on the Poor Law" Locke advocates forced labor for the nonworking poor, therefore indicating that he saw them as having more limited rights to liberty, as I discuss later in relation to Locke's Board of Trade work.

In addition to these legal practices of forced migration and forced labor, demand for workers in the colonies created a market for illegally transporting people and selling them into servitude. Through the practice known as "spiriting" unlucky English people were illegally taken or lured onto ships, transported to American or Caribbean colonies, and sold involuntarily as indentured servants.[74] Spirits used tactics such as kidnapping young children,[75] persuading naive poor people onto the ship by misleading them about the destination and purpose of the voyage, and getting victims drunk so that they could be carried on board.[76] Once victims of spiriting arrived in the colonies and were sold into indentured servitude then their status as servants was usually upheld by colonial courts.[77] One victim named Charles Bayly was spirited from Gravesend in England in 1646, transported to Maryland, and sold into servitude as "the temporary, chattel property of his owner" for seven years—a period that was doubled in punishment when he attempted to escape.[78] In the mid-seventeenth century spiriting became so common that "Barbadoes" was adopted as a verb to describe the practice.[79] After the Restoration the London authorities attempted to stop spiriting by creating a registry office where servants emigrating to the colonies could declare their willingness to travel,[80] but spiriting continued and in 1672 one convicted spirit claimed that hundreds of victims were illegally transported to the colonies each year.[81] The victims of spiriting had not broken natural law, so Locke's *Second Treatise* would suggest that they could not lawfully be coerced or enslaved, and that their illegal coercion justifies the death or enslavement of their captors. The theory of slavery in the *Two Treatises* therefore legitimates some seventeenth-century practices of forced labor and migration such as transportation and penal servitude for convicts and prisoners of war, while prohibiting other practices of forced migration and labor such as spiriting.

PENAL SLAVERY IN LOCKE'S BOARD OF TRADE WORK

Locke not only argued that penal slavery was theoretically legitimate, but advocated its use during his work for the Board of Trade. Locke's support for penal slavery is apparent in three examples of his work for the Board. First, Locke was personally involved in the Board's decision to recommend that fifty female convicts be transported from England to the Leeward Islands in 1697. Secondly, Locke proposes in the "Essay on the Poor Law" that repeated forgers of Poor Law passes "shall be transported to the plantations, as in the case of felony,"[82] which indicates his support for and desire to expand the existing practice of forced migration and forced labor for English criminals. Thirdly, Locke's "Essay on Virginia" argues that English criminals sentenced to hang should instead be transported to Virginia as forced laborers.[83]

In both the "Essay on the Poor Law" and "Essay on Virginia" Locke outlines the practical advantages offered by convict transportation and penal slavery. In the "Essay on the Poor Law" Locke argues that the idle English poor are undermining national prosperity, that the nation will benefit economically and morally if they are forced to work, and that poor people who evade these measures should be punished. In the "Essay on Virginia" Locke explains that transporting criminals and the poor to underpopulated colonies as laborers will make those colonies more prosperous and easier to defend. Read together, these essays make it clear that Locke saw forced migration and forced labor of convicts as economically and politically beneficial to both England and its colonies.

In January 1697 the Board of Trade received a message from King William informing them that Newgate prison held many criminals sentenced to transportation and expressing the hope that "they might be made Serviceable to those Plantations that chiefly wanted Inhabitants."[84] The Board understood this as a request to arrange transportation of the convicts to provide forced labor in English colonies, and responded by considering whether the convicts could be sent to the slave colonies of Jamaica and Barbados. The Board noted that Jamaica merchants had already stated that they did not want to receive convicts because "they can easily make their escape from one Colony to another"[85]—a concern that confirms the transported convicts were not free migrants or laborers. When the Board asked merchants from Barbados if they would take convicts they were told that "there be people here willing to take any numbers of such of them as are able strong Men, fit for Laborious Service; but no Woman, Children or other infirm Persons,"[86] and the Board duly informed the King of this response.[87] Locke's ill health meant that he could not attend meetings in London during the winter and was absent for the Board's discussion of convict transportation in January, but he was present when the Board revisited the issue in July 1697.

On July 1, 1697, the issue of penal slavery returned to the Board's agenda when it received another letter from the King:

> informing their Lordships that about fifty women convicts, now lying in Newgate, for Transportation, are intended accordingly to be Transported at His Majesty's Charge; and requiring their Lordships to consider to what places those Women should be sent, and what Instructions and Directions will be proper to send—along with them, for their being received and disposed of according to their Condition and Circumstances.[88]

The Board duly wrote to representatives of several colonies asking if they were willing to receive the women. Most colonies were unenthusiastic and the reasons that they gave are instructive. The Jamaica merchants again declined the convicts, but this time cited gender as their reason, stating that the women:

will be of no use to us in the Island of Jamaica, nay, we would not Receive 'em unless upon Condition, that we might have at least 150 Male Convicts along with 'em. It is men that we want . . .those women will be onely a Charge and Burden to the people, and Contribute nothing to their Defence. [89]

This reply suggests that the Jamaica merchants did not object to receiving convicts per se, but rejected female convicts on the grounds that their gender made them ill-suited for warfare and profitable work. Similarly, the agents of Barbados replied that they would not take the women because: "no English women are there put to work in the Field: and the People will not be willing to take such as these into their Houses. So that they will be altogether Useless." [90] These replies reveal a great deal about the gendered and racialized division of labor in England's Caribbean colonies. [91] Although the Barbados agents clearly considered it inappropriate to put English women to work in the sugar fields alongside African slaves or as overseers for the slaves, they also believed that Barbados residents would be unwilling to accept convicts as domestic servants. The women's status as convicts was used as grounds to exclude them from the domestic labor done by non-convict white women in Jamaica and Barbados, but gender was used as grounds to exclude them from military activity and slave overseer roles that could be performed by white male convicts. While the presumed immorality of convict women meant they were regarded as of lower social status than non-convict women, their status was clearly seen as distinct from that of the enslaved African women who worked in the sugar fields. In the eyes of the Caribbean planters, crime did not strip white women of racial privilege.

The agent for Virginia and Maryland also declined to take the women convicts, and recommended sending the women to a Caribbean colony where they could not escape because they would be "confined und'r one governm't and enclosed within the Island." [92] A more enthusiastic reply was received from the small sugar colony of the Leeward Islands, who told the Board that "it may not be improper" to send the women to the Leewards where the governor would decide what to do with them. [93] Locke was the most influential of the four Board members present when the Board proposed sending the female convicts to the Leeward Islands, [94] and on July 26, 1697, he was one of the five signatories to the Board's letter advising that the fifty female convicts be sent to the Leewards. [95] In addition to making this recommendation, the Board's letter summarizes the responses that colonial representatives gave about the female convicts, including the gendered division of labor described in Barbados:

We have not found any suitable disposition to receive them in any of the said Colonies Except only the Leeward Islds, some alledge that in Planting they imploy no other whites but men, and are not willg to receive Women of this character into their houses. . . . We therefore most humbly offer to yr Excellencies our opinion, that those women may be sent accordingly to the Leeward Islands. [96]

The responses received from the colonial representatives made it clear that transported convicts were required to work, and the involuntary nature of the convicts' migration and labor was emphasized by the recurrent warnings that they would seek to escape. Despite this, the Board did not provide any recommendations about the type of work that the women should be put to in the Leeward Islands, which suggests that they were not concerned about the status accorded to the convict women. Whereas the Barbados agents sought to uphold racial hierarchy and gender roles, there is no indication that Locke or the other Board members saw female convicts as deserving different treatment than men or different treatment than enslaved African women.

Locke then advocated convict transportation for English criminals in two papers that he wrote for discussion by the Board later that year. Locke's "Essay on the Poor Law" was written in the autumn of 1697, when a Bristol resident named Mr. Cary asked the Board to devise a plan for employing the nonworking poor in Bristol. [97] Cary requested that the Board divide the poor into classes to "regulate their different Employments" by age and ability, [98] and expressed hope "in a little while to make the Poor maintain themselves." [99] In response, the Board decided that each member should draw up proposals and bring them for discussion. [100] Locke and his fellow Board member Mr. Pollexfen brought draft proposals on September 28, and the Board asked them each to "perfect his own modell." [101] On October 19, 1697, the Board's Journal records that "Mr Locke produced to the Board a perfected Draught of the Scheme for the Employment of the Poor throughout England . . . which being read, he was now desired by ye Board to put it into proper forme that it might then be more thoroughly considered Paragraph by Paragraph." [102] On October 26 Locke returned with the details of his scheme finalized, but discussion of his proposals led to conflict: "beginning to read it some other propositions being made, and a debate arising upon that subject, the further consideration thereof was deferr'd to another time." [103] The Board discussed the poor law several more times but deferred a decision until after Locke left London in late November, so he was absent when the Board developed its final advice. [104] Locke was clearly frustrated that his proposals had been rejected, because he wrote to his friend the MP Edward Clarke that "since our Board thought not fit to make use of it" he was sending his proposals about the poor to Clarke for consideration. [105]

Locke's "Essay on the Poor Law" makes it clear that he did not object to forced labor and forced transportation, because he advocates both for the nonworking poor. Locke's opening argument is that the nonworking poor must be compelled to work because they are a "growing burden on the kingdom" [106] and evidence that people have been corrupted by "vice and idleness."[107] The idle poor are therefore presented as both morally deficient and undermining the prosperity of the commonwealth, which Locke proposes to remedy through forced labor for poor men, women, children, the elderly, and the disabled. For able-bodied men without jobs Locke proposes activities including naval service,[108] hard labor in a workhouse,[109] and a working school.[110] For forgers of poor law passes Locke proposes harsher treatment: "whoever shall counterfeit a pass shall lose his ears for the forgery the first time that he is found guilty thereof, and the second time, that he shall be transported to the plantations, as in the case of felony."[111] Locke's presentation of transportation as a more severe penalty than the loss of both ears—a permanent corporal punishment that produced a visible stigma, damaged the offender's hearing, and could kill them if the wounds became infected—indicates that transportation was intended to be extremely punitive. By likening transportation for those who repeatedly forge passes to the existing legal penalty of transportation for felons Locke makes it clear that he is proposing not just forced transportation to the colonies but also forced labor upon arrival.

In the autumn of 1697 Locke also wrote (or co-wrote) "Some of the Cheif Greivances of the Present Constitution of Virginia, with an Essay Towards Remedies Thereof," usually referred to as the "Essay on Virginia."[112] In the late 1690s political power in Virginia was concentrated in the hands of the Governor-General, Sir Edmund Andros, and economic power centered around a few wealthy men who used slaves and indentured servants to grow tobacco on huge areas of land. Leading Whig politicians opposed Andros and this system of rule in Virginia,[113] and as the most influential Whig on the Board Locke sought to investigate and reform the colony. In August 1697 the Board received complaints about the government of Virginia from James Blair,[114] so Locke and the other Whig members took the opportunity to gather information about Andros's mismanagement and wrote to him demanding copies of the colony's accounts.[115] Andros was elderly and unwell, so when he received a hostile letter from the Board in March 1698 he resigned.[116] During the autumn of 1697 Locke began writing the "Essay on Virginia" either with Blair, or without Blair's direct involvement but drawing on the information that he provided.[117] At Locke's suggestion, the Board then appointed Francis Nicholson as the new governor of Virginia in spring 1698,[118] and during the summer of 1698 Locke played the major role in drafting the Board's instructions for Nicholson, which were approved despite fierce Tory opposition.[119]

The first problem that Locke addresses in the "Essay on Virginia" is the "want of people" in the colony.[120] Locke argues that the underpopulation of Virginia has negative political and economic consequences, including lower tobacco production, lower tax revenues for England, the failure to develop other industries that would benefit England such as iron or silk production, and the inability of Virginia to defend itself militarily.[121] Locke attributes these problems to the flawed system of land allocation in Virginia and lack of help for immigrants, which means that poor immigrants "must become Servants for four or five Years to pay for their passage."[122] To remedy these problems Locke proposes reforms to land ownership in Virginia and measures to increase immigration to the colony, including the transportation of English convicts and the poor:

> It might be worth the while to Consider whether multitudes of poor people that are onely a burthen to their parishes at home here in England might not be well spared; as also whither Delinquents had not better be sent to the Plantations (tho' condemned to several years Servitude) than to be sent to Tyburne.[123]

Here, Locke explicitly advocates that English convicts sentenced to death by hanging[124] should be transported as an alternate penalty and then required to provide forced labor for several years. This proposal is consistent with the theory of slavery in the *Second Treatise*, because Locke is proposing forced labor for convicts who would otherwise face the death penalty. However, in the "Essay on Virginia" Locke refers to this forced labor for English convicts as servitude, not slavery, even though it is involuntary. By describing a punitive and involuntary form of subordination as servitude in this passage Locke blurs the distinction that he made in the *Second Treatise* between voluntary servitude and involuntary slavery. Nonetheless, Locke makes it clear that he supports transportation and forced labor for English convicts, and that he saw this practice as economically and politically beneficial both to the Virginian colony and to England.

UNDERSTANDING LOCKE'S ADVOCACY OF FORCED LABOR

In the *Two Treatises* Locke justifies the enslavement of criminals and participants in unjust wars on the grounds that they have forfeited their rights to life and liberty by breaking natural law. Locke's theory of slavery is therefore specifically a theory of penal slavery, and it corresponds to the English state's practice of forcibly transporting English criminals and prisoners of war to English colonies for sale into forced labor. Locke's work on the Board of Trade makes it clear that his advocacy of penal slavery was not just theoretical, because he advocated convict transportation and penal slavery in his writing for the Board and signed the Board's 1697 recommendation that English convicts be sent to a Caribbean colony for forced labor. It is unlikely to be coincidental that the theory of slavery in the *Two Treatises* so closely matches contemporary English practices of forced migration and forced labor for convicts, and Locke's own advocacy of these policies as a Board member. The most obvious explanation for the correspondence between Locke's theoretical views on penal slavery in the *Two Treatises* and the policies he advocated on the Board is that Locke intended his theory of slavery to justify the forced migration and forced labor of English convicts. Reading the theory of slavery in the *Second Treatise* as a justification of penal slavery that includes English criminals means that Locke intended his theory to justify actual practices of forced labor, and that he did not intend slave status to apply solely to non-Europeans or those racialized as non-white. However, this is not to say that Locke's theory of slavery was intended *only* to justify the enslavement of English criminals—on the contrary, Locke's natural law theory is universalistic and extends to all people and all regions of the world. By arguing that lawbreakers could be legitimately enslaved Locke justifies the enslavement of criminals and those engaged in unjust wars in the state of nature and in commonwealths, without exclusions based on gender, race, or ethnicity. It is therefore possible that Locke also intended to justify the enslavement of Native Americans who broke natural law, as James Tully and Brad Hinshelwood argue.[125] The mismatch between Locke's theory of slavery and the practice of African slavery in the Americas does not warrant Farr's conclusion that "Locke, whatever else, was making a case against 'slavery' on his island, not for slavery in the new world,"[126] because there is no contradiction between Locke's opposition to absolutism in England and the desire to legitimize actual coercive practices. Contrary to Farr's claims, the theory of slavery in the *Two Treatises* does justify at least one form of slavery in the Americas: penal slavery for criminals who could have been justly killed, including transported English convicts.

While Locke's views on penal slavery in the *Two Treatises* are consistent with his stance as a member of the Board of Trade it is more difficult to reconcile his views about the freedom of the poor. In the *Two Treatises* Locke argues that law-abiding people have inalienable rights to life and liberty, so coercing them would violate natural law. However, in the "Essay on the Poor Law" and "Essay on Virginia" Locke proposes forced labor and forced transportation for poor English people who have not committed crimes that warrant death, and some of whom may be innocent of any crime. This tension between the *Two Treatises* and Locke's advocacy of coercion for the poor in the "Essay on the Poor Law" has led to debates about Locke's view of poverty. C. B. Macpherson uses Locke's "Essay on the Poor Law" to support his reading of the *Two Treatises* as a text that advocates excluding the poor from political participation on the grounds of their limited freedom and lack of full rationality.[127] A similar reading of Locke is provided by Nancy Hirschmann, who argues that Locke saw the bad living conditions of the poor as preventing them from developing the full rationality needed to participate in politics. Hirschmann concludes that Locke was a believer in class-differentiated rights who denied freedom to alms recipients, beggars, and poor people who worked for wages.[128] Both Macpherson and Hirschmann therefore see Locke's willingness to force the poor to work as an indication that his political theory accords them lesser political rights. Whether or not Locke intended the *Two Treatises* to present a theory of class-differentiated rights, his "Essay on the Poor Law" indicates that he believed the poor had a moral obligation to work and that this justified forcing them to work. By requiring that poor men, women, and children engage in productive labor, and by prohibiting vagrancy and begging, the provisions in Locke's "Essay on the Poor Law" effectively criminalize many poor people. Since Locke argues in the *Two Treatises* that criminals have forfeited their natural rights and can be coerced, the criminalization of the poor provides a potential justification for their enslavement. It is therefore possible to read Locke's views on forced labor in the *Two Treatises* and the "Essay on the Poor Law" as consistent without assuming that he intended to develop a theory of formally class-differentiated rights. According to the *Two Treatises*, criminals who could justly be killed can be enslaved, and death or enslavement is a proportionate punishment for nonviolent crime if a lesser penalty would not deter people from committing the offense. Given that many of the idle poor would be criminalized by the provisions in the "Essay on the Poor Law," anyone whose criminal idleness warrants punishing them with death can be enslaved. The introduction of a requirement for the English poor to work collapses the distinction between criminals and law-abiding poor people without jobs, thereby turning many of the poor into presumptive criminals who have lost their natural right to freedom.

Locke's advocacy of forced migration and forced labor for English criminals is consistent not only with the theory of slavery in the *Two Treatises*, but also with his wider political and economic goals. In England, Locke's *Two Treatises* were intended to condemn absolutist rule and justify political resistance, as studies by scholars such as Laslett, Ashcraft, and Farr have shown.[129] By justifying forced labor and forced migration for those who break natural law Locke provides a penalty that can be used to punish tyrants, and that could potentially be applied to the Stuarts and their supporters. In the Americas, scholars such as Tully and Arneil have shown that Locke sought to promote English appropriation, settlement, and farming of land that was formerly occupied by indigenous peoples.[130] Transporting English criminals to the Americas as forced laborers provided a settler population and a cheap agricultural labor force, thereby enabling Locke's colonial vision. Convict transportation and penal slavery also fit with Locke's goal of promoting national prosperity. In the *Second Treatise* Locke argues that economic production derives largely from labor, and that the low productivity of uncultivated land "shews, how much numbers of men are to be preferd to largenesse of dominions."[131] This means it is not sufficient for states to merely acquire land, because effective rule also requires "the right imploying"[132] of that land, which Locke describes as "the great art of government."[133] In his other political and economic essays Locke restates the benefits of a large population and argues that England should support immigration because "People are the strength of any country or government."[134] However, Locke makes it clear the value of a large population lies in their provision of labor, and argues that idle people such as beggars do not contribute to trade.[135] Locke's recipe for national prosperity therefore involves a large population who are all engaged in productive labor. In his 1676–9 writings titled "Atlantis" outlining the rules for a hypothetical colony, Locke proposes policies to promote both population growth and hard work, including a proposal to send all beggars to a workhouse.[136] Locke continues this point in the "Essay on Virginia," arguing that boosting the population of underpopulated colonies would generate more goods and more tax revenue. Collectively, Locke's writings suggest that penal slavery offers multiple benefits, because it could simultaneously strengthen English colonies and punish those who acted unlawfully. In practice, these goals were combined when Cromwell sold prisoners of war into indentured servitude in Barbados in the 1650s and when James II sold Whig rebels into indentured servitude in Barbados in the 1680s.

Textual, philosophical, and contextual methods of analysis all indicate that the theory of slavery in the *Two Treatises* is a theory of penal slavery that justifies the coercion of English criminals. Textual analysis of the *Two Treatises* shows that Locke proposes slavery only for those who break the law, either individually or collectively, and that this applies in the state of nature and in commonwealths. Philosophical analysis of Locke's claims shows that in a commonwealth the right to enslave criminals belongs to the state, and that the owner of a lawful slave has the right to force the slave to work, dictate their location, and transfer ownership. Contextual analysis shows that the *Two Treatises* were written and published during a period when the English state used forced migration and forced labor for convicts, prisoners of war, and the poor. The theory of penal slavery that Locke presents in the *Two Treatises* therefore justifies practices of state-sponsored coercion that were widely used in seventeenth-century England and continued in the eighteenth century. Further, Locke's work on the Board of Trade shows that he supported the actual use of forced migration and forced labor for English convicts. This close correspondence between Locke's advocacy of penal slavery in the *Two Treatises*, existing practices in England, and his stance on the Board strongly suggests that Locke intended the theory of slavery in the *Two Treatises* to justify forced labor and forced migration for English convicts. While this support for state-sponsored coercion may surprise readers who see Locke as a "proto-liberal,"[137] Locke's views were influenced by seventeenth-century political practices and debates, which included widespread acceptance of multiple systems of forced migration and forced labor. Locke's support for penal slavery reflects the ubiquity of forced labor in early modern Europe, and shows that even defenders of natural rights were willing to justify state coercion in the name of punishing law-breakers, especially if this provided additional benefits such as national prosperity or military defense. This theme of state coercion for the sake of military defense is the focus of the next chapter, where I examine Locke's views about the seventeenth-century practice of forcing English sailors into naval service through impressment.

NOTES

1. GBPRO, *Calendar of State Papers Colonial*, vol. 15, 567 and The National Archives CO 391/10, 172 (original numbering).
2. Locke, *Two Treatises*, II §6 271.
3. *Ibid*, II §10–12 273–4.
4. *Ibid*, II §12 274.
5. *Ibid*, II §17 279.
6. *Ibid*, II §17 280.
7. *Ibid*, II §23 284.
8. *Ibid*, II §24 284.
9. *Ibid*, II §178 387.
10. *Ibid*, II §178 387–8.
11. *Ibid*, II §179 388.
12. *Ibid*, II §182 389.
13. *Ibid*, II §183 390.
14. *Ibid*, II §182 389.
15. *Ibid*, II §183 390.
16. *Ibid*, II §183 390.
17. *Ibid*, II §183 391.
18. *Ibid*, II §23 284. The master's right to kill the slaves enables slaves to commit indirect suicide, see *Ibid*, II §23 284.
19. *Ibid*, II §23 284.
20. *Ibid*, II §85 322.
21. *Ibid*, II §24 285.
22. *Ibid*, II §35 292.
23. *Ibid*, II §12 275.
24. *Ibid*, II §24 284.
25. *Ibid*, II §23 284 and II §182 389.
26. The 1669 *Fundamental Constitutions of Carolina* specify that "Every freeman of Carolina shall have absolute dominion and ownership of his negro slaves," see Locke and others, "Fundamental Constitutions," 180. There is also abundant evidence of Locke's knowledge of African slavery in the records of the Council of Trade and Foreign Plantations in the 1670s, which included jurisdiction over England's Caribbean slave colonies.
27. See Laslett's note in Locke, *Two Treatises*, II §24 284–5.
28. Welchman, "Locke on Slavery."
29. Dunn, *Political Thought of John Locke*, 174–5.
30. Waldron, *God, Locke and Equality*, 206.
31. Farr, "'So Vile and Miserable an Estate,'" and Farr, "Locke, Natural Law, and New World Slavery."
32. Tully, *Approach to Political Philosophy*, 153–4; Hinshelwood, "Carolinian Context."
33. For example, Welchman argues that Locke justifies penal slavery in the state of nature, but overlooks the possibility that Locke may equally be justifying penal slavery within commonwealths, see Welchman, "Locke on Slavery," 67. Similarly, Dilts notes that Locke's theory of slavery is an extension of the right to punish those who break the law, and he notes the

presence of penal slavery in the U.S. Constitution, but does not consider the possibility that Locke intended to justify actual practices of penal slavery, see Dilts, "To Kill a Thief."

34. Alison Games, "Migration" in *The British Atlantic World: 1500–1800*, eds. David Armitage and Michael J. Braddick (New York: Palgrave Macmillan, 2002), 41.

35. Marcus Rediker, Cassandra Pybus, and Emma Christopher, "Introduction" in *Many Middle Passages: Forced Migration and the Making of the Modern World*, eds. Marcus Rediker, Cassandra Pybus, and Emma Christopher (Berkeley and Los Angeles: University of California Press, 2007), 2.

36. See Denver Brunsman, "Men of War: British Sailors and the Impressment Paradox," *Journal of Early Modern History* 14, no. 1 (2010): 22.

37. Abbot Emerson Smith, *Colonists in Bondage: White Servitude and Convict Labor in America, 1607–1776* (New York: Norton & Company, 1971), 233.

38. Hilary McD. Beckles, *A History of Barbados: From Amerindian Settlement to Nation-State* (Cambridge and New York: Cambridge University Press, 1990), 17.

39. *Ibid*, 17–18; Smith, *Colonists in Bondage*, 235–6; Vincent T. Harlow, *A History of Barbados: 1625–1685* (New York: Negro Universities Press, 1969), 304; Jennie Jeppesen, "To Serve Longer According to Law: The Chattel-Like Status of Convict Servants in Virginia" in *Order and Civility in the Early Modern Chesapeake*, eds. Debra Meyers and Melanie Perreault (Lanham, MD: Lexington Books, 2014), 202.

40. Harlow, *A History of Barbados*, 302–3.

41. Peter Wilson Coldham, *Emigrants in Chains: A Social History of Forced Emigration to the Americas of Felons, Destitute Children, Political and Religious Non-Conformists, Vagabonds, Beggars and Other Undesirables, 1607–1776* (Maryland: Genealogical Publishing Co., 1992), 43.

42. Smith, *Colonists in Bondage*, 238–40.

43. Beckles, *History of Barbados*, 19. In Virginia children of indentured servants were sometimes required to serve a period of servitude and their treatment varied by race, see Jeppesen, "To Serve Longer," 198.

44. Beckles, *History of Barbados*, 34.

45. Smith, *Colonists in Bondage*, 232–3; John Donoghue, "'Out of the Land of Bondage': The English Revolution and the Atlantic Origins of Abolition," *The American Historical Review* 115, no. 4 (2010): 945; Jeppesen, "To Serve Longer," 195.

46. Locke, *Two Treatises*, II §24 285 and II §85 322. On Locke's view of indentured servitude see Dunn, *Political Thought of John Locke*, 174.

47. Richard Hakluyt, *Particuler Discourse*, 28.

48. Coldham, *Emigrants in Chains*, 43.

49. Beckles, *History of Barbados*, 298; Gwenda Morgan and Peter Rushton, *Eighteenth-Century Criminal Transportation: The Formation of the Criminal Atlantic* (New York: Palgrave Macmillan, 2004), 10.

50. Smith, *Colonists in Bondage*, 232.

51. Morgan and Rushton, *Eighteenth-Century Criminal*, Appendix VII, 181.

52. David Eltis, "Europeans and the Rise and Fall of African Slavery in the Americas: An Interpretation," *The American Historical Review* 98, no. 5 (1993): 1410.

53. Beckles, *History of Barbados*, 295; Smith, *Colonists in Bondage*, 157.

54. Beckles, *History of Barbados*, 295; Smith, *Colonists in Bondage*, 164.

55. Beckles, *History of Barbados*, 296; Smith, *Colonists in Bondage*, 160–1.

56. Beckles, *History of Barbados*, 118–9.

57. Christopher Hill, *Liberty Against the Law: Some Seventeenth Century Controversies* (London: Penguin Books, 1996), 169; Coldham, *Emigrants in Chains*, 51; Smith, *Colonists in Bondage*, 179.

58. Beckles, *History of Barbados*, 297; Smith, *Colonists in Bondage*, 189–90.

59. Coldham, *Emigrants in Chains*, 101.

60. Locke, *Two Treatises*, II §23 284.

61. *Ibid*, II §178 387.

62. Farr goes even further, stating that "No act of the lawful master can violate the rights of a slave, who, through an earlier act of his own, has no rights," see Farr, "'So Vile and Miserable,'" 273.

63. Locke, *Two Treatises*, II §135 357.

64. *Ibid*, II §153 369.

65. *Ibid*, II §152 369.

66. *Ibid*, I §131 238 and I §130 237.

67. Seymour Drescher, "On James Farr's 'So Vile and Miserable an Estate,'" *Political Theory* 16, no. 3 (1988): 502.

68. Waldron, *God, Locke and Equality*, 202.

69. Locke, *Two Treatises*, I §130 237.

70. Coldham, *Emigrants in Chains*, 41.

71. Hill, *Liberty Against the Law*, 165.

72. Coldham, *Emigrants in Chains*, 46.

73. Charles II, 1662: An Act for the Better Releife of the Poore of this Kingdom. *Statutes of the Realm: Volume 5: 1628–80* (1819), 401–405. Retrieved from http://www.british-history.ac.uk/report.aspx?compid=47315.

74. Donoghue, "'Out of the Land of Bondage,'" 942–74.

75. The term "kidnapped" was coined to describe spiriting, see Nikolas Fryman, "Impressment, Kidnapping and Panyarring" in *The Princeton Companion to Atlantic History*, ed. Joseph C. Miller (Princeton and Oxford: Princeton University Press, 2015), 241.

76. Beckles, *History of Barbados*, 300.

77. Gary Puckrein, *Little England: Plantation Society and Anglo-Barbadian Politics, 1627–1700* (New York and London: New York University Press, 1984), 26; Donoghue, "'Out of the Land of Bondage,'" 944.

78. Donoghue, "'Out of the Land of Bondage,'" 944.

79. Puckrein, *Little England*, 26

80. Smith, *Colonists in Bondage*, 73.

81. *Ibid*, 74.

82. John Locke, "Essay on the Poor Law," 186.

83. Blair, Locke, and Kammen, "Virginia at the Close," 158.

84. The National Archives, CO 391/9, 366 (original numbering).

85. *Ibid*, 367 (original numbering).

86. *Ibid*, 378 (original numbering).

87. *Ibid*, 382 (original numbering); GBPRO, *Calendar of State Papers Colonial*, vol. 15, 341.

88. The National Archives, CO 391/10, 138 (original numbering). For the original letter see The National Archives, CO 323/2, 171 (printed numbering).

89. The National Archives, CO 323/2, 176 (printed numbering). See summary in GBPRO, *Calendar of State Papers Colonial*, vol. 15, 543.

90. The National Archives, CO 323/2, 185 (printed numbering).

91. The gendered and racialized division of labor varied between English colonies in the 1690s, and white women were sometimes put to work in the tobacco fields of Virginia. The Barbados Agents reported this variation in colonial labor practices to the Board of Trade, stating that "in Places where white women work in the Field, as Virginia & Carolina, such Women as these may be useful & acceptable," see The National Archives, CO 323/2, 185.

92. The National Archives, CO 323/2, 175 and GBPRO, *Calendar of State Papers Colonial*, vol. 15, 541.

93. The National Archives, CO 323/2, 174 (printed numbering).

94. The National Archives, CO 391/10, 166–7 (original numbering). On July 20 two merchants from New York also wrote to the Board that the colony would be willing to take the women if they were "young and fitting for labor" to serve between four and seven years, providing that someone was made responsible for providing the women with food and clothing upon arrival, see National Archive, CO 323/2, A68 401. It seems that the Board did not read this letter prior to issuing their order about sending the women to the Leeward Islands.

95. The National Archives, CO 153/6, 86–8.

96. *Ibid*, 86–8.
97. The National Archives, CO 391/10, 263 (original numbering).
98. *Ibid*, 263 (original numbering).
99. *Ibid*, 264 (original numbering).
100. *Ibid*, 282 (original numbering).
101. *Ibid*, 282 (original numbering).
102. *Ibid*, 316 (original numbering).
103. *Ibid*, 326 (original numbering).
104. *Ibid*, 376–9 (original numbering), and Fox Bourne, *Life of John Locke*, vol. 2, 502.
105. De Beer, *Correspondence of John Locke*, vol. 6, 329, No. 2398, February 25, 1698.
106. Locke, "Essay on the Poor Law," 183.
107. *Ibid*, 184.
108. *Ibid*, 185–6.
109. *Ibid*, 186.
110. *Ibid*, 193.
111. *Ibid*, 186.
112. Ashcraft, "Political Theory and Political Reform," 745.
113. *Ibid*, 399.
114. The National Archives, CO 391/10, 215–23.
115. Webb, "William Blathwayt," 400, and Brewer, "Slavery, Sovereignty," 14.
116. Webb, "William Blathwayt," 400.
117. The relative roles of Locke and Blair as authors are disputed, as noted in the previous chapter.
118. See Cranston, *Locke: A Biography*, 422–3; De Beer, *Correspondence of John Locke*, vol. 6, 408–9, No. 2446, May 26, 1698.
119. Brewer, "Slavery, Sovereignty," 17–20.
120. Blair, Locke, and Kammen, "Virginia at the Close," 153.
121. *Ibid*, 153–4.
122. *Ibid*, 155.
123. *Ibid*, 158.
124. Public hangings in London were conducted at Tyburn from the medieval period to the late eighteenth century. The obvious implication of Locke's reference to Tyburn is that he is discussing convicted criminals who have been sentenced to death.
125. Tully, *Approach to Political Philosophy*, 153–4; Hinshelwood, "Carolinian Context," 561–90.
126. Farr, "Locke, Natural Law," 507.
127. Macpherson, *Possessive Individualism*, 282.
128. *Ibid*, 233–34; Nancy J. Hirschmann, *Gender, Class, and Freedom in Modern Political Theory* (Princeton: Princeton University Press, 2007), 84; Hirschmann, "Liberal Conservativism."
129. Laslett, introduction to Locke, *Two Treatises*; Ashcraft, *Revolutionary Politics*; Farr, "Locke, Natural Law."
130. Tully, *Approach to Political Philosophy*; Arneil, *John Locke and America*.
131. Locke, *Two Treatises*, II §42 297.
132. *Ibid*, II §42 298.
133. *Ibid*, II §42 298.
134. Locke, "For a General Naturalisation," 322.
135. Locke, "Trade," 222.
136. Locke, "Atlantis," 255–8.
137. The term "proto-liberal" was coined by Duncan Ivison, see Ivison, "Locke, Liberalism and Empire." For a wider discussion of readings of Locke as a liberal see Duncan Bell, "What Is Liberalism?" *Political Theory* 42, no. 6 (2014): 682–715.

Chapter Five

Locke's Theory on Forced Military Service

Although Locke is famously a proponent of natural rights he also advocated forced labor for the idle poor and served as a leading Board of Trade member for an English government that used forced labor and forced migration. In the previous chapter I argued that the theory of slavery in the *Two Treatises of Government* should be read as a theory of penal slavery that extends to English convicts, and that justifies their transportation to English colonies for sale into forced labor. This chapter examines Locke's views about another form of forced labor that was widely used by the English state during the seventeenth and eighteenth centuries: naval impressment, or the practice of forcing sailors to serve in the navy. The *Second Treatise* clearly justifies penal slavery, but is less clear about whether forced military service is legitimate and, if so, when and why. Forced military service is a difficult topic for Locke because the *Second Treatise* articulates principles of individual rights, and principles of collective sovereignty and preservation, and these sets of principles can come into conflict over military service. On the one hand, Locke's account of natural rights provides grounds to argue that forcing men into military service is an unlawful infringement on individuals' rights to freedom and life. On the other hand, Locke argues that individuals agree to limits on their freedom when they enter into the social contract and that commonwealths should prioritize the defence of the community over the survival of any given individual, which provides grounds to argue that forced military service is justified for the sake of protecting the collective. These conflicting individualist and collectivist principles mean that different passages in the *Two Treatises* can be used to argue both for and against forced military service, which creates ambiguity about Locke's stance on the issue.

My investigation of Locke's views on forced military service begins with a close reading of the *Two Treatises*, but textual analysis alone does not provide a clear answer about his stance. In the *Two Treatises* Locke provides no explicit statement about the legitimacy of forcing men into military service, and his description of contemporary practices of military recruitment conflicts with his account of just warfare. In Chapter Sixteen of the *Second Treatise* Locke argues that men usually volunteer to serve in the military in exchange for receiving land and goods from their conquered foes (i.e., that militaries characteristically attract recruits by promising them shares in the property that will be seized through conquest). However, Locke then imposes stringent restrictions on lawful warfare that prohibit conquerors from seizing property from noncombatants, and that only allow property to be seized from defeated combatants in order to compensate the lawful victors for the costs and damage involved in the war. In effect, Locke's just war theory prohibits the system of military manning that he describes as common practice, but he does not propose an alternate manning policy. Given the lack of explicit statements about how military manning should be conducted, I use philosophical analysis to consider what systems of military manning are consistent with the principles in the *Two Treatises*. I argue that the *Two Treatises* legitimates a manning system in which men voluntarily undertake military service in exchange for pay funded by tax revenue. However, Locke also argues that taxes can only be lawfully levied with the consent of the majority of citizens or their representatives, and this requirement might make it difficult to raise enough tax revenue to pay a volunteer military. If popular opposition to taxes prevented a commonwealth from paying attractive wages to the military then the state might be forced to use a cheaper manning system, such as forcing men to serve. Although forced military service violates individual freedom, some commentators argue that this is justified under certain conditions. Ruth Grant maintains that the *Two Treatises* allows forced military service if it is necessary for the defense of the collective, equitably distributed among citizens, and the war is just.[1] By contrast, Michael Walzer argues that only those who gave express consent to the social contract could be justly forced to serve.[2] Grant and Walzer both express concern about the equitable distribution of military service obligations, but neither acknowledge that forced military service in late seventeenth-century England targeted professional sailors and therefore was not equitably distributed among citizens. Philosophical analysis therefore shows that the *Two Treatises* may allow forced military service under certain conditions, but that this would not justify seventeenth-century naval impressment.

To better understand how Locke applied his theoretical principles to the issue of forced military service I then provide contextual analysis of his wider political writings and Board of Trade activity. Locke's minor writings make it clear that he supported the selective use of forced military service, but his views about who should be forced to serve changed over time. In the "Atlantis" entries written in the late 1670s Locke advocates an exemption from forced military service for married men and parents, thereby implicitly approving forced military service for unmarried and childless men. In the 1697 "Essay on the Poor Law" Locke then advocates three-year terms of forced naval service for nonworking poor men in maritime areas. There is also evidence of Locke's support for selective naval impressment in his work on the Board of Trade, which advised the government about naval policy. In response to concerns about naval impressment in England's Caribbean colonies Locke supported the Board's call for reduced and more regulated impressment in the colonies, which meant that more men would need to be impressed in England. This impressment policy was intended to ensure that England's Caribbean colonies and merchants were adequately defended, and that the colonies were politically and economically stable. However, protecting the status quo in England's Caribbean colonies involved maintaining the systems of forced labor in those colonies, namely African chattel slavery and white indentured servitude. In his Board of Trade work Locke therefore favored a manning policy that increased the number of sailors in England who were forced into naval service, and that helped to uphold forced labor in England's sugar colonies, thus restricting the freedom of both English sailors and Caribbean slaves. Locke's support for the selective use of forced military service is difficult to reconcile with his arguments in the *Two Treatises*, and suggests that there was an inconsistency in Locke's theoretical views about military service.

FORCED MILITARY SERVICE
IN SEVENTEENTH-CENTURY ENGLAND

Before considering Locke's stance on forced military service it is helpful to know a little about the practices of military manning in his historical context, and about the contemporary political debates on the subject. In England, the power to force men into military service was regarded as a form of royal prerogative, and was used from the medieval period onward. During wars in the early modern period it was common for local authorities or military units to seize poor men and compel them to serve in the army or navy, which was known as impressment or pressing. The advantage of impressment from the state's perspective was that it enabled large numbers of men to be engaged for military service quickly and cheaply, whereas voluntary recruitment would have taken longer and/or required the men to be paid higher wages. Unlike twentieth-century practices of conscription, impressment was not designed to be universal or equitably shared among the population. Throughout the seventeenth century the vast majority of impressed men were poor, and on the rare occasions when wealthy men were seized by press gangs they paid for exemptions and were released. During the English Civil War men were pressed into the Royalist and Parliamentarian armies, despite objections from impressed troops.[3] Pressing continued during the Interregnum when Cromwell's government used impressment to provide troops and sailors for its Western Design, but radicals condemned impressment as a form of slavery.[4] After the restoration the English state stopped pressing men into the army but continued pressing men into the navy, so impressment became identified with forcing men into naval service. From the 1660s onward most of those impressed were professional sailors, particularly those who frequented major English ports such as London.

Impressment was repeatedly used to muster sailors in wars against the Dutch and French during the latter half of the seventeenth century, when the naval administrator and diarist Samuel Pepys described London press gangs as "a great tyranny."[5] By the late seventeenth century there were up to 40,000 sailors in England,[6] but this was not enough to fully man both the merchant fleet and the wartime navy.[7] The shortage of English sailors pushed up their wage rates, and wages on merchant ships in wartime were often double those in peacetime.[8] Whereas merchants sought to man their ships in wartime by offering attractive wages, the navy had low wages that were paid unreliably and late.[9] The unattractive wages led many sailors to avoid naval service, and the navy made up the shortfall by forcing sailors to serve through impressment. Professional sailors were in such high demand because early modern sailing ships required a highly skilled and experienced crew. Those serving on navy ships needed to understand the terminology on board, be able to operate ropes, sails, and guns in coordination with other crewmembers, and undertake hard physical work on a moving surface in all weather conditions. Some of the most important roles on a ship were also extremely dangerous: topmen balanced on ropes high above the deck and had to maintain their balance while hauling in sails, even in high winds when the ship rocked wildly. The need for experienced topmen meant that the English navy could not man its fleet with unskilled workers; instead, they used impressment to force experienced sailors into naval service.[10] Between 1660 and 1692 periods of naval impressment usually lasted no more than six months, because naval wars were largely fought in European seas during summer and sailors were released when the fighting season ended. During the period when Locke wrote and first published the *Two Treatises* the normal practice of the English state was to use seasonal naval impressment in wartime. The burden of forced military service was therefore unevenly shared, and it fell largely on the relatively small proportion of young Englishmen who worked as sailors.

Contemporary debates over the legitimacy of impressment are reflected in the political theory produced in England during the seventeenth century, including the work of Hobbes and the Levellers. The Levellers strongly opposed military impressment, arguing that it infringed on individual liberty and was not necessary for successful warfare:

> That the matter of impressing and constraining any of us to serve in the wars is against our freedom; and therefore we do not allow it in our representatives; the rather, because money (the sinews of war) being always at their disposal, they can never want numbers of men apt enough to engage in any just cause. [11]

This reasoning suggests that because Parliament has the power to raise revenue through taxation it can afford to pay high enough wages to induce sufficient men to fight voluntarily in just wars. The Levellers therefore present the decision to impress men as the result of government's choice to pay inadequate wages to the military and/or to engage in unjust wars, and consequently as an unjustified infringement on individual freedom. At first glance Hobbes also seems to oppose impressment, because he argues that if the state forces men to serve in the army then they may "in many cases refuse" or run away from the battle, whereas voluntary recruits are required to fight as commanded. [12] However, Hobbes goes on to argue that the state is justified in forcing men to serve if national defense cannot be ensured with volunteers, and that in such a situation the pressed men are all obliged to fight:

> when the defence of the commonwealth, requireth at once the help of all that are able to bear arms, every one is obliged; because otherwise the institution of the commonwealth, which they have not the purpose, or courage to preserve, was in vain. [13]

Hobbes therefore maintains that men can be legitimately impressed and must comply if their contribution is required immediately to protect the commonwealth, but that they may flee or refuse to fight if their service is not urgently required or a substitute for them could be found. [14] The Levellers and Hobbes therefore disagree about the legitimacy of forced military service because of their divergent views about its necessity: Hobbes argues that in dire situations forced military service is necessary and thus justified, whereas the Levellers claim that just warfare never requires forcing men to serve. These themes of individual freedom, collective defense, and necessity recur in later political debates about impressment and in the secondary literature about military service in Locke's *Second Treatise*.

FORCED MILITARY SERVICE AND THE *TWO TREATISES*

At the beginning of the *Second Treatise* Locke states that all individuals have inalienable rights to life and liberty, [15] and that removing the freedom of an individual inherently threatens their life and therefore deserves severe punishment.[16] In the state of nature individual freedom is restricted only by natural law, but this changes after the social contract. By participating in the social contract individuals transfer their right to enforce natural law to the collective, which consequently has the authority to make and enforce domestic laws and to enforce natural law internationally through "the *power of War and Peace*."[17] Moreover, Locke argues that each participant in the social contract consents for "the Commonwealth to employ his force, for the Execution of the Judgments of the Commonwealth, whenever he shall be called to it,"[18] thereby agreeing to assist the state in these tasks. Domestically, Locke argues that state power is limited by natural law, because the laws passed by a state are "only so far right, as they are founded on the Law of Nature, by which they are to be regulated and interpreted."[19] In the international domain the actions of a state are also limited by natural law, which prohibits aggressive wars[20] but allows a state to defend the lives, liberty, and property of its citizens by using violence against a state that violates those rights. Participants in the social contract authorize their state to engage in lawful warfare, but Locke argues that the people do not authorize unlawful wars because they cannot transfer a right that they do not possess:

> For the People having given to their Governours no Power to do an unjust thing, such as is to make an unjust War, (for they never had such a Power in themselves:) They ought not to be charged, as guilty of the Violence an Unjustice that is committed in an Unjust War, any farther, than they actually abet it.[21]

Since citizens do not authorize unjust wars through the social contract Locke reasons that they are only responsible for unjust wars that they directly participate in. Soldiers and politicians who wage an unjust war can be justly held responsible and punished, but citizens who do not participate in the war must not be punished.[22]

The powers of a legitimate government are also limited by the public good, because Locke argues that its acts must "be directed to no other *end*, but the *Peace, Safety*, and *publick good* of the People" which includes defense against "Inroads and Invasion" by foreigners.[23] Unlawful conquest would threaten the individual and collective rights of the citizenry, so the state's task of protecting the people and pursuing the public good requires it to provide defense against foreign aggression. As further guidance, Locke states that "*the first and fundamental natural Law*, which is to govern even the Legislative it self, is *the preservation of the Society*, and (as far as will consist with the publick good) of every person in it."[24] Here, Locke acknowledges that the preservation of an individual may conflict with the public good, and if that happens then Locke requires the legislative to prioritize the collective over any individual. The state is only required to protect an individual's life if this is consistent with the public good, so it is lawful for the state to risk the lives of some citizens by tasking them with defense of the commonwealth. Moreover, Locke argues that it is lawful for states to restrict the freedom and risk the lives of their troops, because this discipline is necessary for an effective military:

> For the Preservation of the Army, and in it of the whole Commonwealth, requires an *absolute Obedience* to the Command of every Superior Officer, and it is justly Death to disobey or dispute the most dangerous or unreasonable of them . . . Because such a blind Obedience is necessary to that end for which the Commander has his Power, *viz*. the preservation of the rest.[25]

Although Locke outlines the rights possessed by men serving in the military, he does not explain how men should be enlisted for military service. The only point in the *Second Treatise* where Locke discusses military recruitment is in Chapter Sixteen, and this passage raises more questions than it answers. Here, Locke claims that those who fight in wars:

> most commonly they serve upon Terms, and on Condition to share with their Leader, and enjoy a part of the Spoil, and other Advantages that attend the Conquering Sword: or at least have a part of the subdued Country bestowed upon them.[26]

This passage suggests that men usually volunteer for military service in the expectation that they will gain by seizing land or goods from the conquered, but such a practice is inconsistent with Locke's account of lawful conquest. Although Locke maintains that victors in a just war can kill or enslave the combatants that they have defeated, he argues that they do not acquire rights over the lives, liberty, or possessions of those who did not participate in the unjust war.[27] Moreover, Locke argues that just conquerors cannot take the land of defeated combatants[28] and can only take their goods "in order to make reparation for the damages received, and the Charges of the War, and that too with reservation of the right of the innocent Wife and Children."[29] Victors therefore cannot take more of the vanquished army's goods than is needed to cover the cost of the war and repair the damage sustained, and will be unable to take even this compensation if doing so would imperil the families of the defeated army. Under Locke's principles of just warfare there is no legitimate grounds for victors to gain by seizing land or goods from their defeated foes. The only way that a conquering army can lawfully obtain an overall *benefit*, as opposed to compensation for their *losses*, is by enslaving their defeated opponents.

The limitations that Locke imposes on the rights of conquest mean that the legal "Advantages that attend the Conquering Sword"[30] are restricted to the enslavement of combatants and compensatory seizures of their goods. Compliance with these terms would mean that people would only volunteer to participate in a just war in exchange for future spoils if they expected to enslave enough of their defeated enemies to make their military service beneficial. Individuals might volunteer for military service in the expectation of acquiring slaves, but this motivation would hamper military tactics because it would create a strong incentive for combatants to capture their enemies instead of killing them. Designing military tactics around the mass capture of slaves would risk seriously undermining national defense, thereby sacrificing the common good of the commonwealth to the financial interests of its military. Since Locke argues that natural law requires the preservation of the society it seems highly unlikely that he would allow the military to prioritize their own enrichment over the security of the populace. This tension between the military tactics required for the public good and the tactics required for the military to be paid solely in captured slaves shows the need for a different system of military recruitment. Regrettably, Locke provides no indication of what this manning system would be and therefore the *Second Treatise* leaves the question of military recruitment unresolved.

In practice, the English state used two systems of military recruitment during the seventeenth century: recruiting volunteers by paying them adequate wages, and forcing men to serve through impressment.[31] A military composed of volunteers who received wages funded by taxation would ensure that men were not subjected to military authority without their consent, and would comply with Locke's restrictions on seizing property from the conquered. However, Locke argues that lawful taxation requires the consent of the majority of the people or their representatives,[32] so the English populace and/or Parliament would need to approve taxes to pay the military. If the legislative and/or the public supported taxes that enabled the state to pay high enough wages to attract sufficient volunteers then the state could achieve a system of national defense that maintained individual freedom. Conversely, if the public and legislative objected to paying higher taxes in order to fund a volunteer military then the required taxes could not be lawfully raised, so the state would need to use a cheaper manning policy, such as impressment. On the issue of military service two tenets of Locke's theory are therefore liable to come into conflict: individual rights to life and liberty, and the collective rights of the majority to have government and taxation based on their consent. Paying sailors high enough wages to induce them to volunteer during wars would have significantly increased the cost of warfare for the English state, because it would probably have more than doubled the English navy's wage bill.[33] The navy was very expensive even when it paid low wages and the English Parliament was already reluctant to impose the taxes necessary to fund it,[34] so a call for higher taxes to pay for voluntary naval manning would not have received legislative support. It is also highly doubtful whether the

English citizenry would have approved higher taxes to fund the navy. In the early seventeenth century Charles I encountered widespread popular opposition when he imposed a tax known as Ship Money that was partly intended to fund the navy, and grievances over Ship Money contributed to hostility toward the King during the English Civil War. Locke's argument that taxation could only be raised with the consent of the majority or their representatives was intended to prevent unpopular taxes such as Ship Money. However, this principle of taxation by consent empowered the English public and Parliament to refuse to pay for a volunteer navy, thus requiring a cheaper manning system. By making it difficult to raise taxes Locke increased the likelihood that the state would be unable to pay for a volunteer military and would consequently need to infringe on individual freedom in order to provide national defense.

If the legislative and the majority of citizens decide that forced military service is the best way to preserve the collective and enable the public good, then does this make it legitimate? Answering this question requires assessing the balance between the individualist and collectivist aspects of Locke's political theory. The individualist element of Locke's theory specifies that a government breaks natural law if it removes the freedom or threatens the lives of its subjects.[35] Compelling an individual to serve in the military infringes on his liberty and threatens his life, so arguably a government that forced men into military service would be beginning a state of war with the impressed men. Michael Walzer follows this reasoning by arguing that compelling men to serve in the military conflicts with Locke's premises about individual rights.[36] Even if the reasons why individuals entered the social contract were consistent with an obligation to undertake military service in defense of the collective then Walzer argues that the obligation to serve would only extend to those who expressly consented to the social contract, and not to the many who gave tacit consent.[37] If Locke supported forced military service for men who had not expressly consented then Walzer suggests that this indicates a double standard whereby Locke saw the poor as having less moral value than the rich.[38] In making this argument Walzer assumes that those forced to serve in the military would be young, male, and poor,[39] but he does not mention that the main defining characteristic of those forced into military service in late seventeenth-century England was that they were sailors. Although most sailors were young and poor the fact that very few non-sailors were impressed shows that the primary grounds for impressment was occupation, not age or social class. While Walzer's suggestion that Locke viewed the poor as having a lesser moral value might explain the allocation of differential rights based on socioeconomic class it does not explain why it is legitimate for poor sailors to bear a higher burden of military service than poor non-sailors.

Alongside Locke's commitment to individual rights there is a collectivist element to the *Two Treatises*. Locke argues that the legislative must preserve the society and act in the public good, but that it is not required to preserve any given individual, which suggests that forced military service might be legitimate if it was necessary to ensure the "*Peace, Safety*, and *publick good* of the People*."*[40] This collectivist reading of the *Two Treatises* is adopted by Ruth Grant who argues that participants in the social contract agree to limit their natural freedom and abide by collective decision-making,[41] which makes forced military service legitimate provided that three conditions are met. First, Grant suggests that the infringement on individual rights to life and liberty through forced military service is only justified if it serves to preserve the collective: "the price of the protection of the community may be the ultimate sacrifice, since the community cannot maintain itself without the right to demand this of its members."[42] Grant therefore defends forced military service on the grounds that it is sometimes necessary to defend the commonwealth. Secondly, Grant maintains that the normative justification for forced military service applies only to just wars, so the state can never legitimately compel men to participate in an unjust war.[43] Thirdly, Grant argues that political obligations under the Lockean social contract are just because they are equitably distributed, which suggests that the obligation to serve in the military must be equitably shared:

> If you wish to enjoy the benefits of social life, you must be willing to make the necessary sacrifices. If you expect others to be willing to make those sacrifices, you must be willing to do the same. The bargain is necessary to obtain the benefit you seek and just in the sense that it is equitable.[44]

Unfortunately, Grant does not explain what constitutes an equitable distribution of obligations, so it is unclear if she would see it as equitable to impose obligations of military service only on citizens with a particular skill or profession, as occurred with naval impressment. Perhaps Grant would argue that if collective defense requires military service by citizens with a particular set of skills then it is equitable for the state to require only citizens with those skills to serve. Alternately, Grant might argue that the equitable distribution of political obligations requires the use of broader criteria, such as age or health, and that skill-based impressment is inequitable. Either way, Grant's reading of the *Two Treatises* suggests that forced military service is only justified if the state is fighting a just war, forced military service is required to preserve the collective, and the obligation to serve is distributed equitably. Even if one assumes that the wars fought by the English state were just then it is doubtful if seventeenth-century naval impressment meets Grant's criteria. English naval warfare sometimes involved defending the English coastline from foreign attack, and in these cases naval service arguably ensured the preservation of the collective. However, naval ships were also assigned to protect English merchants and to defend English colonies from foreign militaries, privateers, and pirates. It is not clear that the defense of colonies such as Jamaica was necessary to preserve the collective citizenry of England, and even less likely that the protection of English merchant ships in distant seas was necessary for collective survival. Moreover, naval impressment placed the obligation of forced military service almost solely on the small minority of the English population who were professional sailors, which is arguably inequitable. Even among sailors the burden of military service was inequitably shared, because some were forced to serve continuously for years while others avoided impressment entirely. Late seventeenth-century naval impressment therefore does not seem to meet Grant's criteria for the legitimate use of forced military service under the principles articulated in the *Two Treatises*.

The *Two Treatises* provides no explicit answer about the appropriate way to enlist men for military service and major principles in the text come into conflict over the issue, which creates ambiguity about Locke's stance. Opponents of impressment can use Locke's account of individual rights to argue that forced military service is illegitimate because it violates natural rights to life and liberty, as Walzer suggests. This reading of the *Two Treatises* would suggest that naval impressment is an unjustified infringement on individual rights. Alternately, supporters of impressment can argue that the social contract established consent to collective decision-making and the prioritization of collective preservation over any individual, which Grant uses to claim that the *Two Treatises* authorizes forced military service under certain conditions. However, late seventeenth-century practices of naval impressment did not meet the criteria of necessity and equitableness that Grant identifies, which means that naval impressment would be illegitimate according to her reading of the *Two Treatises*. The English state's use of naval impressment therefore seems to be unjustified according to both individualist and collectivist interpretations of how the principles in the *Two Treatises* apply to military service. In short, philosophical analysis of the *Two Treatises* suggests that if Locke was fully consistent in his political views then he would oppose naval impressment in his other writings and his work for the Board of Trade.

LOCKE'S BOARD OF TRADE WORK
ON FORCED MILITARY SERVICE

When the Board of Trade was created in May 1696 England was fighting the Nine Years War against France, which was seriously hampering English trade and causing conflict over impressment. At the start of the war in 1688 the English government placed an embargo on most colonial trade in order to make more sailors available for the navy. Once the embargo was lifted the French navy and privateers began to inflict serious losses on English merchants. The English navy responded by providing merchants with protective convoys, but they found it difficult to coordinate the timing of convoys with seasonal conditions and numerous merchants traveling to a variety of destinations. These logistical problems meant that some merchants sailed independently of the convoys, and many were captured. In 1692 the French attacked the Smyrna fleet of English merchants and managed to seize ships and cargo worth thirty million livres, to the fury of the English Parliament. [45] By 1692 it was also clear that the traditional English practice of impressing sailors from spring to autumn during wars was insufficient because the French were attacking English merchant ships not only in Europe, but also in the Caribbean, North America, and Asia. Defending English merchants and colonies required warships to be sent to distant oceans where the return voyages took many months or years, so naval campaigns beyond Europe required sailors to serve for longer periods. Beginning in the winter of 1692 the English navy began requiring impressed men to serve year-round, which provoked protests, riots, and mutinies by sailors. [46] Whereas seasonal impressment meant that impressed seamen served only a few months and could expect to be home by November, year-round impressment meant that "an impressed seaman remained in the navy until he died, he escaped, or a particular war ended—whichever came first."[47] Sailors objected to these long, unpredictable periods of impressment and the author of the 1699 pamphlet *The State of the Navy Consider'd* complained that English sailors were being unlawfully enslaved:

> The Sailors Case is indeed deplorable . . . tho as good and brave Englishmen as any; are altogether enslaved, and without any Law that I ever heard of imprest, their Liberty taken from them, which when gone they are effectual Slaves; imprison'd on board Ship, caned and kick'd by Commanders just dropt from behind a Coach at *WhiteHall* into the Service of the Navy, miserably abus'd in being turn'd over from one Ship to another (contrary to the Rules of Humanity, and the Custom of the Navy) so that after they have been at Sea several years, are hurried out again without Liberty so much as to see their Relations. [48]

Long periods of impressment during voyages to the Americas or Asia made naval service more dangerous because sailors were exposed to scurvy and tropical diseases, such as yellow fever. So many sailors fell ill on warships in the Caribbean that captains were often left without enough healthy men to operate the ship, [49] which created continual pressure to acquire more men by impressing people from the local ships and colonies. Protests by sailors led to the suspension of year-round impressment in 1694, but the English government struggled to develop an alternate system of naval manning. [50]

In early 1696 Parliament attempted to solve the problem of naval manning by passing the Act for the Increase and Encouragement of Seamen, which created a voluntary national registry for sailors. This scheme was inspired by the French *inscription maritime*, which involved a compulsory national registry of French sailors who were then called up in rotation during wars.[51] English sailors who registered under the 1696 Act agreed to serve in the navy when needed in exchange for annual payments, eligibility for medical treatment at Greenwich Hospital, and pensions for their widows if the sailors died in naval service.[52] Around twenty thousand men volunteered for the registry, but their annual payments went unpaid and the widows' pensions proved inadequate, so the system quickly collapsed and the navy resumed its reliance on year-round impressment.[53] Unfortunately, impressment did not ensure the protection of English merchant ships. Over the course of the Nine Years War French privateers seized around four thousand English ships,[54] and Parliament became increasingly angry about the mounting losses. In 1695–6 Parliament responded by voting to establish a Board of Trade under their authority, which would be tasked with collecting information and issuing recommendations about naval convoys and the protection of trade.[55] By seeking to appoint a Board with these powers Parliament hoped to reduce the economic damage caused by the war and increase their influence over naval policy, thereby challenging the powers of the King and Admiralty. In response, King William appointed his own Board of Trade, which preserved his control over naval policy while responding to Parliament's demands for more attention to English mercantile interests. The Board's mission of promoting English trade quickly drew them into debates over naval policy, because they received numerous appeals for more warships to defend the colonies, and for colonists to be exempt from impressment. The navy was resistant to pleas from colonial authorities and merchants, but the Board largely sympathized with their concerns and advocated for them to the King and Admiralty. By the end of 1696 the Board had developed new plans for naval manning in the colonies and persuaded the King to transfer the power of impressment from naval captains to colonial governors. The Board clearly thought these contributions were significant, because when the House of Commons asked them in 1700 to outline their achievements the Board's reply stated:

> We have upon several occasions proposed to His Majesty the appointing of convoys for the Plantations and of ships of war necessary to protect their trade, and upon the complaints of the inhabitants there or merchants in England of hardships in the pressing of men and otherwise by Captains of men of war in those parts, we have presented unto His Majesty regulations therein, which have had a good effect.[56]

Jamaica and Barbados were viewed as England's most important colonies during the 1690s, and this is reflected in the Board of Trade's proposed impressment policy. The Caribbean was strategically important because the trade winds and currents meant that nearly all ships sailing from Europe to the Americas passed through the area. As a result, the Spanish, French, Dutch, and English had all seized islands in the Caribbean, and these colonies were vulnerable to attack by other European states. The Caribbean was also economically important because it grew sugar for European markets, and by 1700 Caribbean products constituted 13 percent of England's annual imports.[57] Caribbean sugar transformed the English diet, including by sweetening other colonial products such as cocoa, coffee, and tea, and it provided a profitable source of re-exports to other European states.[58] However, England's Caribbean colonies relied on merchant ships to export their products, supply them with food and goods, and provide them with slaves.[59] In wartime the Caribbean colonies and their shipping were vulnerable to attack, and there was an ever-present possibility of slave uprisings. By the 1690s Jamaica and Barbados were populated by tens of thousands of enslaved Africans who were controlled by a few thousand white colonists. The colonial authorities in Jamaica and Barbados worried constantly about whether the islands had enough white occupants to stop slave revolts, and they opposed the impressment of white colonists on the grounds that reducing the white population increased the risk of a slave uprising. The Caribbean planters and merchants formed a powerful lobby in England, so the Board of Trade and English government were responsive to their concerns.

From its creation in May 1696 until the end of the war in September 1697 the Board received repeated reports that the English navy was causing harm by impressing too many men from Jamaica and Barbados. In June 1696 Governor Beeston of Jamaica complained the island was becoming depopulated because:

> No people come in, many die, some get away from fear, others because they are in debt, and many are pressed into the King's ships, which also frightens others away, so by many ways we decrease, which disheartens those that have interest and makes them talk of removing.[60]

In July 1696 the Council of Jamaica recorded that the number of white men on the island had fallen by over a thousand in the past year, and argued that the remaining population could not "defend it against a foreign enemy or secure it from a domestic one if the slaves should make any attempt, for . . . the slaves number close on forty thousand."[61] To remedy these problems the Council asked King William to send men and warships for their protection, give Governor Beeston the power to command navy ships stationed at the island, stop impressment in Jamaica, and send more sailors on each warship from England.[62] Beeston promptly repeated these complaints to the Board, stating that "seamen have left us because the men-of-war press and harass them so that they run away as fast as they can, and, even though they venture their lives by swimming from the ships, they get out of the country to other parts."[63] Beeston and the Jamaican colonists also complained that the navy was wrongly pressing indentured servants and Jamaicans who were not sailors.[64] The criticism of impressment by Jamaican authorities did not stem from an objection to forced labor, because they refer uncritically to slavery and indentured servitude on the island. Instead, powerful Jamaicans objected to impressment because it removed indentured servants from the island, thereby depriving masters of the servants' labor, and because impressment reduced the population of white colonists and they believed that this made slave revolts more likely. The Jamaican governor, Council, planters, and merchants therefore opposed forced naval service for poor, white men in Jamaica because they saw it as a threat to their favored systems of forced labor, namely African slavery and white indentured servitude.

In September 1696 the Lords Justices instructed the Board of Trade to compose a report about how to provide naval convoys for the Caribbean merchant fleet,[65] but when the Board asked the merchants for their input they also received complaints about impressment. The Jamaica merchants requested that the navy ships carry extra men and "be strictly commanded not to press any either seamen from the Merchant Ships, or Inhabitants on Land."[66] Moreover, the merchants reported that the fear of naval impressment was leading sailors to flee Jamaica and become pirates, thereby contributing to the surge in piracy:

> Pressing has not only lost to the Island those who have been taken away but has frighted away five times as many more, part to Providence and other places, part to Curaçoa, some to the French at Petit Guavos, while a great many have turned pirates and gone to the Red Sea.[67]

To reinforce their message several Jamaica merchants spoke at the Board's meeting on September 18, 1696, when they claimed that the excessive pressing in Jamaica occurred because colonial governors did not have the power to command nearby naval captains.[68] The Barbados merchants echoed these requests by asking for their crews to be exempted from impressment.[69] More unusually, the Board also received complaints from several impressed sailors who had been seized from Jamaica by the navy, carried to England, and then discharged without pay or a way of getting home.[70] Locke seems to have been particularly involved in the Board's discussion of Caribbean impressment in the autumn of 1696, because on September 21 the Board's Journal reports that "Mr Locke delivered to the Board a short Memorial which he received from the Jamaica Merchants, dated this day, in explanation of their former of the 18th."[71]

Locke was among the five attendees on September 30, 1696, when the Board composed its report to the Lords Justices about naval convoys and impressment, and on October 1 when the report was signed.[72] The report makes several recommendations about naval policy in English colonies. First, the Board proposes that "men-of-war bound to the West Indies should carry a larger complement than usual, so as to be provided against the accidents of death while guarding the Islands."[73] This would require the navy to anticipate the number of sailors likely to die on a voyage to the Caribbean and ensure that their ships left England carrying enough extra sailors that they would have a full crew once the expected deaths occurred. Secondly, the Board suggests sending additional navy seamen on merchant ships traveling to the Caribbean so that those sailors could join shorthanded navy ships. Given that naval manning in England relied on impressment these first two suggestions effectively call for an increase in the number of men impressed in England in order to offset a steep fall in impressment in the Caribbean colonies. Thirdly, the Board proposes that naval ships in the colonies should be under the command of the relevant colonial governor. Finally, the Board recommends that the power to impress men in the colonies should belong to colonial governors, not naval commanders, and that if naval ships become very shorthanded then the governors should either impress men or authorize naval captains to do so.[74] This last proposal makes it clear that the Board saw impressment as legitimate, but believed colonial governors were better judges than the navy of when impressment was necessary and of whom should be impressed.

On October 22, 1696, the King responded by ordering that "Captains of King's ships, who are in want of men, must apply to the Governor of the Colony to assist them, and if he fail to do so, then the Captain may impress men."[75] The Board saw this as inadequate, and in December they wrote to the King repeating their suggestions that extra seamen be sent to the Caribbean and that the power to impress men in the colonies should belong only to colonial governors.[76] The King responded by ordering that five impressed Jamaicans who had been carried to England should be released, paid, and returned home,[77] and that the power of impressment in English colonies be given only to colonial governors:

> when any Capt or Commander of any of his Majties Ships of Warr in any of His Majties Plantations shall have Occasion for Seamen to Serve on Board His Majties Ships under their Command, they do make their Application to the Governour or Commander in Chiefe of His Majties Plantations respectively to whom (as Viceadmiralls) his Majtie is pleased to Committ the Sole Power of Impresting Seamen in any of his Majties Plantations in America, or, in sight of any them, such Governours or Commanders in Chiefe being hereby required

upon such Application to take Care that His Majties said Ships of Warr be Furnished with the Number of Seamen that may be Necessary for His Majties Service on board the said Ships from time to time. [78]

This order requires shorthanded naval captains to receive permission from colonial governors before impressing men in the colonies, but also requires the governors to supply warships with enough men. In early 1697 the Board duly informed the colonial governors that the King had given them the sole power of impressing sailors, [79] but they knew that this would not remove the need for impressment or resolve the problems that it caused. The Board therefore continued to recommend that extra sailors be sent to the Caribbean so that warships there could be fully manned without impressing local inhabitants. These requests for extra sailors were firmly opposed by the Admiralty, who told the Board in January that sending additional navy seamen to the colonies on merchant ships would be too costly and that "the men, being pressed men, will desert the merchant-ships at the first opportunity, whereby the service abroad will receive no benefit." [80] Nonetheless, the Board repeated their requests for more sailors to be sent to Jamaica, [81] and persuaded the King to order that a hundred extra sailors be sent there. [82] The Admiralty issued orders that the next two warships to the Caribbean should include a hundred extra men, [83] but Governor Beeston later reported that those ships arrived without extra sailors. [84]

As the Board had expected, transferring the power of impressment to governors was no panacea. In July 1697 Governor Beeston complained that "the order about impressing will signify very little if the Governors of these Colonies must be obliged to impress the people whenever the captains say that they want men." [85] When asked to use his new powers to impress sailors, Beeston proved reluctant and two naval captains soon protested that he had refused their requests for impressed men. [86] Beeston countered that the warships had brought no extra men, that Jamaica had no men to spare, and that impressment was impossible because "men cannot be impressed where they are not, nor can any be impressed by the Government here but the inhabitants, which would force men from their families, probably never to see them again, besides weakening the country." [87] In September 1697 the Treaty of Ryswick ended the war with France, but the Caribbean colonies requested that the navy continue sending warships to the islands. [88] The Board accepted this suggestion and in October 1697 Locke signed the Board's recommendation that warships be sent annually to Jamaica, Barbados, and the Leeward Islands. [89] Although the end of the war meant that impressment was no longer used in England, ongoing naval patrols in the Caribbean and high disease rates on navy ships in that region made it likely that the navy would continue seeking to impress men in the Caribbean colonies.

Conflict between the Jamaican authorities and the navy continued throughout Locke's term on the Board, because Governor Beeston was unwilling to impress men when asked and the navy retaliated by impressing men itself, contrary to the King's orders. Beeston then complained that the navy was impressing Jamaicans illegally and that "ships of war, when they get so far from England, believe themselves lawless, and that nobody has any authority but themselves."[90] These disputes came to the attention of the King in late 1699 and the Board wrote to him reiterating their view that only governors should have the power to impress men in the colonies, and that if warships left England with enough sailors then they would not be short-handed upon arrival in the Caribbean.[91] The King ordered that the Admiralty be instructed to implement the Board's proposals,[92] and the Board promptly informed the colonial governors. By 1699 Locke and the other Board members had therefore created a system whereby navy warships were supposed to have enough men to be fully manned upon arrival in the Caribbean colonies, but often did not, and colonial governors were supposed to impress men for the navy if needed, but often did not. The Board lacked the authority to make the navy comply with this system, and in practice they had limited enforcement power over the colonial governors. This system for impressment in English colonies was still in place when Locke retired from the Board in June 1700, and the principle of restricting naval impressment in English colonies continued for much of the eighteenth century. Nonetheless, ongoing opposition to impressment in English colonies led to sporadic anti-impressment riots such as the 1747 Knowles Riot in Boston, and later contributed to support for the American Revolution.

Two themes are notable in the Board of Trade's activity on impressment in the colonies. First, it is clear that the Board's impressment policy was developed in response to the concerns of wealthy Caribbean authorities and merchants, and not in response to the views of sailors. Many English sailors criticized impressment as an infringement on their freedom, but there is no evidence that Locke or the other Board members questioned the legitimacy of forcing men into naval service. The Board's discussion of impressment addressed the questions of where, by whom, and over whom impressment should be used, but presumed throughout that forcing men into military service was legitimate and should continue. The Jamaican and Barbadian authorities were concerned about naval impressment in the Caribbean because they saw it as a threat to their interests, but they also demanded naval defense of their islands and raised no objection to impressment in England. The Board was highly receptive to the wishes of the Caribbean authorities and responded by advocating significant reductions in impressment in the Caribbean, and the transfer of impressment powers to colonial governors. However, the Board's favored policy of maintaining naval patrols in the Caribbean while reducing local impressment meant that more sailors must be sent from England, which required impressing more Englishmen. The navy told the Board bluntly that their suggestions would require sending more impressed men from England, but the Board seemed unconcerned and repeated their calls for more English sailors to be sent to the Caribbean. In their work on impressment the Board consistently prioritized the economic interests of the Caribbean planters and merchants over the freedom or interests of English sailors. Second, the Board's impressment policy was not designed to reduce forced military service or forced labor, but to amend the English government's use of forced military service in order to protect the systems of forced labor in the Caribbean colonies. The letters received by the Board make it clear that the Caribbean authorities, planters, and merchants objected to impressment because they believed that the loss of white residents through impressment might enable a successful slave revolt, and because the navy sometimes impressed their indentured servants and this imposed an economic loss on the masters. The Board's recommendations led to changes in policy that prohibited the navy from impressing men in the colonies without permission from colonial governors (who could prevent the impressment of servants), and the Board worked hard to reduce the numbers of men impressed from the Caribbean colonies. These policy changes may have prevented naval impressment from restricting the freedom of some Caribbean residents, but they also helped to preserve systems of African slavery and white indentured servitude. Whatever views Locke personally held about the practice of African slavery, the Board's impressment policy was designed to enable the continuation of racialized coercion, hierarchy, and exploitation in the Caribbean. By protecting racialized chattel slavery in the Caribbean the Board indirectly contributed to the expansion of slavery and the slave trade that occurred in English colonies during the eighteenth century.

LOCKE'S MINOR WRITINGS ON FORCED MILITARY SERVICE

In addition to signing Board of Trade reports approving naval impressment for English sailors, Locke expressed support for forced military service in two of his minor political writings: the "Atlantis" journals written between 1676 and 1679, and his 1697 "Essay on the Poor Law." In "Atlantis" Locke outlines a series of proposals for the governance of a hypothetical colony, including policies about tax, crime, marriage, and forced military service. In a 1678 journal entry Locke suggests "He that is married or has a child shall not be pressed to the wars,"[93] thereby exempting married men and parents from forced military service. Then in a 1679 entry Locke proposes "No man that has a wife [and] children shall be bound to serve in arms without the bounds of his country."[94] This second proposal exempts married men and parents from military service abroad or at sea, but implies that they can be forced to serve within the borders of their homeland. Although Locke does not explicitly argue that impressment is legitimate, his proposals clearly imply that unmarried and childless men can be justifiably pressed and required to serve in the military abroad or at sea. The reasoning behind these proposals is not stated overtly, but one of the major themes in Locke's "Atlantis" entries is that the proper regulation of family life will boost the population and prosperity of the colony.[95] In the context of Locke's claims about the political and economic significance of the family we can infer that his reasons for exempting married men and parents from military impressment are probably the desire to encourage healthy, numerous children, and to prevent conflict between men's political and familial obligations.[96] Several of the themes in "Atlantis" recurred in Locke's later work on the Board of Trade,[97] but his reluctance to force married men and parents into military service presumably waned over the years because he took a different approach to selective impressment in the "Essay on the Poor Law."

Locke's "Essay on the Poor Law" was written in 1697 after a merchant asked the Board to develop a plan for employing the poor in Bristol.[98] Bristol was one of England's busiest and most important ports, so it is not surprising that Locke's proposals begin with measures aimed at the poor in coastal areas. Locke's first suggestion is that able-bodied beggars in maritime areas be required to serve in the navy for three years:

> That all men sound of limb and mind, above 14 and under 50 years of age, begging in maritime counties out of their own parish without a pass . . . be sent to the next seaport town, there to be kept at hard labour, till some of his majesty's ships, coming in or near there, give an opportunity of putting them on board, where they shall serve three years under strict discipline, at soldier's pay (subsistence money being deducted for victuals on board), and be punished as deserters if they go on shore without leave.[99]

Locke then repeats this proposal of a three-year period of forced naval service for any unemployed poor man in a maritime county who refuses work.[100] Locke's prioritization of naval service for able-bodied men in shipping areas suggests that he saw the navy as particularly important, which is understandable given that his proposals were developed in the autumn of 1697 when the Board was arguing that warships to the Caribbean should carry extra sailors so that they could avoid impressing Caribbean residents. Bristol was the point of departure for many ships to the Caribbean, so it appears that Locke sought to solve two problems simultaneously: forcing able-bodied poor men in Bristol into the navy meant those men would no longer be idle, and Caribbean warships would have extra men. Locke's proposals show a good understanding of the manning needs of the English navy, including the need for experienced sailors to serve year-round. Recommending naval impressment for able-bodied poor men throughout England would have yielded more men, but this would have filled the navy with inexperienced men who would be unable to perform many tasks on board.[101] By recommending forced naval service only for the poor in maritime counties Locke increased the likelihood that those impressed would have the sailing experience to be useful in the navy. Moreover, Locke's stipulation that poor men serve three years in the navy ensured periods of service that were long enough for return voyages to the Caribbean, Americas, or Asia. In addition, Locke proposes a system of nine-year naval apprenticeships for poor boys:

> That every master of any of the king's ships shall be bound to receive without money, once every year (if offered him by the magistrate or other officer of any place within the bounds of the port where his ship shall be), one boy, sound of limb, above 13 years of age, who shall be his apprenticeship for nine years.[102]

Locke does not suggest any other system of apprenticeships in the "Essay on the Poor Law," so the navy seems to have been singled out for special treatment. Although many naval captains already took on apprentices they often expected payment from the boy's family, which tended to exclude indigent children. Requiring the navy to accept apprentices without receiving payment would have created a career track for the poorest youths to become experienced sailors with the skills to be topmen or even officers. If all naval captains took on an apprentice annually as Locke proposed then hundreds of poor boys would have become skilled sailors and the number of sailors in England would probably have risen, thereby making it easier to man the navy in wartime.[103] Increasing the number of sailors might also have benefited England's economy by providing more men to crew merchant ships, as Locke argued in the essay "Trade."[104]

In the "Essay on the Poor Law" Locke prioritizes naval service by advocating that nonworking, able-bodied men in maritime areas serve in the navy for three years instead of doing forced labor on land, and by proposing naval apprenticeships for poor boys but not any other form of apprenticeship. These proposals to engage the English poor in naval service are a clever attempt to address two problems that were within the remit of the Board of Trade: naval manning in English colonies, and the employment of the nonworking poor. However, Locke's proposals in the "Essay on the Poor Law" do not differentiate forced military service from forced labor in general, because the justification that he provides for forcing men into the navy is the same as for forcing them into other kinds of work. In the essay, Locke advocates forced labor for all poor men, women, and children who are capable of productive activity, and his reasons refer not to national security, but to morality and economics: that the nonworking poor are lazy, drunken, immoral,[105] and a growing burden on taxpayers.[106] Whereas Grant suggests that the *Two Treatises* legitimate forced military service if it is equitably distributed and necessary for the preservation of the collective, Locke's "Essay on the Poor Law" justifies forced naval service on nondefensive grounds and targets the nonworking poor in a way that is arguably inequitable. The proposals in the "Essay on the Poor Law" therefore seem to violate the criteria for legitimate use of forced military service that Grant identified in the *Two Treatises*. Instead, Locke's advocacy of naval impressment in the "Essay on the Poor Law" seems to reflect his beliefs that the poor are required to work and that by refusing work they forfeit their full natural rights, thereby justifying their compulsion. In short, the "Essay on the Poor Law" suggests that it is legitimate to force idle poor men into naval service because idleness is wrong and should be remedied, and not because their contribution is required for defense of the commonwealth.

UNDERSTANDING LOCKE'S SUPPORT
FOR FORCED MILITARY SERVICE

Locke's *Two Treatises* are ambiguous about the legitimacy of forced military service, but his support for selective naval impressment is clear from his minor writings and his work on the Board of Trade. In "Atlantis" Locke prohibits the impressment of married men and those with children, and this stance seems to be driven by his goals of population growth and the proper management of family life. The "Atlantis" entries are very broad in scope, so by explicitly exempting married men and parents from impressment Locke provides implicit approval of impressment for unmarried and childless men. Locke's proposals in "Atlantis" therefore suggest that it is legitimate to force men into military service during wartime, except when military service would conflict with the obligations that men owe to their dependent family members. In practice, most English sailors were young and unmarried, so implementation of these proposals would have protected a minority of sailors from impressment while allowing the English state to impress large numbers of skilled men for its wartime navy. Locke's "Essay on the Poor Law" also proposes the selective use of forced military service, but a different group is targeted for impressment. Here, Locke advocates the impressment of idle, able-bodied poor men in maritime areas, and his stated reasons center on the political, economic, and moral imperatives for the poor to work. In the "Essay on the Poor Law" Locke does not differentiate between the military service obligations of married and unmarried men, or between parents and childless men; instead, his selection criteria are gender, age, physical ability, and location. Locke's proposals in the "Essay on the Poor Law" all relate to unemployed poor people, so it is not possible to draw firm inferences about his views on forced military service for those who are employed or wealthy.

However, it is notable that Locke does not propose forced service in the navy for poor people who are female, disabled, less than fourteen years old, more than fifty years old, or who live in non-maritime areas. In practice, members of these groups were generally viewed as incapable of naval service and were rarely, if ever, impressed, so exempting them from impressment would have had little impact on the practice of naval impressment in late seventeenth-century England.

Locke's support for the selective use of naval impressment is confirmed by his activity on the Board of Trade. As a member of the Board Locke was closely involved in drafting English impressment policy, and he repeatedly advocated both a reduction in impressment in England's Caribbean colonies and an increase in the number of English sailors sent to the Caribbean. The Admiralty explained in the clearest terms that sending more sailors to the Caribbean would require impressing more sailors within England, so Locke would surely have understood that his favored policies involved both condoning and expanding the impressment of English sailors. Physical location was therefore the explicit criterion for impressment in the policies that Locke promoted on the Board: people residing in England could be impressed, but people in the Caribbean colonies should not be impressed. In practice, the navy also used other criteria such as occupation, gender, age, and physical ability, and the Board raised no objection to these criteria. It is worth nothing that there is a significant point of overlap between the principles behind the Board's work on impressment and Locke's arguments in "Atlantis," because both stress the advantages of a large population in colonies. Just as the fear of a dwindling white population in the Caribbean led the Board of Trade to advocate local exemption from impressment, it is likely that Locke's "Atlantis" proposal to exempt parents from impressment was driven by the desire to promote population growth in his hypothetical colony. While archival records do not tell us whether Locke's support for the Board of Trade's impressment policy was enthusiastic or reluctant, they do make it clear that he supported the policy in situations when he could have withheld support. There is no evidence in the Board of Trade records, "Atlantis," or the "Essay on the Poor Law" that Locke was concerned about how forced military service restricted the freedom of impressed men, or that he questioned the legitimacy of impressment as a whole. Instead, Locke's contributions on the issue of impressment involve a series of proposals about who should or should not be impressed, while consistently operating on the assumption that some form of impressment was legitimate.

The support that Locke expresses for the selective use of forced military service in his minor writings and Board of Trade work is in tension with his arguments in the *Two Treatises*. According to the *Two Treatises* it is a violation of natural rights to coerce men who have not committed crimes, and impressment clearly threatens men's rights to freedom, health, and life. In

Chapter Two of the *Second Treatise* Locke argues that removing the liberty of non-criminals constitutes unlawful enslavement, so one might expect him to agree with the author of *The State of the Navy Consider'd* that impressed men were being unlawfully enslaved. Alternately, one can read the *Two Treatises* as a more collectivist text in which the principles of collective sovereignty and societal preservation justify forced military service under certain conditions, as Grant suggests. However, this reading of the *Two Treatises* does not resolve the tension in Locke's stance on forced military service, because the various impressment selection criteria that Locke proposed in his minor writings bear no resemblance to the conditions identified by Grant for the legitimate use of impressment according to the principles in the *Two Treatises*. Whereas Grant suggests that forced military service is justified only if the war is just, the obligation to serve is equitably distributed, and it is necessary to preserve the collective, the selection criteria that Locke proposes in "Atlantis" and the "Essay on the Poor Law" center on marital and reproductive status, socioeconomic class, gender, age, and location. How are we to understand this inconsistency between the *Two Treatises* and Locke's other positions on forced military service?

If the only evidence of Locke's support for impressment was his activity on the Board of Trade then one might suspect that Locke simply deviated from his theoretical views when required to make government policy. After all, the Board members were appointed at a time when England was fighting a long and costly war against a powerful foreign state. Moreover, the Board began its work shortly after Parliament's efforts to redesign English naval manning had failed due to the lack of funds with which to pay those who volunteered for naval service. In this context it might be understandable for Locke to prioritize the national interest over the rights of English sailors and, practically speaking, it is very unlikely that he could have persuaded the English state to abolish impressment. Although Locke's Board of Trade work on impressment could perhaps be explained by the idea that the pressures of war prompted him to deviate from his normative principles, this cannot explain his proposals about military service in "Atlantis." Many of Locke's suggestions in "Atlantis" involve restricting individual freedom for the collective good,[107] so the text has been interpreted as indicating a republican aspect to Locke's political views.[108] Whatever ideological significance one attaches to the "Atlantis" entries, it seems clear that the entries were not written for immediate practical application and therefore that the differences between Locke's arguments in "Atlantis" and the *Two Treatises* cannot be explained in terms of the gap between theory and practice. Instead, a comprehensive view of Locke's writings shows that there are tensions between the theoretical principles that he articulates in different passages and texts, including between the collectivist principles in "Atlantis" and his articulation of individual rights in the *Two Treatises*. Overall, Locke expressed repeated

support for the selective use of forced military service in contributions spanning twenty years: two journal entries that precede his authorship of the *Two
Treatises*, a text that follows his publication of the *Two Treatises*, and his
policymaking activity. By contrast, the *Two Treatises* makes no explicit
statement about the legitimacy of forced military service, and the principles
that Locke advocates in the text can be interpreted as either opposing forced
military service or as allowing it under highly restrictive conditions that bear
no resemblance to the selective criteria that Locke advocated elsewhere.
Given Locke's repeated support for selective impressment it seems possible
that the reason the *Two Treatises* makes no explicit statement about the
legitimacy of forced military service is because Locke knew that his views
on impressment were in tension with the principles he was articulating in the
Two Treatises. In short, Locke's silence about forced military service in the
Two Treatises may reflect his awareness of a theoretical inconsistency between the principles in that text and his long-standing support for the selective use of forced military service.

Locke's contribution to England's policy on naval impressment has not
been widely recognized, but this activity had a greater practical impact than
most of his suggestions in the "Essay on the Poor Law." By giving colonial
governors control over naval impressment in the colonies and proposing that
more English sailors be sent to the Caribbean Locke and the other Board
members sought to provide effective naval defense of English colonies while
protecting colonial systems of forced labor. Despite Locke's advocacy of
natural rights, his favored naval policy was designed to expand impressment
for English sailors and uphold forced labor for African slaves and white
indentured servants in the Caribbean, and it probably went some way toward
achieving these goals. Locke's practical contribution to English naval policy
therefore enabled the expansion of English trade and empire at the expense
of individual freedom for sailors and slaves. In the 1720s the system of naval
impressment that Locke had helped to develop directly enabled the Atlantic
slave trade by protecting slavers from pirates that seriously threatened the
profitability of the trade.[109] By the end of the long eighteenth century more
than a hundred and fifty thousand UK residents had been forced into naval
service through impressment,[110] and their forced labor facilitated British imperial expansion and rule. The historical connection between English naval
impressment and the enslavement of Africans shows that Locke's implication in practices of racialized chattel slavery goes far beyond his ownership
of shares in the Royal African Company. Moreover, the English government's use of naval impressment to protect and maintain English slave colonies, slave traders, and merchants carrying slave-produced goods shows the
complex and tragic relationships between multiple systems of forced labor
during the early modern period.

NOTES

1. Ruth W. Grant, *John Locke's Liberalism* (Chicago and London: University of Chicago Press, 1987), 129–35.

2. Michael Walzer, *Obligations: Essays on Disobedience, War, and Citizenship* (Cambridge, MA: Harvard University Press, 1970), 77–119.

3. See Several Hands, "An Agreement of the People for a Firm and Present Peace Upon Grounds of Common Right and Freedom," in *The English Levellers*, ed. Andrew Sharp (Cambridge: Cambridge University Press, 1998), 94; John Lilburne and others, "Petition of 11 September 1648," in *English Levellers*, 136.

4. See John Donoghue, "Unfree Labour, Imperialism, and Radical Republicanism in the Atlantic World, 1630–1661," *Labor: Studies in Working-Class History of the Americas* 1, no. 4 (2004): 47–68.

5. Samuel Pepys, *The Diary of Samuel Pepys*, online at http://www.gutenberg.org/cache/ epub/3331/pg3331.html.

6. N. A. M. Rodger, *The Command of the Ocean: A Naval History of Britain, 1649–1815* (New York and London: W. W. Norton & Company, 2005), 206.

7. In peacetime the navy employed around three thousand to five thousand men, but in wars this surged to over thirty thousand men, see Brunsman, "Men of War," 16.

8. Brunsman, *Evil Necessity*, 57.

9. Rodger, *Command of the Ocean*, 129.

10. By the 1720s the navy estimated that ships usually needed at least a third of the crew to be able seamen with around two years of sailing experience, a third to be ordinary seamen with a year of experience, and the remainder could be unskilled men, see N. A. M. Rodger, *The Wooden World: An Anatomy of the Georgian Navy* (London: W. W. Norton & Company, 1986), 26.

11. Several Hands, "Agreement of the People," 94.

12. Hobbes, *Leviathan* (Oxford: Oxford University Press, 1998), Chapter XXI, 145.

13. *Ibid*, Chapter XXI, 145.

14. For more detailed discussions of Hobbes's views of self-preservation in relation to military service see Deborah Baumgold, "Subjects and Soldiers: Hobbes on Military Service," *History of Political Thought* 4, no. 1 (1983): 43–65; Susanne Sreedhar, "Defending the Hobbesian Right of Self-Defense," *Political Theory* 36, no. 6 (2008): 781–802.

15. Locke, *Two Treatises*, II §6 270–1.

16. *Ibid*, II §17 279.

17. *Ibid*, II §88 324.

18. *Ibid*, II §88 325.

19. *Ibid*, II §12 275.

20. *Ibid*, II §176 385.

21. *Ibid*, II §179 388.

22. *Ibid*, II §179 388.

23. *Ibid*, II §131 353.

24. *Ibid*, II §134 355–6.

25. *Ibid*, II §139 362.

26. *Ibid*, II §177 387.

27. *Ibid*, II §179 388.

28. *Ibid*, II §184 392.

29. *Ibid*, II §182 390.

30. *Ibid*, II §177 387.

31. During wars the English state also licensed privateers to attack and seize the ships of enemy states, and men who volunteered to serve on privateers did so in anticipation of receiving a share of the value of any foreign ships that they captured. However, privateers were not part of the national military and the practice of privateering is incompatible with Locke's account of lawful warfare. According to Locke only defensive wars are lawful and the rights of legal conquest are restricted to enslaving one's vanquished foes and a restricted right to seize their property in compensation. Applying this theory to naval warfare would mean that the

seizure of nearly all foreign merchant ships would be prohibited, thereby undermining the system of prize capture.

32. Locke, *Two Treatises*, II §140 362.

33. In wartime, the wage rates for sailors on merchant ships were around twice those for sailors in the navy. If the English navy had matched the wages paid on merchant ships then this would have put further upward pressure on the market wage for sailors, thus pushing the navy to either match those higher wages or face a lack of volunteers.

34. Rodger, *Command of the Ocean*, 197.

35. Locke, *Two Treatises*, II §172 382 and II §204 402.

36. Walzer, *Obligations*, 89.

37. *Ibid*, 110.

38. *Ibid*, 110–1.

39. *Ibid*, 110.

40. Locke, *Two Treatises*, II §131 353.

41. Grant, *John Locke's Liberalism*, 130–5.

42. *Ibid*, 133.

43. *Ibid*, 130.

44. *Ibid*, 136.

45. Rodger, *Command of the Ocean*, 153.

46. Brunsman, "Men of War," 31, and Rodger, *Command of the Ocean*, 206.

47. Brunsman, "Men of War," 17.

48. Anon, *The State of the Navy Consider'd in Relation to the Victualling, Particularly in the Straits, and the West Indies. With Some Thoughts on the Mismanagements of the Admiralty for Several Years past; and a Proposal to prevent the like for the future*, Second edition (London: Printed for A. Baldwin in Warwick Lane, 1699), 4.

49. On some voyages the mortality rates exceeded 80 percent. For example, in the 1725 Caribbean expedition 4,000 sailors out of 4,750 died within two years, see Rodger, *Wooden World*, 98–9.

50. Brunsman, "Men of War," 31.

51. Brunsman, *Evil Necessity*, 7 and 35.

52. William III, 1695–6: An Act for the Increase and Encouragement of Seamen. In *Statutes of the Realm: Volume 7, 1695–1701*, ed. John Raithby, 98–102. Accessed at http://www.british-history.ac.uk/statutes-realm/vol7/pp98-102.

53. Brunsman, *Evil Necessity*, 31.

54. Rodger, *Command of the Ocean*, 158.

55. J. R. Jones, "Limitations of British Sea Power in the French Wars, 1689–1815," in *The British Navy and the Use of Naval Power in the Eighteenth Century*, eds. Jeremy Black and Philip Woodfine (Atlantic Highlands, NJ: Humanities Press International, 1988), 41.

56. GBPRO, *Calendar of State Papers Colonial*, vol. 18, 131–2.

57. Joyce Chaplin, "The British Atlantic," in *The Oxford Handbook of the Atlantic World, c. 1450–c. 1850*, eds. Nicholas Canny and Philip Morgan (Oxford: Oxford University Press, 2011) 228.

58. In 1700 more than a third of English sugar imports were re-exported, see Sidney W. Mintz, *Sweetness and Power: The Place of Sugar in Modern History* (New York: Penguin Books, 1986), 39.

59. In England's Caribbean colonies the mortality rate for slaves exceeded the reproduction rate, see Chaplin, "The British Atlantic," 228.

60. GBPRO, *Calendar of State Papers Colonial*, vol. 15, 23.

61. *Ibid*, 41–2.

62. *Ibid*, 41–2.

63. *Ibid*, 44–5.

64. *Ibid*, 46–7 and 123.

65. The National Archives, CO 391/9, 87–8 (original numbering); GBPRO, *Calendar of State Papers Colonial*, vol. 15, 92.

66. The National Archives, CO 391/9, 116 (original numbering).

67. GBPRO, *Calendar of State Papers Colonial*, vol. 15, 123.

68. The National Archives, CO 391/9, 116–7 (original numbering).
69. The National Archives, CO 391/9, 97 (original numbering); *Calendar of State Papers Colonial*, vol. 15, 153.
70. National Archive, CO 391/9, 152 (original numbering). The King later ordered that five men pressed by the navy from Jamaica should be paid and returned there, see National Archive, CO 391/9, 291 (original numbering).
71. National Archive, CO 391/9, 120 (original numbering).
72. National Archive, CO 391/9, 149–51 (original numbering). The Board's May 1696 commission from the King stipulated that five Board members were required to sign any representations to the Privy Council. Only five members were in attendance on October 1 when the representation was signed, and Locke was among them, which confirms that he was a signatory.
73. GBPRO, *Calendar of State Papers Colonial*, vol. 15, 168.
74. *Ibid*, 168.
75. *Ibid*, 183.
76. *Ibid*, 235.
77. *Ibid*, 236, and The National Archives, CO 391/9, 291 (original numbering).
78. The National Archives, CO 323/2, 230–1 (original numbering).
79. GBPRO, *Calendar of State Papers Colonial*, vol. 15, 313, 342–5, and 362–3.
80. *Ibid*, 297–8.
81. *Ibid*, 321–2.
82. The National Archives, 232/2, A36 258 (original numbering).
83. The National Archives, 232/2, A36 266 (original numbering); GBPRO, *Calendar of State Papers Colonial*, vol. 15, 332.
84. GBPRO, *Calendar of State Papers Colonial*, vol. 15, 554.
85. *Ibid*, 554.
86. GBPRO, *Calendar of State Papers Colonial*, vol. 16, 31–5.
87. *Ibid*, 57–8.
88. *Ibid*, 3.
89. *Ibid*, 3.
90. GBPRO, *Calendar of State Papers Colonial*, vol. 18, 17–21.
91. GBPRO, *Calendar of State Papers Colonial*, vol. 17, 515–6.
92. *Ibid*, 540.
93. Locke, "Atlantis," 255.
94. *Ibid*, 259.
95. *Ibid*, 255.
96. Concern about how impressment impacted men's families was well founded, because military service abroad or at sea took men away from their families, and the low, irregular military pay often left their families destitute.
97. On the overlap between "Atlantis" and the "Essay on the Poor Law" see Goldie's comments in *Locke: Political Essays*, 253; and Vicki Hsueh, "Unsettling Colonies: Locke, 'Atlantis' and New World Knowledges," *History of Political Thought* 29, no. 2 (2008): 316.
98. The National Archives, CO 391/10, 263 (original numbering).
99. Locke, "Essay on the Poor Law," 185.
100. *Ibid*, 188.
101. To avoid pressing inexperienced men press gangs on land were most active in major ports such as London, Bristol, and Liverpool, where many inhabitants were sailors.
102. Locke, "Essay on the Poor Law," 198.
103. A system of naval apprenticeships for poor boys set up in the mid eighteenth century by the Marine Society sent over ten thousand men and boys to sea during the Seven Years War, and contributed at least 5 percent of navy recruits in the period, see Rodger, *Wooden World*, 162. The success of the Marine Society scheme suggests that Locke's idea for a system of naval apprenticeships might have helped to mitigate the shortage of sailors in wartime.
104. Locke, "Trade," 222.
105. Locke, "Essay on the Poor Law," 186.
106. *Ibid*, 185.

107. Mark Goldie comments "the Atlantis entries are arresting for the extent to which Locke argues for intrusions into people's lives," see "Atlantis," 253.

108. Hsueh, "Unsettling Colonies," 318.

109. Pirates in the 1710s and 1720s attacked slave ships to steal the ships themselves and in some cases (notably the career of Howell Davies) attacked and destroyed slave forts. The prospect of living as a pirate also encouraged the crews of slave ships to mutiny against the poor conditions, thereby disrupting labor relations on board, see Rediker, *Villains of All Nations*, 137–45.

110. Brunsman, "Men of War," 22.

Conclusion

Maritime Political Thought, Then and Now

With this work, I have sought to show that ideas about law and political power at sea were central to Locke's political thought. In the *Two Treatises of Government* Locke conceptualizes the oceans as the common property of mankind,[1] which means there are universal rights to use the oceans for lawful purposes such as travel and fishing. Locke does not explicitly state that the oceans will always remain the common property of all humans, but his theory of property makes it practically impossible to appropriate a region of the oceans, thus justifying continued common ownership. Locke also argues that exclusive state jurisdiction extends only over regions that are the private property of particular individuals or groups,[2] so common ownership of the oceans puts them outside the territory or exclusive jurisdiction of any state. The *Two Treatises* therefore contributes to early modern theories of maritime law by providing a normative justification of free seas, and a rebuttal of the closed sea arguments presented by Selden and Filmer. This free seas theory provides one of the legal foundations for Locke's advocacy of English colonization of the Americas,[3] because the legitimacy of English colonialism depended in part on the legality of travel across the oceans. Locke's free seas theory also underpins his belief in the legitimacy of England's maritime trade, which he advocates in texts including the *Two Treatises*, the 1674 essay "Trade," the 1691 paper "Some Considerations of the Consequences of the Lowering of Interest and Raising the Value of Money," and the 1693 essay "For a General Naturalisation."[4] Maritime trade was central to Locke's conceptions of English national interest and empire, which he argued should involve extending political power overseas through trade, not conquest. Praise for English merchant shipping and mercantile empire run through much of Locke's work, from early texts such as the 1654 poem celebrating the end of the Dutch war[5] to later writings such as the 1691 paper on recoinage where he argued that English rulers "have found the enlarging their Power by Sea, and thus securing our Navigation and Trade, more the Interest of this Kingdom than Wars or Conquests."[6] In short, Locke's vision of both English politics and international politics depended on his theory of law and political power at sea.

Locke's *Two Treatises* also makes it clear that the oceans are governed by natural law, which prohibits infringements of individual rights to life, liberty, and property.[7] Theft or violence at sea are violations of natural law, and Locke confirms this by repeatedly stating that piracy is unlawful.[8] However, Locke also argues that it is difficult to enforce natural law in the state of nature,[9] which suggests that it would be difficult to apprehend and punish pirates. The first difficulty in punishing pirates is the complexity of law and legal jurisdiction on the oceans, because the *Two Treatises* suggests that oceans are governed both by natural law that exists in the state of nature and by national legislation that governs the conduct of citizens at sea. The co-existence of natural law and national laws means that the citizenships of the pirates and victims determine who has the right to punish an act of piracy, and under what law. The system of law enforcement at sea outlined in the *Two Treatises* empowers England to prosecute and punish its own citizens under national anti-piracy laws, but does not empower England to try or punish foreign pirates under those laws. Instead, England would only be able to punish foreign pirates by seeking a remedy for a violation of natural law in the international state of nature, which would require it to use foreign policy against the state(s) of which the pirates were citizens. Practical difficulties would also arise, because states might refuse to punish their own citizens for crimes against foreigners at sea, and because the vast scale of the oceans makes it virtually impossible for any single state to enforce law effectively across the whole area. In the *Two Treatises* Locke therefore provides a clear explanation of why piracy is prohibited, but he does not present an effective strategy for maritime law enforcement.

As a member of the Board of Trade Locke played a prominent role in making English economic policy and overseeing the governance of English colonies, including by contributing to policies on many issues that are related to his arguments in the *Two Treatises*. In this book I have considered Locke's Board of Trade writing and activity about three maritime issues: piracy, penal slavery, and naval impressment. In his Board of Trade work on piracy Locke applied the principles of natural law outlined in the *Two Treatises* by arguing that pirates were violating the law and should therefore be tried and severely punished, but he also modified his views about how to enforce law against pirates. Whereas Locke argues in the *Two Treatises* that piracy can be punished under natural law in the international state of nature or under national laws applying to citizens, he proposes in "Pyracy 97" that Europe's major maritime states should create an international piracy treaty. Locke suggests that the treaty should include agreements not to harbor pirates, to prosecute and punish any citizens who commit future acts of piracy, and to either punish foreign pirates or "send them to their respective countries to receive there the sentence due."[10] In "Pyracy 97" Locke therefore seeks to develop more effective law enforcement against pirates, including by using an international treaty to create written maritime law that could be consistently applied by multiple states, and by suggesting that states can punish acts of piracy committed by noncitizens. The international piracy treaty that Locke proposed was not created during his time on the Board. However, Locke successfully argued for a new English piracy law that imposed severe punishments for pirates and that applied to all English jurisdictions and the world's oceans. This law authorized the English navy to seize, try, and execute pirates anywhere at sea, and Locke also advocated the deployment of English warships to fight pirates off the coast of Asia, Africa, and the Americas. During the 1690s Locke therefore advocated the extension of English law and naval power across the world's oceans in order to more effectively punish pirates for breaking the natural law outlined in the *Two Treatises*.

Locke's Board of Trade work about forced migration and forced labor also provides an opportunity to examine the relationship between his practical and theoretical work on these issues. In the *Second Treatise* Locke argues that those who break natural law by committing a violent crime or participating in an unjust war have forfeited their natural rights, and can therefore be legitimately killed or enslaved.[11] This forfeiture of natural rights means that lawbreakers are the only group who can be lawfully coerced, so the theory of slavery in the *Second Treatise* is specifically a theory of penal slavery. On the Board, Locke applied this theory of penal slavery by advocating that English convicts be transported to English colonies and sold into forced labor. Locke's written support for convict transportation and penal slavery is evident in his "Essay on the Poor Law" and "Essay on Virginia," and Locke also voted in favor of transporting female convicts from England to the Leeward Islands for forced labor.[12] Locke's support for the forced migration and forced labor of English convicts as a member of the Board is consistent with his arguments in the *Two Treatises*, but there is less consistency in his views about the poor. In the *Two Treatises* Locke argues that all individuals have a natural right to liberty, so it is a violation of natural law to coerce any law-abiding individual.[13] However, in his Board of Trade writings Locke proposes forced migration and forced labor for the nonworking English poor, which suggests that Locke either modified his theoretical position in the *Two Treatises* by exempting the nonworking poor from the natural right to liberty, or that he believed the poor should be legally required to work and therefore saw the idle poor as presumptive criminals who could be justly punished with deprivation of their liberty.

There also seems to be inconsistency between Locke's arguments in the *Two Treatises* and his other writing and activity about forced military service. In the *Two Treatises* Locke makes no explicit statement for or against the legitimacy of forced military service, but the normative principles in the text seem relevant to this issue. In the *Second Treatise* Locke argues that individuals have natural rights to freedom, life, and health, and since forcing individuals to serve in the military would threaten these rights it is arguable that the *Two Treatises* prohibits forced military service. Alternately, Ruth Grant provides a more collectivist reading of the *Two Treatises* under which forced military service is legitimate provided that it is equitably distributed among citizens, necessary for the defense of the collective, and part of a just war.[14] Depending on how one interprets the *Two Treatises*, the text therefore either prohibits forced military service or allows forced military service provided that very restrictive conditions are met. However, in other writings and his Board of Trade work Locke advocates the selective use of forced military service in ways that do not seem consistent with the principles in the *Two Treatises*. In his 1678–9 "Atlantis" entries Locke implies that it is legitimate to force unmarried and childless men to serve in the military,[15] and in the "Essay on the Poor Law" he proposes three-year terms of forced naval service for nonworking poor men in maritime areas.[16] As a member of the Board of Trade Locke also helped to develop policies that sought to reduce and regulate the impressment of Caribbean residents, while increasing the number of English sailors who would be impressed and sent on warships to the Caribbean.[17] Locke's reasoning for forced military service in "Atlantis" and the "Essay on the Poor Law" seems to be primarily economic: he seeks to ensure that colonies are prosperous and populous by ensuring that men were not taken from their families, and wanted the idle poor to work productively instead of being a burden on taxpayers. The Board of Trade's policy on forced military service was also economically motivated, because the Board sought to ensure naval defense of English colonies and merchants while maintaining the profitable systems of white indentured servitude and African slavery in those colonies. Locke's advocacy of universal natural rights in the *Two Treatises* sits in tension with his support for the selective use of forced military service in "Atlantis," and as a member of the Board.

The wealth of archival records about Locke's work on the Board of Trade provides a valuable opportunity to see how he applied, amended, or deviated from his normative principles when engaged in the practical task of making English government policy. In this work, I have shown examples of Locke deploying all three of these tactics, singly and in combination. In relation to piracy Locke both applied and amended his theoretical arguments in the *Two Treatises*: he applied his theory of natural law, which prohibited piracy, but amended his views about the enforcement of natural law at sea. On the issue of penal slavery Locke also applied his theoretical ideas: the theory of slavery in the *Two Treatises* legitimates enslavement only as a punishment for breaking the law, and in his Board of Trade work Locke advocated forced labor and migration for English convicts. By contrast, Locke deviated from the theoretical principles in the *Two Treatises* in his Board of Trade activity about forced military service, because the principles in the *Two Treatises* suggest that forced military service is either illegitimate, or legitimate only under very restrictive conditions, whereas Locke supported a different use of forced military service in his work on the Board. The policy proposals that Locke drafted for the Board and the decisions that he supported at Board meetings were sometimes consistent with the theoretical principles that he advocated in the *Two Treatises*, and sometimes in tension with those principles. Where there were implicit or explicit tensions between Locke's Board of Trade work and the arguments in the *Two Treatises* then analysis of Locke's wider writings sometimes reveals deeper tensions in his theory. For example, Locke expressed support for the selective use of forced military service in his 1678–9 "Atlantis" entries as well as in his work on the Board, which suggests that there was an inconsistency between the views of individual freedom and political obligation that he expressed in different texts. Overall, it is striking how often Locke's actions on the Board of Trade in relation to piracy, penal slavery, and forced military service overlapped with ideas that he had expressed in writing, either in the *Two Treatises* or in minor texts. It is also noteworthy that Locke's writings often interweave ideas about politics, economics, law, and morality, such that a paper about interest rates also discusses vice[18] and a paper about trade condemns legal complexity and arbitrary government.[19] Locke's writings show that he saw politics and economics as interrelated, and that his views about both were shaped by his conception of natural law. Scholars seeking to understand Locke's political thought may therefore find it valuable to consult his economic work, instead of assuming that Locke's economic views were disconnected from or irrelevant to his political thought.

MARITIME POLITICAL THOUGHT TODAY

Current patterns of maritime activity, trade, and migration are very different from those that existed in the seventeenth century, but many of the issues that arise in Locke's maritime political thought are still relevant today. In the seventeenth century rival theorists of maritime law debated whether seas were commonly owned and therefore available for peaceful use by all, or if the seas were the exclusive jurisdiction and property of particular states. Whereas Selden argued that England governed and owned her coastal seas,

Locke categorizes the oceans as a common with universal rights of access. These competing conceptions of closed and open seas have both shaped twenty-first-century maritime law, because the United Nations Convention on the Law of the Sea (UNCLOS) divides the world's oceans into the regions where specific states have sovereignty, partial legal jurisdiction, or property rights, and the regions that are international spaces governed by international law. Under UNCLOS, states that border on an external sea or ocean are entitled to claim exclusive possession and sovereignty over waters that extend up to 12 nautical miles (13.8 miles) from their coast or from their reefs or shoals. States can also claim some rights over three further oceanic zones: limited law enforcement powers over a "contiguous zone" extending up to 24 nautical miles (27.6 miles) from their coast; ownership of natural resources in a "Exclusive Economic Zone" of up to 200 nautical miles (230 miles) from their coast; and rights to undersea resources in the continental shelf extending from their state, which may reach up to 350 nautical miles from their coast (402 miles). All other areas of the world's seas and oceans are classified as an international space that UNCLOS describes as part of the "common heritage of mankind."[20] Current maritime law therefore reflects a compromise between the views of Locke and Selden: the open oceans are conceptualized as free seas, whereas the coastal waters surrounding states are conceptualized as closed seas where states have various rights of political jurisdiction and ownership.

Seventeenth-century debates about the legal status of the seas were influenced by concerns about the scarcity of marine resources, and these concerns also apply today. The ecologist Garrett Hardin argues that common ownership and access to natural resources leads to a "tragedy of the commons" where resources are overused and depleted, whereas private ownership would enable the imposition of limits to make resource use more sustainable.[21] This theoretical approach suggests that Locke's proposal of universal access to oceanic fisheries is liable to cause overfishing and declining fish stocks. By contrast, Selden advocated exclusive ownership and use of coastal fisheries, which he argued would prevent overextraction. Concerns about the sustainability of oceanic fisheries led to political conflict during the twentieth century, and fishing rights may become even more contentious as fish stocks continue to dwindle. The current legal principles for determining jurisdiction and ownership of extractable marine resources are reflected in UNCLOS, but both the content of these agreements and the political clashes surrounding them show the continued salience of debates about the principles of maritime law. The first UNCLOS agreement in 1956 outlined the powers that states possess in their territorial waters, but agreement on the extent of territorial waters and exclusive resource rights was not reached until 1982. While the negotiations over UNCLOS were ongoing, Britain and Iceland were engaged in a fierce dispute over North Sea fisheries that has become known as the Cod Wars.

In 1952 Iceland asserted that foreign ships were prohibited from fishing within four miles of its coast, which it claimed as territorial waters. The cod fishery surrounding Iceland's coast was extremely valuable and British ships had been fishing in the area for centuries, so Iceland's announcement angered the British and they responded with an embargo on Icelandic fish.[22] In response to the embargo, Iceland signed a trade treaty with the Soviet Union and began supplying them with fish.[23] In the face of continued overfishing by foreign fleets Iceland soon extended these restrictions: in 1958 they prohibited foreign fishing within twelve nautical miles of the Icelandic coast, in 1972 they extended the limit to fifty nautical miles, and in 1975 extended the limit again to two hundred nautical miles. Each extension of the fishing limit was strenuously opposed by Britain, and British trawlers continued fishing in waters claimed by Iceland. The Cod Wars led to Iceland jailing British fishermen, British fishing boats ramming Icelandic coast guard ships, the Icelandic coast guard cutting British fishing nets, and the British navy being deployed in waters that Iceland had claimed. This conflict over fishing rights led to significant tensions within NATO in the midst of the Cold War: Iceland repeatedly threatened to resign from NATO, asked the U.S. to put pressure on Britain, threatened to expel U.S. forces from a military base in Iceland if the British navy entered its exclusive fishing zone, and finally cut off diplomatic relations with Britain.[24] The Cod Wars showed the continued salience of theoretical disagreements about the legal status of the seas. In Iceland's view, conceptualizing coastal fishing areas as common waters meant that foreign fleets caught an unsustainable number of fish and depleted the fish stocks. By contrast, establishing that Iceland had exclusive rights to fisheries near its coastline empowered Iceland to exclude foreign fishing boats and to limit fishing in those waters, thereby restricting catches to a more sustainable level. The 1982 UNCLOS agreement later legitimated Iceland's claims by allowing states to claim an exclusive economic zone with sole fishing rights extending up to two hundred nautical miles from their coast.

Despite UNCLOS, political disputes over fishing rights have continued. In Europe, the European Union (EU) sought to standardize fishing rights between their members through the Common Fisheries Policy, which gives each EU member state exclusive fishing rights within twelve nautical miles of its coastline but grants ships from any EU state equal fishing rights in the area between twelve and two hundred nautical miles of the coast. Compared to UNCLOS, the Common Fisheries Policy gives EU ships more rights to fish near the coast of other EU states. However, this policy has caused conflict because citizens of some EU states have complained that people from other EU states are unjustly taking "their" fish. In the 1980s a dispute arose between Britain and Spain, because Britain argued that Spanish boats were illegally fishing in British waters, while the Spanish fishermen argued that British efforts to exclude them were contrary to EU law.[25] The Common Fisheries Policy is widely regarded as enabling destructive levels of overfishing in EU waters,[26] and has been described as an exemplary case of the tragedy of the commons.[27] Moreover, the unpopularity of the Common Fisheries Policy has caused criticism of the EU and even encouraged opposition to EU membership. Prior to the June 2016 British referendum on EU membership some British politicians and fishermen advocated leaving the EU so that Britain would regain control of coastal fisheries and could prioritize domestic fishermen over foreign ships.[28] Conflict over fisheries has also arisen between the EU and other states, including the disagreement with Canada over turbot catches in the North Atlantic during the 1990s, which some refer to as the Turbot War.[29]

Overfishing is a widespread problem, and many of the world's saltwater fisheries are becoming depleted. The UN Food and Agriculture Organization (UNFAO) estimates that in 2011 28.8 percent of marine fish stocks were overfished and 61.3 percent were being fished at the maximum sustainable level, meaning that careful monitoring and management were needed to prevent overfishing.[30] The depletion of marine fisheries threatens the livelihoods of the millions of people globally who work as fishers,[31] and the collapse of regional fisheries has devastated local economies such as the traditional fishing towns in Newfoundland. Overfishing can cause unwelcome changes in the marine ecosystem, as occurred when overfishing of sardines near Japan led to a surge in the numbers of huge poisonous jellyfish.[32] Moreover, overfishing poses a risk to food supplies and human health. The UNFAO calculates that in 2010 fish provided over 16 percent of animal protein globally,[33] and more than half of the animal protein consumed in low-income coastal states such as Bangladesh, Ghana, and Indonesia.[34] Fish are also rich in essential nutrients such as vitamins D, A, and B, iodine, calcium, and omega-3 fatty acids,[35] which is why cod liver oil has long been a popular dietary supplement. The depletion of marine fish stocks will reduce the availability of nutritious food, so the UN Environment Program has argued that "the world cannot achieve . . . hunger eradication without improving fisheries management."[36] The difficulty of preserving the world's fisheries is directly linked to legal constructions of ownership and jurisdiction at sea, because restricting fishing in shared waters requires international agreements and enforcement. In practice, restrictions on fishing have been more difficult to achieve at an international level, with the result that "the probability of a fish stock being over- (under-)utilised rises (falls) with the number of countries sharing the stock."[37] The historical legacy of early modern theories of free seas is not only the expansion of maritime trade, but also the ongoing problem of destructive overfishing.

Most early modern disputes over the ownership of extractable marine resources centered on fish, but many recent disputes are over undersea resources such as oil and natural gas. Globally, more than a quarter of conventional oil reserves are in offshore areas such as the North Sea and the Gulf of Mexico, and more than a third of conventional natural gas is in offshore areas such as the Persian Gulf.[38] Locke did not anticipate the discovery of undersea resources so he does not discuss them in the *Two Treatises*, but we can consider how his theory of property would apply.[39] Locke characterizes the oceans as the common property of all humans and argues that using one's labor to catch a fish establishes one's ownership of that fish, but not of the surrounding ocean. Under Locke's theory of property, people are only entitled to claim exclusive ownership of a region if they use their labor to improve the value or productivity of the region in a manner akin to how farming increases the productivity of land.[40] Building an oil platform makes it possible to extract undersea oil, but it does not increase the amount of oil so the region is no more productive than it was before. Absent a way to greatly increase the productivity of an undersea oil field, people would only be able to claim ownership of the oil extracted through their labor. Under Locke's theory of property the extraction of undersea oil therefore seems to be like picking apples or catching fish: it establishes private ownership of a pre-existing good that was formerly owned in common, but does not establish ownership of the region in which the good was found. Such a system of Lockean property rights beneath the seabed would probably cause a rush to extract oil and natural gas, and perhaps conflict over dwindling supplies. Instead, UNCLOS gives states the right to claim ownership of undersea resources in an Exclusive Economic Zone extending up to 200 nautical miles from their coast and in the continental shelf extending from their state for up to 350 nautical miles. This system has enabled states such as the United States, Brazil, and Norway to establish exclusive rights to offshore oil and natural gas fields and to extract the resources, but conflict can arise when multiple states claim the same region. In particular, there is potential for conflict over the Arctic where large undersea energy reserves are expected to become accessible as climate change causes polar ice to melt, and where the United States, Canada, Denmark, and Russia have all asserted claims.[41]

Historically the oceans have been major trade routes, and a high proportion of international goods still travel by sea. The merchant shipping industry has an annual turnover of over $400 billion and moves more than seven billion tons of cargo each year,[42] ranging from crude oil to grain, metal ores, and manufactured goods such as computers. Most of these goods travel on huge oil tankers, bulk carriers, and container ships where the vast size of the ship helps to reduce transportation costs, thus making it cost-efficient to carry goods over long distances.[43] The adoption of shipping containers since the 1960s has also led to sharp falls in the cost of transporting goods internationally, which contributed to trends such as the decline of manufacturing in North America and Western Europe, and the rise in manufacturing in Asia.[44] Despite having the world's longest undefended land border, the United States transported international merchandise worth $1,700 billion by water in 2014,[45] comprising almost half of U.S. imports and a third of exports by value, and a majority of both imports and exports by weight.[46] America's most important trade gateways are ports such as New York and Los Angeles, each of which received over $150 billion in imported goods during 2014.[47] In early 2015 the economic importance of ports became even clearer when a labor dispute at West Coast ports led to delays that impacted businesses across the United States, and beyond.[48]

The high volume and value of goods transported by sea means that ships are still attractive targets for criminals. In 2016 the International Criminal Court (ICC)'s International Maritime Bureau recorded 191 pirate attacks globally,[49] and this represents a decline since 2011 when there were more than 400 attacks.[50] From 2008 to 2011 there was a surge in piracy based in Somalia, and the ICC recorded over a thousand attacks on ships in the Gulf of Aden, the Red Sea, and off the Somali coastline,[51] which led to dozens of ships being hijacked.[52] The pirates often targeted oil tankers that passed the Somali coast as they traveled from the Persian Gulf to markets in Europe and North America, so the attacks showed the vulnerability of global oil supplies.[53] Perhaps the most infamous of these Somali pirate attacks was the boarding of the U.S.-registered MV *Maersk Alabama* in April 2009, when pirates held the Captain hostage for several days before he was rescued by the U.S. military. The attack and rescue of the *Maersk Alabama* have since been described in a best-selling book by the captive Richard Phillips[54] and in the 2013 film *Captain Phillips*, starring Tom Hanks. Somali piracy has dwindled in recent years, but there has been a rise in piracy targeting oil tankers in the Gulf of Guinea.[55] Since 2011 the ICC has recorded over a hundred pirate attacks off the Nigerian coast,[56] and their most recent report states, "All waters in/off Nigeria remain risky. Vessels are advised to be vigilant."[57] These ongoing pirate attacks show both the economic importance of shipping and the vulnerability of ships due to the minimal law enforcement on much of the world's oceans. The absence of effective law enforcement at sea also enables offenses such as human trafficking, smuggling, forced labor, and illegal pollution. For example, reporting by the *New York Times* showed that a cargo ship named the *Donna Liberta* committed a range of offenses over a three-year period, including mistreating its sailors, illegally dumping oil, and abandoning two stowaways on a raft in the Atlantic.[58]

Despite the expansion in air travel, the oceans continue to provide a route for human migration. In 2015 over 790,000 people arrived in Europe by sea after fleeing conflicts in areas such as Syria and Iraq,[59] and over 180,000 more people made the journey in the first four months of 2016.[60] The ships making this journey are often unseaworthy and overcrowded, which has led to many vessels capsizing or sinking, and thousands of refugees have drowned. In 2016 the International Organization for Migration estimates that over five thousand migrants died in the Mediterranean and Aegean Sea,[61] and the fatalities continued unabated in early 2017.[62] These accidents have led to debates about whether the EU or coastal states have a responsibility to patrol the seas and rescue people on unsafe vessels, but there has not been consistent support for such efforts. In October 2013 the Italian navy introduced a marine rescue program called Mare Nostrum after more than four hundred people died in shipwrecks near the island of Lampedusa, but the program was canceled the following year.[63] Unfortunately, the Mediterranean is not the only region where refugees make dangerous journeys by ship. In Southeast Asia over 88,000 people have fled states such as Myanmar, Bangladesh, Indonesia, and Sri Lanka by ship since 2014, leading to more than a thousand drownings.[64] The numbers of migrants who drown during ocean crossings show that the promise of international mobility offered by the seas continues to come at a high price.

Both in the seventeenth century and today, the oceans are spaces where law is imposed and where political, economic, and military power is exercised, but they are also spaces that offer a measure of freedom, including free movement for migration and trade. In the *Two Treatises* Locke presents a free seas argument that builds on earlier theories of maritime law, and on the Board of Trade Locke sought to ensure the freedom to travel peaceably at sea through his efforts to punish pirates. Locke's vision of freedom at sea is therefore one of responsible behavior that conforms to natural law, and where English citizens and the occupants of English colonies are expected to obey English laws that Locke saw as consistent with natural law and the public good, such as the 1700 Piracy Act. In short, Locke's conception of freedom on the oceans rests on the distinction that he draws in the *Two Treatises* between law-abiding liberty and uncontrolled "Licence."[65] However, Locke's work on the Board provides glimpses of the very different conceptions of freedom held by some of the groups he sought to regulate. Disagreements about the meaning of freedom are evident in the actions of the pirates from the American colonies who challenged Locke's model of law, property rights, and trade. Challenges to Locke's vision of freedom are also visible among the American colonists who supported piracy, some of whom argued for local political autonomy instead of the imposition of colonial law and governance from London. Even the most disadvantaged groups actively resisted forms of legalized coercion, as we see in the "Essay on the Poor Law" where Locke describes how paupers forged poor law passes in order to move freely within England.[66] Innumerable examples of subaltern resistance can be found in the records of the Board of Trade, including English sailors fleeing press gangs, escapes by indentured servants, and rebellions by

African slaves. Locke's view of regulated freedom was therefore challenged by other liberatory ideas and practices: by pirates, slaves, and sailors seeking escape from exploitation and domination, by American colonists protesting English imperial rule, and by the constant risk of mutiny or revolution. Seventeenth-century debates about maritime political thought serve as a reminder that current conceptions of maritime law are also subject to challenge and change, and that people—from pirates to refugees—will continue to reimagine the meaning of freedom at sea.

NOTES

1. Locke, *Two Treatises*, II §30 289.
2. *Ibid*, II §35 292.
3. See *Ibid*, II §36 293, II §37 294, II §41 296–7, II §49 301, Blair, Locke, and Kammen, "Virginia at the Close," and much of Locke's colonial writing and activity.
4. See Locke, *Two Treatises*, II §43 298; Locke, "Trade," 222; Locke, "Some Considerations of the Consequences of the Lowering of Interest and Raising the Value of Money," in Kelly, ed., *Locke on Money, Volume 1*, 222–3 and 292; and Locke, "For a General Naturalisation," 323–4.
5. Locke, "Verses on the Dutch War," 202.
6. Locke, "Some Considerations," 232.
7. Locke, *Two Treatises*, II §6 271.
8. *Ibid*, I §81 203, II §176 385, and II §228 416–7.
9. *Ibid*, II §13 276, II §124–6, 350–1.
10. MS Locke c. 30, fol. 62, Bodleian Library, Oxford.
11. Locke, *Two Treatises*, II §23 284.
12. Locke, "Essay on the Poor Law," 186; Blair, Locke, and Kammen, "Virginia at the Close," 158; The National Archives, CO 153/6, 86–8.
13. Locke, *Two Treatises*, II §17 279.
14. Grant, *John Locke's Liberalism*, 129–35.
15. John Locke, "Atlantis," 255 and 259.
16. Locke, "Essay on the Poor Law," 185 and 188.
17. The National Archives, CO 323/2, 230–1 (original numbering).
18. Locke, "Some Considerations," 231.
19. Locke, "Trade," 222.
20. "Preamble" in United Nations Division for Ocean Affairs and the Law of the Sea, "United Nations Convention on the Law of the Sea of 10 December 1982" (1982), retrieved from http://www.un.org/Depts/los/convention_agreements/texts/unclos/preamble.htm.
21. Hardin, "Tragedy of the Commons."
22. Guðmundur J. Guðmundsson, "The Cod and the Cold War," *Scandinavian Journal of History* 31, no. 2 (2006): 97–118.
23. *Ibid*, 98.
24. *Ibid*, 100–6.
25. See *R (Factortame Ltd) v Secretary of State for Transport*, in which Britain's highest court ruled that the U.K. must comply with the EU Common Fisheries Policy.
26. Emily Self, "Who Speaks for the Fish? The Tragedy of Europe's Common Fisheries Policy," *Vanderbilt Journal of Transnational Law* 48, no. 2 (2015): 577–607.
27. Rouba Al-Fattal, "The Tragedy of the Commons: Institutions and Fisheries Management at the Local and EU Levels," *Review of Political Economy* 21, no. 4 (2009): 537–47.
28. This argument was prominently made by George Eustice, Conservative MP and Minister for Agriculture, Fisheries and Food in "The Fishing Industry and Brexit" at https://www.georgeeustice.org.uk/news/fishing-industry-and-brexit, retrieved on February 1, 2017,

and at http://www.bluemarinefoundation.com/2016/05/02/leave-europe-george-eustice-uks-fisheries-minister-puts-marine-case-brexit/, retrieved on February 1, 2017. Some fishermen also advocated Brexit on the grounds that Britain would regain control of coastal fisheries, see Kimiko De Freytus-Tamura, "In Brexit Debate English Fishermen Eye Waters Free of E.U.," *New York Times*, April 14, 2016, retrieved from http://www.nytimes.com/2016/04/15/business/international/many-in-british-fishing-port-want-eu-out-of-their-waters.html.

29. Donald Barry, "The Canada-European Union Turbot War Internal Politics and Transatlantic Bargaining," *International Journal* 53, no. 2 (1998): 253–84.

30. United Nations Food and Agriculture Organization (UNFAO), "The State of World Fisheries and Aquaculture" (2014), 37. Retrieved from http://www.fao.org/3/a-i3720e.pdf.

31. *Ibid*, 28.

32. Jellyfish blooms then interfere with the fishery by competing with fish for food, eating fish eggs or larvae, killing fish, and tangling in fishing nets. Some jellyfish have stings that can be fatal to humans, so jellyfish surges can lead to further problems such as beach closures. See Anthony J. Richardson et al., "The Jellyfish Joyride: Causes, Consequences and Management Responses to a More Gelatinous Future," *Trends in Ecology and Evolution* 24, no. 6 (2009): 312–22.

33. UNFAO, "State of World Fisheries," 66.

34. *Ibid*, 66.

35. *Ibid*, 104–5.

36. United Nations Environment Program, "Challenges to International Waters—Regional Assessments in a Global Perspective" (2006), 9. Retrieved from http://www.unep.org/dewa/giwa/publications/finalreport/giwa_final_report.pdf.

37. Stephanie F. McWhinnie, "The Tragedy of the Commons in International Fisheries: An Empirical Examination," *Journal of Environmental Economics and Management* 57, no. 3 (2009): 322.

38. See Thomas Bosch et al. (Cluster of Excellence), *World Oceans Review: Living with the Oceans* (Berlin: Maribus, 2010), 143–5. The description of oil or gas reserves as "conventional" means that the industry considers them relatively affordable and easy to extract with current technology. By contrast, unconventional oil reserves include tar sands where oil extraction is more difficult and costly, and unconventional natural gas reserves include shale gas that can be extracted through fracking.

39. For a brief discussion of Locke's theory of property and undersea mineral resources see Robert Goldwin, "Locke and the Law of the Sea," *Commentary* 71, no. 6 (1981): 46–50.

40. As discussed earlier, Locke argues that private appropriation of land is justified because most of the value and productivity of land derives from labor and only a small proportion from the natural resource, see Locke, *Two Treatises*, II §32 290, II §37 294, and II §40 296.

41. Wojciech Janicki, "Why Do They Need the Arctic? The First Partition of the Sea," *Arctic* 65, no. 1 (2012): 87–97; Christoph Humrich, "Fragmented International Governance of Arctic Offshore Oil: Governance Challenges and Institutional Improvement," *Global Environmental Politics* 13, no. 3 (2013): 79–99.

42. Martin Stopford, *Maritime Economics 3rd Edition* (Hoboken, NY: Taylor and Francis, 2009), 48.

43. *Ibid*, 75–78.

44. See Marc Levinson, *The Box: How the Shipping Container Made the World Smaller and the World Economy Bigger* (Princeton and Oxford: Princeton University Press, 2006).

45. United States Department of Transportation, "Freight Facts and Figures 2015," 16. Retrieved from http://www.rita.dot.gov/bts/sites/rita.dot.gov.bts/files/FF%26F_complete.pdf on February 10, 2016.

46. *Ibid*, 16.

47. *Ibid*, 14.

48. See Henning Gloystein, "U.S. port strike pushed up freight rates with ships held offshore," *Reuters*, February 16, 2015, retrieved from http://www.reuters.com/article/us-usa-ports-west-asia-idUSKBN0LK0A420150216 on February 10, 2016, and Cole Stangler, "West Coast Port Slowdown: Port Dispute Hits U.S. Economy Hard," *International Business Times*,

February 18, 2015, retrieved from http://www.ibtimes.com/west-coast-port-slowdown-labor-dispute-hits-us-economy-hard-1820740 on February 10, 2016.

49. International Criminal Court (ICC) International Maritime Bureau, "Piracy and Armed Robbery Against Ships, Report for the Period 1 January 2016–31 December 2016" (London: ICC International Maritime Bureau, 2017), 5. Retrieved from https://www.icc-ccs.org/upload report/2016-Annual-IMB-Piracy-Report.pdf, on February 1, 2017.

50. ICC International Maritime Bureau, "Piracy and Armed Robbery Against Ships, Report for the Period 1 January 2011–31 December 2011" (London: ICC International Maritime Bureau, 2012), 5–6. Retrieved from https://www.icc-ccs.org/uploadreport/2011_Annual_IMB_ Piracy_Report.pdf, on April 2, 2016.

51. *Ibid*, 5.

52. Somali pirates hijacked twenty-eight ships in 2011 alone, *Ibid*, 8.

53. See BBC News, "Somali Piracy Threatens Global Oil Supplies," February 10, 2011. Retrieved from http://www.bbc.com/news/world-africa-12412488 on April 16, 2016.

54. See Richard Phillips, *A Captain's Duty: Somali Pirates, Navy SEALS and Dangerous Days at Sea* (New York: HarperCollins Publishers, 2010).

55. Sandra L. Hodgkinson, "Current Trends in Global Piracy: Can Somalia's Successes Help Combat Piracy in the Gulf of Guinea and Elsewhere?" *Case Western Reserve Journal of International Law* 43 (2003): 145–60.

56. ICC International Maritime Bureau, "Piracy and Armed Robbery 2016," 5.

57. *Ibid*, 18.

58. Ian Urbina, "Stowaways and Crimes Aboard a Scofflaw Ship," *New York Times*, July 17, 2015. Retrieved from http://www.nytimes.com/2015/07/19/world/stowaway-crime-scofflaw-ship.html on July 20, 2015.

59. United Nations High Commissioner for Refugees (UNHCR), "Global Appeal 2016–17," 54. Retrieved from http://www.unhcr.org/564da0e5a.html on February 11, 2016. The International Organization for Migration provides a higher estimate of over a million migrants arriving in Europe by sea in 2015, see International Organization for Migration, "Mediterranean Update. Migration Flows Europe: Arrivals and Fatalities," 1. Retrieved from http://missingmigrants.iom.int/sites/default/files/Mediterranean_Update_09_February_2016_0.pdf on February 11, 2016.

60. Data from International Organization for Migration Missing Migrants Project, http://missingmigrants.iom.int/mediterranean-migrant-arrivals-2016–181476-deaths-1232, retrieved on April 28, 2016.

61. International Organization for Migration, "Mixed Migration Flows in the Mediterranean and Beyond, 2016," 12, retrieved from http://migration.iom.int/docs/2016_Flows_to_Europe_ Overview.pdf, on February 1, 2017.

62. The International Organization for Migration Missing Migrants Project reports that over 250 people died crossing the Mediterranean in January 2017, see "Mediterranean" at http://missingmigrants.iom.int/mediterranean, retrieved February 1, 2017.

63. See Alessio Patalano, "Nightmare Nostrum? Not Quite," *The RUSI Journal* 160, no. 3 (2015): 14–9.

64. See UNHCR, "Bay of Bengal and Andaman Sea Initiative: Enhancing Responses and Seeking Solutions" (2015), 5. Retrieved from http://www.unhcr.org/cgi-bin/texis/vtx/home/opendocPDFViewer.html?docid=557ad6a59&query=bay%20of%20bengal, on February 11, 2016. The International Organization for Migration Missing Migrants Project provides a higher estimate of 94,000 people on these routes since 2014, see http://missingmigrants.iom.int/migrant-routes-southeast-asia-6-october-2015, retrieved on February 16, 2016.

65. Locke, *Two Treatises*, II §6 270.

66. Locke, "Essay on the Poor Law," 186.

Bibliography

Al-Fattal, Rouba. "The Tragedy of the Commons: Institutions and Fisheries Management at the Local and EU Levels." *Review of Political Economy* 21, no. 4 (2009): 537–47.

Anon. *The State of the Navy Consider'd in Relation to the Victualling, Particularly in the Straits, and the West Indies. With Some Thoughts on the Mismanagement of the Admiralty for Several Years past; and a Proposal to prevent the like for the future.* Second edition. London: Printed for A. Baldwin in Warwick Lane, 1699.

Armitage, David. *The Ideological Origins of the British Empire.* Cambridge: Cambridge University Press, 2000.

Armitage, David. "John Locke, Carolina, and the *Two Treatises of Government.*" *Political Theory* 32, no. 5 (2004): 602–627.

Armitage, David. "John Locke's International Thought." In *British International Thinkers from Hobbes to Namier*, edited by Ian Hall and Lisa Hill, 33–48. New York: Palgrave Macmillan, 2009.

Armitage, David. "John Locke: Theorist of Empire?" In *Empire and Modern Political Thought*, edited by Sankar Muthu, 84–111. Cambridge: Cambridge University Press, 2012.

Armitage, David and Michael J. Braddick, eds. *The British Atlantic World 1500–1800*, New York: Palgrave Macmillan, 2002.

Arneil, Barbara. *John Locke and America: The Defence of English Colonialism.* New York: Oxford University Press, 1996.

Ashcraft, Richard. "Political Theory and Political Reform: John Locke's Essay on Virginia." *Political Research Quarterly* 22, no. 4 (1969): 742–58.

Ashcraft, Richard. *Revolutionary Politics and Locke's Two Treatises of Government.* Princeton, NJ: Princeton University Press, 1986.

Augustin. *St. Augustin's City of God and Christian Doctrine*, trans. Philip Schaf. Grand Rapids, MI: Christian Classics Ethereal Library, 1890.

Barker, Ernest, ed. *Social Contract: Essays by Locke, Hume, and Rousseau.* London: Oxford University Press, 1947.

Barry, Donald. "The Canada-European Union Turbot War: Internal Politics and Transatlantic Bargaining." *International Journal* 53, no. 2 (1998): 253–84.

Baumgold, Deborah. "Subjects and Soldiers: Hobbes on Military Service." *History of Political Thought* 4, no. 1 (1983): 43–65.

Beckles, Hilary McD. *A History of Barbados: From Amerindian Settlement to Nation-State.* Cambridge and New York: Cambridge University Press, 1990.

Bell, Duncan. *The Idea of Greater Britain: Empire and the Future of World Order, 1860–1900.* Princeton, NJ: Princeton University Press, 2007.

Bell, Duncan. "What Is Liberalism?" *Political Theory* 42, no. 6 (2014): 682–715.

Bieber, Ralph Paul. "The British Plantation Councils of 1670–4." *The English Historical Review* 40, no. 157 (1925): 93–106.

Black, Jeremy and Philip Woodfine, eds. *The British Navy and the Use of Naval Power in the Eighteenth Century*. Atlantic Highlands, NJ: Humanities Press International, 1988.

Black, Jeremy. *The British Seaborne Empire*. New Haven, CT and London: Yale University Press, 2004.

Blair, James, John Locke, and Michael Kammen, ed. "Virginia at the Close of the Seventeenth Century: An Appraisal by James Blair and John Locke." *The Virginia Magazine of History and Biography* 74, no. 2 (1966): 141–69.

Blakemore, Richard J. "The Legal World of English Sailors, c. 1575–1729." In *Law, Labour and Empire: Comparative Perspectives on Seafarers, c.1500–1800*, edited by Maria Fusaro, Bernard Allaire, Richard Blakemore, and Tijl Vanneste, 100–20. New York: Palgrave Macmillan, 2015.

Bolster, W. Jeffrey. "Putting the Ocean Back in Atlantic History: Maritime Communities and Marine Ecology in the Northwest Atlantic, 1500–1800." *The American Historical Review* 113, no. 1 (2008): 19–47.

Bosch, Thomas, et al. (Cluster of Excellence). *World Oceans Review: Living with the Oceans*. Berlin: Maribus, 2010.

Brewer, Holly. "Slavery, Sovereignty, and 'Inheritable Blood': The Struggle over Locke's Virginia Plan of 1698 in the Wake of the Glorious Revolution" (unpublished working paper).

Brunsman, Denver. "Men of War: British Sailors and the Impressment Paradox." *Journal of Early Modern History* 14, no. 1 (2010): 9–24.

Brunsman, Denver. *The Evil Necessity: British Naval Impressment in the Eighteenth-Century Atlantic World*. Charlottesville and London: University of Virginia Press, 2013.

Buchan, Bruce. "The Empire of Political Thought: Civilization, Savagery and Perceptions of Indigenous Government." *History of the Human Sciences* 18, no. 2 (2005): 1–22.

Burgess, Douglas R. "A Crisis of Charter and Right: Piracy and Colonial Resistance in Seventeenth-Century Rhode Island." *Journal of Social History* 45, no. 3 (2012): 605–22.

Canny, Nicholas and Philip Morgan, eds. *The Oxford Handbook of the Atlantic World, c. 1450–c. 1850*. New York and Oxford: Oxford University Press, 2011.

Chaplin, Joyce. "The British Atlantic." In *The Oxford Handbook of the Atlantic World, c. 1450–c. 1850*, edited by Nicholas Canny and Philip Morgan, 219–34. Oxford: Oxford University Press, 2011.

Cicero. *De Re Publica & De Legibus*, trans. Clinton Walker Keyes. Cambridge, MA: Harvard University Press, 1928.

Coldham, Peter Wilson. *Emigrants in Chains: A Social History of Forced Emigration to the Americas of Felons, Destitute Children, Political and Religious Non-Conformists, Vagabonds, Beggars and Other Undesirables, 1607–1776*. Maryland: Genealogical Publishing Co., 1992.

Cordingly, David. *Under the Black Flag: The Romance and the Reality of Life Among the Pirates*. New York: Random House, 1995.

Cranston, Maurice. *John Locke: A Biography*. London: Longmans, Green & Co. Ltd., 1968.

De Beer, E. S., ed. *The Correspondence of John Locke, Volume 6*. Oxford: Clarendon, 1981.

De Beer, E. S., ed. *The Correspondence of John Locke, Volume 7*. Oxford: Clarendon, 1982.

Dilts, Andrew. "To Kill a Thief: Punishment, Proportionality, and Criminal Subjectivity in Locke's *Second Treatise*." *Political Theory* 40, no. 1 (2012): 58–83.

Donoghue, John. "Unfree Labour, Imperialism, and Radical Republicanism in the Atlantic World, 1630–1661." *Labor: Studies in Working-Class History of the Americas* 1, no. 4 (2004): 47–68.

Donoghue, John. "'Out of the Land of Bondage': The English Revolution and the Atlantic Origins of Abolition." *The American Historical Review* 115, no. 4 (2010): 943–74.

Drescher, Seymour. "On James Farr's 'So Vile and Miserable an Estate.'" *Political Theory* 16, no. 3 (1988): 502–3.

Dunn, John. *The Political Thought of John Locke: An Historical Account of the Argument of the "Two Treatises of Government."* Cambridge: Cambridge University Press, 1969.

Eltis, David. "Europeans and the Rise and Fall of African Slavery in the Americas: An Interpretation." *The American Historical Review* 98, no. 5 (1993): 1399–423.

Farr, James. "'So Vile and Miserable an Estate': The Problem of Slavery in Locke's Political Thought." *Political Theory* 14, no. 2 (1986): 263–69.

Farr, James. "Locke, Natural Law, and New World Slavery." *Political Theory* 36, no. 4 (2008): 495–522.

Farr, James. "Locke, 'Some Americans,' and the Discourse on 'Carolina.'" *Locke Studies* 9 (2009). Retrieved from lockestudies.org/wp-content/uploads/2013/10/FarrLS9.pdf.

Filmer, Robert. *Patriarcha and Other Political Works of Sir Robert Filmer*, ed. Peter Laslett. Oxford: Basil Blackwell, 1949.

Fox Bourne, H. R. *The Life of John Locke, Volume 1*. New York: Harper and Brothers Publishers, 1876.

Fox Bourne, H. R. *The Life of John Locke, Volume 2*. New York: Harper and Brothers Publishers, 1876.

Friedman, Milton. *Capitalism and Freedom: Fortieth Anniversary Edition*. Chicago: University of Chicago Press, 2002.

Fryman, Nikolas. "Impressment, Kidnapping and Panyarring." In *The Princeton Companion to Atlantic History*, edited by Joseph C. Miller. Princeton and Oxford: Princeton University Press, 2015.

Fusaro, Maria, Bernard Allaire, Richard Blakemore, and Tijl Vanneste, eds. *Law, Labour and Empire: Comparative Perspectives on Seafarers, c.1500–1800*. New York: Palgrave Macmillan, 2015.

Games, Alison. "Migration." In *The British Atlantic World: 1500–1800*, edited by David Armitage and Michael J. Braddick, 31–50. New York: Palgrave Macmillan, 2002.

Glausser, Wayne. "Three Approaches to Locke and the Slave Trade." *Journal of the History of Ideas* 51, no. 2 (1990): 199–216.

Goldwin, Robert. "Locke and the Law of the Sea." *Commentary* 71, no. 6 (1981): 46–50.

Grant, Ruth W. *John Locke's Liberalism*. Chicago and London: University of Chicago Press, 1987.

Great Britain Public Record Office. *Calendar of State Papers Colonial: America and West Indies, Volume 7, 1669–1674*, ed. W. Noel Sainsbury. London, 1889.

Great Britain Public Record Office. *Calendar of State Papers Colonial: America and West Indies, Volume 14, 1693–1696*, ed. J. W. Fortescue. London, 1903.

Great Britain Public Record Office. *Calendar of State Papers Colonial: America and West Indies, Volume 15, 1696–1697*, ed. J. W. Fortescue. London, 1904.

Great Britain Public Record Office. *Calendar of State Papers Colonial: America and West Indies, Volume 16, 1697–1698*, ed. J. W. Fortescue. London, 1905.

Great Britain Public Record Office. *Calendar of State Papers Colonial: America and West Indies, Volume 17, 1699 and Addenda*, ed. J. W. Fortescue. London, 1908.

Great Britain Public Record Office. *Calendar of State Papers Colonial, America and West Indies, Volume 18, 1700*, ed. Cecil Headlam. London, 1910.

Great Britain Public Record Office. *Calendar of State Papers Domestic: William III 1698*, ed. Edward Bateson. London, 1933.

Grotius, Hugo. *The Freedom of the Seas, or the Right Which Belongs to the Dutch to Take Part in the East Indian Trade*, trans. Ralph van Deman Magoffin. New York: Oxford University Press, 1916.

Guðmundsson, Guðmundur J. "The Cod and the Cold War." *Scandinavian Journal of History* 31, no. 2 (2006): 97–118.

Haddad, Brent M. "Property Rights, Ecosystem Management, and John Locke's Labor Theory of Ownership." *Ecological Economics* 46, no. 1 (2003): 19–31.

Hakluyt, Richard. *A Particuler Discourse Concerning the Greate Necessitie and Manifolde Commodyties that are Like to Growe to This Realm of England By the Westerne Discoueries Lately Attempted*, eds. David B. Quinn and Alison M. Quinn. London: Hakluyt Society, 1993.

Hall, Ian and Lisa Hill, eds. *British International Thinkers from Hobbes to Namier*. New York: Palgrave Macmillan, 2009.

Hanna, Mark G. *Pirate Nests and the Rise of the British Empire, 1570–1740*. Chapel Hill: University of North Carolina Press, 2015.

Harcourt, Bernhard. *The Illusion of Free Markets: Punishment and the Myth of Natural Order*. Cambridge, MA: Harvard University Press, 2011.

Hardin, Garrett. "The Tragedy of the Commons." *Science* 162, no. 3859 (1968): 1243–48.

Harlow, Vincent T. *A History of Barbados: 1625–1685*. New York: Negro Universities Press, 1969.

Harrison, John and Peter Laslett. *The Library of John Locke*. Oxford: Oxford University Press, 1965.

Hayes, Peter. "Pirates, Privateers and the Contract Theories of Hobbes and Locke." *History of Political Thought* 29, no. 3 (2008): 461–84.

Heidbrink, Ingo Klaus. "The Oceans as the Common Property of Mankind from Early Modern Period to Today." *History Compass* 6, no. 2 (2008): 659–72.

Heller-Roazen, Daniel. *The Enemy of All: Piracy and the Law of Nations*. New York: Zone Books, 2009.

Her Majesty's Stationery Office. *House of Lords Journal Volume 16, 1696–1701*. London, 1767–1830.

Hill, Christopher. *Liberty Against the Law: Some Seventeenth Century Controversies*. London: Penguin Books, 1996.

Hinshelwood, Brad. "The Carolinian Context of John Locke's Theory of Slavery." *Political Theory* 41, no. 4 (2013): 562–90.

Hirschmann, Nancy J. "Liberal Conservativism, Once and Again: Locke's 'Essay on the Poor Law' and Contemporary US Welfare Reform." *Constellations* 9, no. 3 (2002): 335–55.

Hirschmann, Nancy J. *Gender, Class, and Freedom in Modern Political Theory*. Princeton: Princeton University Press, 2007.

Hirschmann, Nancy J. and Kirstie M. McClure, eds. *Feminist Interpretations of John Locke*. University Park, PA: Pennsylvania State University Press, 2007.

Hobbes, Thomas. *Leviathan*. Oxford: Oxford University Press, 1998.

Hodgkinson, Sandra L. "Current Trends in Global Piracy: Can Somalia's Successes Help Combat Piracy in the Gulf of Guinea and Elsewhere?" *Case Western Reserve Journal of International Law* 43 (2003): 145–60.

Hsueh, Vicki. "Cultivating and Challenging the Common: Lockean Property, Indigenous Traditionalisms, and the Problem of Exclusion." *Contemporary Political Theory* 5, no. 2 (2006): 193–214.

Hsueh, Vicki. "Unsettling Colonies: Locke, 'Atlantis' and New World Knowledges." *History of Political Thought* 29, no. 2 (2008): 295–319.

Hsueh, Vicki. *Hybrid Constitutions: Challenging Legacies of Law, Privilege, and Culture in Colonial America*. Durham and London: Duke University Press, 2010.

Hume, David. "Of the Original Contract." In *Social Contract: Essays by Locke, Hume, and Rousseau*, ed. Ernest Barker. London: Oxford University Press, 1947.

Humrich, Christoph. "Fragmented International Governance of Arctic Offshore Oil: Governance Challenges and Institutional Improvement." *Global Environmental Politics* 13, no. 3 (2013): 79–99.

International Criminal Court International Maritime Bureau. "Piracy and Armed Robbery Against Ships, Report for the Period 1 January–31 December 2011." London: ICC International Maritime Bureau, 2012. Retrieved from https://www.icc-ccs.org/uploadreport/2011_Annual_IMB_Piracy_Report.pdf.

International Criminal Court International Maritime Bureau. "Piracy and Armed Robbery Against Ships, Report for the Period 1 January–31 December 2016." London: ICC International Maritime Bureau, 2017. Retrieved from https://www.icc-ccs.org/uploadreport/2016-Annual-IMB-Piracy-Report.pdf.

International Organization for Migration. "Mediterranean Update. Migration Flows Europe: Arrivals and Fatalities." 2016. Retrieved from http://missingmigrants.iom.int/sites/default/files/Mediterranean_Update_09_February_2016_0.pdf.

International Organization for Migration. "Mixed Migration Flows in the Mediterranean and Beyond, 2016." 2017. Retrieved from http://migration.iom.int/docs/2016_Flows_to_ Europe_Overview.pdf.

International Organization for Migration. *Missing Migrants Project* at http://missingmigrants. iom.int/.

Ivison, Duncan. "Locke, Liberalism and Empire." In *The Philosophy of John Locke: New Perspectives*, edited by P. Anstey, 86–105. London and New York: Routledge, 2003.

Janicki, Wojciech. "Why Do They Need the Arctic? The First Partition of the Sea." *Arctic* 65, no. 1 (2012): 87–97.

Jeppesen, Jennie. "To Serve Longer According to Law: The Chattel-Like Status of Convict Servants in Virginia." In *Order and Civility in the Early Modern Chesapeake*, edited by Debra Meyers and Melanie Perreault, 198–210. Lanham, MD: Lexington Books, 2014.

Jones, J. R. "Limitations of British Sea Power in the French Wars, 1689–1815." In *The British Navy and the Use of Naval Power in the Eighteenth Century*, edited by Jeremy Black and Philip Woodfine, 33–49. Atlantic Highlands, NJ: Humanities Press International, 1988.

Kelly, Patrick Hyde, ed. *Locke on Money, Volume 1*. Oxford: Clarendon Press, 1991.

Kelly, Patrick Hyde, ed. *Locke on Money, Volume 2*. Oxford: Clarendon Press, 1991.

Kohn, Margaret and Daniel I. O'Neill. "A Tale of Two Indias: Burke and Mill on Empire and Slavery in the West Indies and America." *Political Theory* 34, no. 2 (2006): 192–228.

Laslett, Peter. "John Locke, the Great Recoinage, and the Origins of the Board of Trade: 1695–1698." *The William and Mary Quarterly* 14, no. 3 (1957): 370–402.

Lebovics, Hermann. "The Uses of America in Locke's *Second Treatise of Government*." *Journal of the History of Ideas* 47, no. 4 (1986): 567–81.

Leeson, Peter T. *The Invisible Hook: The Hidden Economics of Pirates*. Princeton, NJ: Princeton University Press, 2009.

Levinson, Marc. *The Box: How the Shipping Container Made the World Smaller and the World Economy Bigger*. Princeton and Oxford: Princeton University Press, 2006.

Lilburne, John and others. "The Petition of 11 September 1648." In *The English Levellers*, ed. Andrew Sharp (Cambridge: Cambridge University Press, 1998), 131–9.

Lindberg, Erik. "From Private to Public Provision of Public Goods: English Lighthouses Between the Seventeenth and Nineteenth Centuries." *The Journal of Policy History* 25, no. 4 (2013): 538–56.

Locke, John. *Two Treatises of Government*, ed. Peter Laslett. Cambridge: Cambridge University Press, 1988.

Locke, John. "Some Considerations of the Consequences of the Lowering of Interest and Raising the Value of Money." In *Locke on Money, Volume 1*, edited by Patrick Hyde Kelly, 207–342. Oxford: Clarendon Press, 1991.

Locke, John. "An Essay on the Poor Law." In *Locke: Political Essays*, by John Locke and edited by Mark Goldie, 182–98. Cambridge: Cambridge University Press, 1997.

Locke, John. "Atlantis." In *Locke: Political Essays*, by John Locke and edited by Mark Goldie, 252–9. Cambridge: Cambridge University Press, 1997.

Locke, John. "For a General Naturalisation." In *Locke: Political Essays*, by John Locke and edited by Mark Goldie, 322–26. Cambridge: Cambridge University Press, 1997.

Locke, John. "Some Thoughts Concerning Reading and Study for a Gentleman." In *Locke: Political Essays*, by John Locke and edited by Mark Goldie, 348–55. Cambridge: Cambridge University Press, 1997.

Locke, John. "Trade." In *Locke: Political Essays*, by John Locke and edited by Mark Goldie, 221–2. Cambridge: Cambridge University Press, 1997.

Locke, John. "Verses on Cromwell and the Dutch War." In *Locke: Political Essays*, by John Locke and edited by Mark Goldie, 201–2. Cambridge: Cambridge University Press, 1997.

Locke, John. *Locke: Political Essays*, ed. Mark Goldie. Cambridge: Cambridge University Press, 1997.

Locke, John and others. "The Fundamental Constitutions of Carolina." In *Locke: Political Essays*, by John Locke and edited by Mark Goldie, 160–81. Cambridge: Cambridge University Press, 1997.

Macpherson, C. B. *The Political Theory of Possessive Individualism: Hobbes to Locke*. Don Mills, ON: Oxford University Press, 2011.

Markley, Robert. "'Land Enough in the World': Locke's Golden Age and the Infinite Extension of 'Use.'" *The South Atlantic Quarterly* 98, no. 4 (1999): 817–37.

Matar, Nabil. "The Barbary Corsairs, King Charles I and the Civil War." *The Seventeenth Century* 16, no. 2 (2001): 239–58.

McWhinnie, Stephanie F. "The Tragedy of the Commons in International Fisheries: An Empirical Examination." *Journal of Environmental Economics and Management* 57, no. 3 (2009): 321–33.

Mehta, Uday Singh. *Liberalism and Empire: A Study in Nineteenth Century British Liberal Thought*. Chicago and London: University of Chicago Press, 1999.

Miller, Joseph C., ed. *The Princeton Companion to Atlantic History*. Princeton, NJ, and Oxford: Princeton University Press, 2015.

Mills, Charles. *The Racial Contract*. Ithaca: Cornell University Press, 1997.

Milton, J. R. "Dating Locke's *Second Treatise*." *History of Political Thought* 16, no. 3 (1995), 356–90.

Mintz, Sidney W. *Sweetness and Power: The Place of Sugar in Modern History*. New York: Penguin Books, 1986.

Morefield, Jeanne. *Covenants Without Swords: Idealist Liberalism and the Spirit of Empire*. Princeton, NJ: Princeton University Press, 2005.

Morgan, Gwenda and Peter Rushton. *Eighteenth-Century Criminal Transportation: The Formation of the Criminal Atlantic*. New York: Palgrave Macmillan, 2004.

Muthu, Sankar. *Enlightenment Against Empire*. Princeton, NJ: Princeton University Press, 2003.

Muthu, Sankar, ed. *Empire and Modern Political Thought*. Cambridge: Cambridge University Press, 2012.

Neff, Stephen C., ed. *Hugo Grotius: On the Law of War and Peace*. Cambridge: Cambridge University Press, 2010.

Neocleous, Mark. "War on Waste: Law, Original Accumulation and the Violence of Capital." *Science & Society* 75, no. 4 (2011): 506–28.

Nicholls, Mark and Penry Williams. *Sir Walter Raleigh in Life and Legend*. London and New York: Continuum Books, 2011.

Nozick, Robert. *Anarchy, State, and Utopia*. Oxford: Blackwell, 1974.

Nutting, Bradley P. "The Madagascar Connection: Parliament and Piracy, 1690–1701." *The American Journal of Legal History* 22, no. 3 (1978): 205–15.

O'Neill, Daniel I. "Rethinking Burke and India." *History of Political Thought* 30, no. 3 (2009): 492–523.

Parekh, Bhikhu. "Liberalism and Colonialism: A Critique of Locke and Mill." In *Decolonization of Imagination*, edited by Jan Nederveen Pieterse and Bhikhu Parekh, 81–96. London, UK: Zed Books, 1995.

Patalano, Alessio. "Nightmare Nostrum? Not Quite." *The RUSI Journal* 160, no. 3 (2015): 14–9.

Pateman, Carole. *The Sexual Contract*. Stanford, CA: Stanford University Press, 1988.

Phillips, Richard. *A Captain's Duty: Somali Pirates, Navy SEALS, and Dangerous Days at Sea*. New York: Harper Collins Publishers, 2010.

Pitts, Jennifer. *A Turn to Empire: The Rise of Liberal Imperialism in Britain and France*. Princeton and Oxford: Princeton University Press, 2005.

Puckrein, Gary. *Little England: Plantation Society and Anglo-Barbadian Politics, 1627–1700*. New York and London: New York University Press, 1984.

Rediker, Marcus. *Between the Devil and the Deep Blue Sea: Merchant Seamen, Pirates, and the Anglo-American Maritime World, 1700–1750*. New York: Cambridge University Press, 1987.

Rediker, Marcus. *Villains of All Nations: Atlantic Pirates in the Golden Age*. London: Verso Books, 2004.

Rediker, Marcus, Cassandra Pybus, and Emma Christopher, eds. *Many Middle Passages: Forced Migration and the Making of the Modern World*. Berkeley and Los Angeles: University of California Press, 2007.

Rediker, Marcus, Cassandra Pybus, and Emma Christopher. "Introduction." In *Many Middle Passages: Forced Migration and the Making of the Atlantic World*, edited by Marcus Rediker, Cassandra Pybus, and Emma Christopher, 1–19. Berkeley and Los Angeles: University of California Press, 2007.

Richardson, Anthony J., et al. "The Jellyfish Joyride: Causes, Consequences and Management Responses to a More Gelatinous Future." *Trends in Ecology and Evolution* 24, no. 6 (2009): 312–22.

Ritchie, Robert C. *Captain Kidd and the War Against the Pirates*. Cambridge, MA: Harvard University Press, 1986.

Rodger, N. A. M. *The Wooden World: An Anatomy of the Georgian Navy*. London: W. W. Norton & Company, 1986.

Rodger, N. A. M. *The Command of the Ocean: A Naval History of Britain, 1649–1815*. New York and London: W. W. Norton & Company, 2005.

Rogers, Nicholas. *The Press Gang: Naval Impressment and Its Opponents in Georgian Britain*. London and New York: Continuum Books, 2007.

Saunders Webb, Stephen. "William Blathwayt, Imperial Fixer: Muddling Through to Empire, 1689–1717." *The William and Mary Quarterly* 26, no. 3 (1969): 373–415.

Scott, Jonathan. "Maritime Orientalism, or the Political Theory of Water." *History of Political Thought* 35, no. 1 (2014): 70–90.

Selden, John. *Mare Clausum: The Right and Dominion of the Sea*, trans. Marchmont Nedham and ed. J. H. Grant. London, 1663.

Self, Emily. "Who Speaks for the Fish? The Tragedy of Europe's Common Fisheries Policy." *Vanderbilt Journal of Transnational Law* 48, no. 2 (2015): 577–607.

Several Hands. "An Agreement of the People for a Firm and Present Peace Upon Grounds of Common Right and Freedom." In *The English Levellers*, edited by Andrew Sharp, 92–101. Cambridge: Cambridge University Press, 1998.

Shanks, Torrey. *Authority Figures: Rhetoric and Experience in John Locke's Political Thought*. University Park, PA: Pennsylvania State University Press, 2014.

Sharp, Andrew, ed. *The English Levellers*. Cambridge: Cambridge University Press, 1998.

Sharp, Nonie. *Saltwater People: The Waves of Memory*. Toronto, ON: University of Toronto Press, 2002.

Smith, Abbot Emerson. *Colonists in Bondage: White Servitude and Convict Labor in America, 1607–1776*. New York: Norton & Company, 1971.

Sreedhar, Susanne. "Defending the Hobbesian Right of Self-Defense." *Political Theory* 36, no. 6 (2008): 781–802.

Steele, I. K. "The Board of Trade, the Quakers, and Resumption of Colonial Charters, 1699–1702." *The William and Mary Quarterly* 23, no. 4 (1966): 596–619.

Steinberg, Philip E. *The Social Construction of the Ocean*. Cambridge: Cambridge University Press, 2001.

Stern, Philip J. "British Asia and British Atlantic: Comparisons and Connections." *William and Mary Quarterly* 63, no. 4 (2006): 693–712.

Stern, Philip. *The Company State: Corporate Sovereignty and the Early Modern Foundation of the British Empire in India*. New York: Oxford University Press, 2011.

Stopford, Martin. *Maritime Economics 3rd Edition*. Hoboken, NY: Taylor and Francis, 2009.

Thornton, Helen. "John Selden's Response to Hugo Grotius: The Argument for Closed Seas." *International Journal of Maritime History* 18, no. 2 (2006): 105–27.

Tuck, Richard. *The Rights of War and Peace: Political Thought and the International Order from Grotius to Kant*. Oxford: Oxford University Press, 1999.

Tuckness, Alex. "John Locke and Public Administration." *Administration and Society* 40, no. 3 (2008): 253–70.

Tuckness, Alex. "Punishment, Property, and the Limits of Altruism: Locke's International Asymmetry." *The American Political Science Review* 102, no. 4 (2008): 467–79.

Tully, James. *An Approach to Political Philosophy: Locke in Contexts*. Cambridge and New York: Cambridge University Press, 1993.

Tyrrell, James. *Patriarcha Non Monarcha. The Patriarch Unmonarch'd*. London, 1681. Retrieved from http://oll.libertyfund.org/titles/2168.

United Nations Division for Ocean Affairs and the Law of the Sea. "United Nations Convention on the Law of the Sea of 10 December 1982." 1982. Retrieved from http://www.un.org/Depts/los/convention_agreements/texts/unclos/UNCLOS-TOC.htm.

United Nations Environment Program. "Challenges to International Waters—Regional Assessments in a Global Perspective." 2006. Retrieved from http://www.unep.org/dewa/giwa/publications/finalreport/giwa_final_report.pdf.

United Nations Food and Agriculture Organization. "The State of World Fisheries and Aquaculture." 2014. Retrieved from http://www.fao.org/3/a-i3720e.pdf.

United Nations High Commissioner for Refugees. "Bay of Bengal and Andaman Sea Initiative: Enhancing Responses and Seeking Solutions." 2015. Retrieved from http://www.unhcr.org/cgi-bin/texis/vtx/home/opendocPDFViewer.html?docid=557ad6a59&query=bay%20of%20bengal.

United Nations High Commissioner for Refugees. "Global Appeal 2016–17." 2016. Retrieved from http://www.unhcr.org/564da0e5a.html.

United States Department of Transportation. "Freight Facts and Figures 2015." 2016. Retrieved from http://www.rita.dot.gov/bts/sites/rita.dot.gov.bts/files/FF%26F_complete.pdf.

van Ittersum, Martine Julia. "Hugo Grotius in Context: Van Heemskerck's Capture of the *Santa Catarina* and Its Justification in *De Jure Praedae* (1604–1606)." *Asian Journal of Social Sciences* 31, no. 3 (2003): 511–48.

van Ittersum, Martine Julia. *Profit & Principle: Hugo Grotius, Natural Rights Theories and the Rise of Dutch Power in the East Indies, 1595–1615*. Leiden and Boston: Brill Academic Publishers, 2006.

van Ittersum, Martine Julia. "*Mare Liberum* Versus the Propriety of the Seas? The Debate Between Hugo Grotius (1583–1645) and William Welwood (1552–1624) and Its Impact on Anglo-Scotto-Dutch Fishery Disputes in the Second Decade of the Seventeenth Century." *Edinburgh Law Review* 10 (2006): 239–76.

van Ittersum, Martine Julia. "The Long Goodbye: Hugo Grotius' Justification of Dutch Expansion Overseas, 1615–1645." *History of European Ideas* 36, no. 4 (2010): 386–411.

Waldron, Jeremy. *God, Locke and Equality: Christian Foundations of John Locke's Political Thought*. Cambridge and New York: Cambridge University Press, 2002.

Walzer, Michael. *Obligations: Essays on Disobedience, War, and Citizenship*. Cambridge, MA: Harvard University Press, 1970.

Welchman, Jennifer. "Locke on Slavery and Inalienable Rights." *Canadian Journal of Philosophy* 25, no. 1 (1995): 67–81.

Woolhouse, Roger. *Locke: A Biography*. New York: Cambridge University Press, 2007.

Index

About the Author

Sarah Pemberton is a political theorist who works on issues of law, freedom, and state power from the early modern period to the present. Her training includes a BA in Philosophy, Politics, and Economics from Merton College, Oxford, and a PhD in Political Science from the University of British Columbia, Vancouver. She has taught at the University of South Florida, Ohio University, and the University of British Columbia. Her research has appeared in the *Oxford Handbook of Feminist Theory*, in journals including *New Political Science* and *SIGNS: Journal of Women in Culture and Society,* and at conferences in North America and Europe. Sarah has received several prestigious fellowships and awards, including a Commonwealth Scholarship, Canada Memorial Fellowship, and the Western Political Science Association's 2011 Betty Nesvold Women and Politics Award.

www.ingramcontent.com/pod-product-compliance
Lightning Source LLC
Chambersburg PA
CBHW021819270326
41932CB00007B/247